RESEARCHING LEGISLATIVE INTENT

Researching Legislative Intent
A PRACTICAL GUIDE

SUSAN BARKER AND ERICA ANDERSON

Researching Legislative Intent: A Practical Guide
© Irwin Law, 2019

Published in 2019 by

Irwin Law Inc
Suite 206, 14 Duncan Street
Toronto, ON   M5H 3G8
www.irwinlaw.com

ISBN: 978-1-55221-513-5 e-book ISBN: 978-1-55221-514-2

Library and Archives Canada Cataloguing in Publication

Title: Researching legislative intent : a practical guide / Susan Barker and Erica Anderson.

Names: Barker, Susan (Susan Marion), author. | Anderson, Erica, 1973– author.

Description: Includes bibliographical references and index.

Identifiers: Canadiana (print) 20190132590 | Canadiana (ebook) 20190132604 | ISBN 9781552215135 (softcover) | ISBN 9781552215142 (PDF)

Subjects: LCSH: Law—Canada—Interpretation and construction. | LCSH: Legal research—Canada. | LCSH: Legislative histories—Canada.

Classification: LCC KE482.S84 B37 2019 | LCC KF425 .B37 2019 kfmod | DDC 348/.7102—dc23

Printed and bound in Canada.

1 2 3 4 5   23 22 21 20 19

Summary Table of Contents

Detailed Table of Contents

✶ CHAPTER TWO

Understanding Statutes: The Process of a Bill 36

  CHAPTER THREE

Intrinsic Aids to Statutory Interpretation   73

 ❦ CHAPTER SIX

Extrinsic Aids to Statutory Interpretation: Other Sources   112

&ar; CHAPTER SEVEN
How to Trace the Legislative Evolution of a Statute

❦ CHAPTER EIGHT

How to Trace the Legislative History of a Statute   173

❦ CHAPTER NINE

Interpretation of Treaties with Indigenous Peoples   184

๏ CHAPTER TEN
Statutory Instruments, Royal Prerogative, and Delegated Legislation   197

List of Illustrations

Acknowledgements

First, we would like to thank our families for their love, support, and understanding during the long process of writing this book. We also owe a debt of gratitude to our work colleagues who provided us with some great ideas and feedback, and to the Toronto Association of Law Libraries and the Association of Parliamentary Libraries in Canada, both of which gave us our first opportunity to showcase our research. Many thanks to our fellow law librarians at the Canadian Association of Law Libraries who supported our project by awarding us the Michael Silverstein Prize for an early version of Chapter 1 that was published as an article in the *Canadian Parliamentary Review*. There were also some individuals who guided and encouraged us while we were writing this book: thanks to Anver Emon, from the University of Toronto Faculty of Law, for allowing us to audit his Statutory Interpretation class at the very beginning when we were just learning the ropes; to Rich Sage, Lorraine Luski, and Jeanette Bosschart, who were kind enough to read our first draft and offer gentle critiques and suggestions for improvement that we happily took on board. And finally, we would like to thank our bosses, Wendy Reynolds, Mary Saulig, and Vicki Whitmell from the Legislative Assembly of Ontario and its library, and Gian Medves and John Papadopoulos from the Bora Laskin Law Library. Thank you all.

Susan and Erica

Introduction

> Statutory interpretation is the Cinderella of legal scholarship. Once
> scorned and neglected, confined to the kitchen, it now dances in the
> ballroom.[1]

Researching legislative intent can be a labour-intensive and time-
consuming task for legal researchers: we are often required to find
discussion about — and the meaning or intent of — a particular word
within a mountain of debate and reports. This type of research involves
tracing how a piece of legislation evolved over time and then finding
out what legislators said about the change(s) in *Hansard* and in committee. This kind of research can also involve finding the material that
inspired the legislation: law reform commission reports, royal commissions or government reports, and many other materials.

Legislative intent is generally discerned by looking at the legislative evolution (changes over time) and legislative history ("everything
that relates to [the] conception, preparation and passage ... from the
earliest proposals to royal assent")[2] of a particular statute or section
thereof. You could say that researching legislative intent is like

---

1   WM Eskridge Jr, *Dynamic Statutory Interpretation* (Cambridge, MA: Harvard Uni-
    versity Press, 1994) at 1.
2   Ruth Sullivan, *Sullivan on the Construction of Statutes*, 6th ed (Markham, ON: Lexis-
    Nexis, 2014) at 679.

Cinderella, pre-ball. The research can be a grind—with librarians and researchers toiling away in the library stacks.

Researching legislative intent is part of the larger field of statutory interpretation, which has been described as

> the unsung workhorse of the law. All but ignored by the law schools, lacking the high profile of constitutional interpretation, the interpretation of statutes is, nevertheless, the most common task of the courts and administrative tribunals. Common, yes; but essential, too.[3]

As statutory interpretation is an essential and common task required by courts today, it follows that the materials used to discern legislative intent, in support of statutory interpretation, should be accessible to everyone, and the research process should be taught to law students and legal researchers. Because there are so many materials available that go into the making of legislation, it is difficult to know when legislative intent research ends and which materials are important. The aim of this book is to support this area of legal research by describing those resources and the ways to find them.

In law libraries, locating resources that show the legislative intent behind a statute is a growing source of many substantial research questions. Librarians work hard to answer these questions and we are fascinated to see how this research is being used in the legal profession. The kinds of questions that law librarians get that require researching intent can range from the fairly straightforward:

- Can I have the *Hansard* and committee debate on this bill and the predecessor bills?
- What did the legislature mean by this phrase in this statute?
- When and why was this section added to the statute?
- Can I have a legislative history of this statute?
- When was this legislation first introduced and how long did it take to pass?

---

3   Paul Mitchell, "Just Do It! Eskridge's Critical Pragmatic Theory of Statutory Interpretation" (Book review of *Dynamic Statutory Interpretation* by William Eskridge) (1996) 41 *McGill Law Journal* 713 at 713.

to the vastly more complicated. Here are a couple of recent questions we have received in our libraries, with the particular details removed:

- *Question*: I would like you to search *Hansard*, policy papers, committee *Hansard* for all discussion surrounding the Act X, dating all the way back in time to when the predecessor of this legislation was introduced, which I believe was prior to 1900. We are interested to determine the meaning of "Y" and if it includes "A and B."
- *Question*: The Act was enacted in 1971. The original Act defined "A" as "B." In 1982 the definition was adjusted to include "C." The effect of this was that the interpretation was "D." This interpretation was not available under the original wording, and it would seem obvious that the Parliament did not intend to change its effect when it enacted the 1982 amendment. I am looking for House or Committee debates at the time of enactment of the original Act, and the amendment, which might show the intention of the legislature when the Act and the amendment were passed. For example, anything that would show the intention was "B" and that the 1982 Act was not intended to change the interpretation to "D" and that they were merely cleaning up the definition to bring it in line with other Acts.

In addition to doing this research, law librarians teach people how to find and use legislative intent materials. Librarians provide training to lawyers and students on finding bills, tracing legislative evolution, searching *Hansard*, and using legislature and parliamentary websites. Librarians teach the process of researching legislative intent in legal librarianship courses, as well as law school legal research and writing, and statutory interpretation courses.

In addition, beyond researching legislative intent, legislative history materials can be used by researchers for information beyond the courtroom. Legislative history is a rich source of information about broad government policy, as well as about local subjects for those legislators who may want to propose their own private bills. Legislative history resources can help people looking for current awareness about an issue and, further, they are a source of historical information about a jurisdiction, local topics, and even word use.

It is from law library research questions, teaching on this topic, and then having a conversation one day, that we began to wonder why we were getting so many of these questions and what happened to the research? We felt that these types of questions, looking for the intent of Parliament, were increasing in law and legislative libraries. We wanted to take this a bit further, peek on the other side of these questions, and see why and how this legislative intent research is used in court.

We found that, while law librarians have become very skilled at researching legislative intent and have been doing it more frequently, very often researchers were left wondering if they had completed the research properly, that they lacked any practical guidance or resources that would enable them to be sure they had done a thorough job. We decided that by looking deeper into these questions about legislative intent, we would be able to help our clients become better at statutory interpretation research, and in turn we would become better legal researchers ourselves. We are excited about this topic and this research and, like Cinderella, we want to "go to the ball," and bring to light the details, processes, and places for researching legislative intent to aid legal researchers. We hope this book addresses this gap and will be a guide for this essential legal research skill.

Susan and Erica

chapter one

Researching Legislative Intent

A. WHY RESEARCH LEGISLATIVE INTENT?

Finding the intent behind a legislative provision is an important part of the process of researching statutory interpretation. The judicial interpretation of the meaning or intent of a few words in a statute can change the outcome of a case and affect someone's life and legal rights.[1] Knowing how to work with and research statutes and the intent behind them will help lawyers become better in the courtroom and help judges make appropriate decisions.

B. DEFINING TERMS IN LEGISLATIVE INTENT

Librarians, judges, and lawyers often use the term "legislative history," but with very little consistency. They could be using one of three meanings. The first could be tracking a piece of legislation back in time to find when a section was added or amended and what those additions or amendments looked like. The second could refer to a collection of all the materials that surround the creation of a piece of legislation, for example, debates and committee reports. And the third could be using

---

1   Stephen F Ross, "Statutory Interpretation in the Courtroom, the Classroom, and Canadian Legal Literature" (1999–2000) 31 *Ottawa Law Review* 39.

the term generically to mean both tracing legislation back in time and finding the materials surrounding its creation.

Peter Hogg describes the common understanding of the term legislative history as

> [t]he term "legislative history" does not have a precise meaning . . . . I use the term to mean the documentary evidence of the events that occurred during the drafting and enactment of a statute. It may include the following elements:
>
> 1. the report of a royal commission or law reform commission or parliamentary committee recommending that a statute be enacted;
> 2. a government policy paper (whether called a white paper, green paper, budget paper or whatever) recommending that a statute be enacted;
> 3. a report or study produced outside government which existed at the time of the enactment of the statute and was relied upon by the government that introduced the legislation;
> 4. earlier versions of the statute, either before or after its introduction into Parliament or the Legislature;
> 5. statements by ministers or members of Parliament and testimony of expert witnesses before a parliamentary committee charged with studying the bill; and
> 6. speeches in the Parliament or Legislature when the bill is being debated.[2]

Using the term legislative history as an all-encompassing term to describe both the evolution of a statute and the materials that went into its drafting can be confusing for legal researchers. In *Sullivan on the Construction of Statutes*, Ruth Sullivan provides clear, authoritative, and useful definitions that distinguish legislative evolution and legislative history as separate terms, each with a precise meaning and research process. It is these definitions that we will be using as the foundation for our discussion and that we will rely on to describe the process of researching legislative intent.

---

2   Peter Hogg, *Constitutional Law of Canada*, 5th ed (Toronto: Thomson Reuters, 2016) (loose-leaf updated 2016, release 1) at 60.1(b) 1–2.

Legislative evolution is "the evolution of a legislative provision consist-[ing] of successive enacted versions from inception to the version in place when the relevant facts occur."[3]

Legislative history includes "everything that is related to [a statute's] conception, preparation and passage … from the earliest proposals to royal assent. This includes reports of law reform commissions; … departmental and committee studies and recommendations; proposals and memoranda submitted to Cabinet; the remarks of the minister responsible for the bill; materials tabled or otherwise brought to the attention of the legislature during the legislative process, such as explanatory notes, materials published by the government during the legislative process, such as explanatory papers or press releases, legislative committee hearings and reports; debates …; the records of motions to amend the bill; regulatory impact analysis statements; and more. It also includes the record of previous attempts to enact similar or identical legislation that died on the order paper."[4]

Both the legislative evolution and the legislative history of a statute are intertwined and used by lawyers and judges to determine the intention of Parliament. The evolution of a piece of legislation or a particular legislative enactment will point the researcher to the appropriate time period to investigate in order to gather relevant legislative history. Legislative evolution has a more linear research process, while legislative history research is more challenging.

C. AIDS TO STATUTORY INTERPRETATION OTHER THAN LEGISLATIVE INTENT

Legislative intent is just one aspect of statutory interpretation. Although this text will focus on researching legislative intent, it is important to understand all the tools that judges use to interpret statutes. These tools can be described as either intrinsic or extrinsic, depending on their relationship to the text of the statutory provision.

---

3   Ruth Sullivan, *Sullivan on the Construction of Statutes*, 6th ed (Markham, ON: LexisNexis Canada, 2014) at 660 [Sullivan, *Construction*, 6th].
4   *Ibid* at 679.

1) Intrinsic Aids to Statutory Interpretation

Researchers should be aware that indications of legislative intent may be found in intrinsic aids that appear in the text of the statute or regulation. These might include titles, preambles, marginal notes, headings, punctuation, and schedules.[5] Judges will look at these intrinsic aids first for indications of legislative intent. If they are unable to discern intent from these aids, then they look outward to the extrinsic aids listed below as their next step.

2) Extrinsic Aids to Statutory Interpretation

Extrinsic aids are generally defined as any source beyond the actual text of a statute or regulation that can be used to aid statutory interpretation.[6] Legislative evolution and legislative history are the two types of extrinsic aids to statutory interpretation that are the focus of this guide. It is also important to know that legislative evolution and legislative history materials are known as extrinsic aids in the process of statutory interpretation. Even though legislative evolution refers to textual changes within a statute or regulation itself, Sullivan still classifies legislative evolution as an extrinsic aid to interpretation and we will do the same in this text.[7]

There are other important extrinsic aids that require their own research techniques that we will not cover in this text but that still may influence a judge's decision making:

- *judicial interpretation*, which relies on cases that have previously considered particular statutes, these cases are an important aid to statutory interpretation as well as a cornerstone of the common law legal system;[8]
- *administrative interpretation*, which looks at administrative guidelines such as Canada Revenue Agency Interpretation

---

5 Pierre-André Côté, *The Interpretation of Legislation in Canada*, 4th ed (Carswell: Toronto, 2011).

6 Sullivan, *Construction*, 6th, above note 3 at 657.

7 *Ibid* at 661.

8 *Ibid* at 714.

Bulletins, or other administrative (not judicial) interpretations of statutes;[9] and finally

- *scholarly interpretation*, which relies on guidance from scholarly texts or articles.[10]

D. STATUTORY INTERPRETATION GENERALLY

When interpreting the meaning of a statute, it is the judge's responsibility to discover and give effect to the intention of the legislature as applied to the facts of a particular case.[11] As noted above, sometimes this meaning is clear and can be discerned by simply reading the text of an Act or by interpreting the words without recourse to examining legislative intent. In order to make this process relatively consistent there are a number of components of statutory interpretation, called "rules," that are used for judicial analysis.[12] These aids to statutory interpretation supply lawyers and judges with a vocabulary that enables them to formulate arguments and determine case outcomes.[13] Although this book is focused on researching legislative intent, legislative intent is only one facet of statutory interpretation and is generally used only if intention cannot be discerned by looking at the intrinsic sources of statutory interpretation.

E. RULES OF STATUTORY INTERPRETATION

Although all jurisdictions have interpretation Acts that provide guidelines as to how statutes should be interpreted generally,[14] there are additional principles and approaches that have been defined in the common law.[15] These rules of statutory interpretation are not set

---

9   *Ibid* at 704.

10   *Ibid* at 701.

11   Ruth Sullivan, *Statutory Interpretation*, 3d ed (Toronto: Irwin Law, 2016) at 31 [Sullivan, *Interpretation*].

12   *Ibid* at 40–48.

13   *Ibid* at 30.

14   Gerald L Gall, *The Canadian Legal System*, 5th ed (Toronto: Thomson Carswell, 2004) at 479.

15   Sullivan, *Interpretation*, above note 11 at 31.

in stone, but are more like techniques, principles, or approaches that judges use to interpret the meaning of a statute. Statutory interpretation is a subjective process.[16] Different judges use different approaches that may result in different interpretations, as they are guided but not bound by the following rules or principles. In Canada, *Sullivan on the Construction of Statutes* provides a detailed overview on the use and application of these principles. Here is a brief overview of common approaches to statutory interpretation:

Ordinary meaning: Ordinary meaning, in the words of Gonthier J, is "the natural meaning which appears when the provision is simply read through."[17] Sullivan notes that ordinary meaning is often used inconsistently and confused with dictionary meaning or literal meaning, among other things. Simply put, ordinary meaning is the reader's first impression of the meaning.[18]

Technical and legal meaning: Technical terms are specialized words used in particular fields such as science and medicine, or in the case of legal meaning, the field of law. When specialized technical words are used in a legislative provision many interpretive issues can arise, for instance the words may have both technical and ordinary meaning and may be read differently by the specialist as opposed to the general public. Generally, the courts have favoured an ordinary meaning rather than a technical meaning.[19]

Bilingual and bijural meaning: In Canada legislation is drafted in both French and English and both versions are official. Citizens are able to rely on either version but neither version is paramount. There are interpretive principles that have developed in the courts to address and resolve bilingual issues in legislation. Similarly, there are principles that apply to issues surrounding the two types of legal systems

---

16   Gall, above note 14 at 479.
17   *Canadian Pacific Airlines Ltd v Canadian Air Line Pilots Association*, [1993] 3 SCR 724 at 735, cited in Sullivan, *Construction*, 6th, above note 3 at 30.
18   Sullivan, *Construction*, 6th, *ibid*.
19   *Ibid*.

in Canada — the civil system in Quebec and the common law system for the rest of Canada.[20]

Original meaning: In regular legislation the original meaning rule seeks to provide guidance on understanding a legislative provision in accordance with the original legislators' understanding of the legislation.[21] Used on its own, original meaning may be an issue, because taken to its extreme the original meaning approach may discourage courts from interpreting a statute for modern circumstances.[22]

Plausible meaning: In statutory analysis, when departing from the ordinary meaning and looking to the intentions of a legislature, the interpretation may only be adopted if the statute's words are "reasonably capable of bearing" the particular meaning.[23]

Textual analysis: A textualist approach to statutory interpretation considers the text of the legislation above any external aids. This approach also acknowledges that legislation has its own set of conventions, its own style and prose, so it also provides guidance to courts on these legislative conventions.[24]

Purposive analysis: This type of analysis is favoured by Canadian courts today and is a cornerstone of Driedger's modern principle of statutory interpretation. A purposive approach to statutory interpretation looks at the underlying purpose of the legislation. This approach does not require that there is ambiguity or absurdity in the legislation that is being examined; it can be used in any case. Most interpretation Acts in Canada promote a purposive interpretation;[25] the federal *Interpretation Act*, for example, directs courts to give every enactment "such fair,

---

20 *Ibid.*

21 *Ibid.*

22 Cameron Hutchison, *The Fundamentals of Statutory Interpretation* (Markham, ON: LexisNexis, 2018) at 34 [Hutchison, *Fundamentals*].

23 *R v McIntosh*, [1995] 1 SCR 686 cited in Sullivan, *Construction*, 6th, above note 3 at 192.

24 Sullivan, *Construction*, 6th, *ibid.*

25 See, for example, *Legislation Act, 2006*, SO 2006, c 21, Schedule F, ss 46–50 or the federal *Interpretation Act*, RSC 1985, c I-21.

large and liberal construction and interpretation as best ensures the attainment of its objects."[26]

Consequential analysis: If, after applying a legislative provision to a particular case, the outcome is thought to be against the norms of justice or not reasonable, it is called absurdity. Consequential analysis developed to assist courts with how to treat an absurd outcome. This type of analysis is often discussed with the "golden rule," which is the presumption that an absurd outcome is not desirable.[27]

Entire context: Another important aspect of Driedger's modern principle is that the words of the statute being interpreted must be looked at in their entire context. The entire context includes the whole statute, the legal context, and external context. The entire context rule provides guidance to courts on how to assess and interpret these different aspects of context.[28]

F. DRIEDGER'S MODERN PRINCIPLE OF STATUTORY INTERPRETATION

The Supreme Court of Canada has frequently quoted Elmer A Driedger's modern principle when identifying their preferred approach to statutory interpretation.[29] According to the modern principle:

> Today there is only one principle or approach, namely, the words of an Act are to be read in their entire context and in their grammatical and ordinary sense harmoniously with the scheme of the Act, the object of the Act, and *the intention of Parliament* [emphasis added].[30]

In the context of Driedger's modern principle, legislative intent or "the intention of Parliament" can be defined as "the meaning the legislature

---

26 *Ibid*, s 11.

27 Sullivan, *Construction*, 6th, above note 3.

28 Sullivan, *Interpretation*, above note 11.

29 Stéphane Beaulac & Pierre-André Côté, "Driedger's Modern Principle at the Supreme Court of Canada: Interpretation, Justification, Legitimization" (2006) 40 *Revue juridique Thémis* 131.

30 Elmer A Driedger, *The Construction of Statutes*, 2d ed (Toronto: Butterworths, 1983) at 67 [Driedger].

wished to embody in the legislative text or the purpose it sought to accomplish by enacting the legislation."[31] Since the Supreme Court of Canada adopted the modern principle as the appropriate standard for statutory interpretation, courts are more frequently referring to legislative intent as one of the tools in their decision-making repertoire.[32]

The modern principle establishes a hierarchy under which these rules should be applied, starting with the textual and then moving on to the purposive if textual analysis is not sufficient. Driedger further fleshes out the purposive aspect of interpretation by defining the object of the Act as the "Social Objective,"[33] the scheme of the Act is the "draftsman's legislative scheme"[34] or "framework or outline of the individual statutory provisions that are required to give effect to the social, economic or other plan,"[35] and the intention of parliament being "the ideas that are embodied in the words of the Act."[36]

Today in Canada, the modern principle of statutory interpretation is known as a "sound methodology of interpretation that balances multiple legitimate inputs relevant to a determination of legislative intent, and where necessary the rational development of the law."[37]

G. HISTORY OF THE RULES OF STATUTORY INTERPRETATION

As noted above, the rules of statutory interpretation are not set in stone but are principles and guidelines established in common law and, as such, have come into and gone out of favour over time. For

31   Sullivan, *Interpretation*, above note 11 at 32.
32   John James Magyar, "The Evolution of Hansard Use at the Supreme Court of Canada: A Comparative Study in Statutory Interpretation" (2012) 33:3 *Statute Law Review* 363.
33   Driedger, above note 30 at 54.
34   *Ibid.*
35   *Ibid* at 53.
36   *Ibid* at 54.
37   Hutchison, *Fundamentals*, above note 22 at 35. Hutchison examines the modern principle and suggests refinements for its use in Canada: when two or more interpretations appear to justify legislative intent, Hutchison suggests courts should use a contextual approach to resolve the ambiguity or difference in interpretations.

instance, from the early eighteenth century until the late twentieth century, judges in England and Canada as well as in other commonwealth countries were not able to consider legislative intent or legislative history when interpreting the meaning of a statute; aids to interpretation, like *Hansard*, were not considered admissible. This rule, known as the exclusionary rule, required that judges examine the meaning of an enactment based on its text alone. But, by the late twentieth century, the exclusionary rule was dropped in Britain and Canada. To understand the changes that occurred in statutory interpretation it is necessary to first look into the history of the exclusionary rule.

H. THE HISTORY OF THE EXCLUSIONARY RULE

Legislative intent was barred from consideration by the courts in England for over 200 years. The exclusionary rule, like other rules of interpretation, is not explicitly set out in a statute but rather was a common law principle established and upheld by caselaw. It is not even *the* exclusionary rule—there are a number of exclusionary rules (often relating to evidence). Under the exclusionary rule, "the legislative history of an enactment was not permissible to assist in interpretation"[38] and "could not be used as direct evidence of legislative intent."[39] This principle was followed by the courts in the United Kingdom (UK) from its first articulation in 1769[40] until 1992.

In 1992, the UK House of Lords, rather controversially, decided that if the meaning of a legislative provision is ambiguous then the court can consider statements made by legislators in either House with respect to that provision as an aid to interpreting its meaning.[41]

In Canada, as in England, the exclusionary rule was followed for many years. But by the late 1990s it was put to bed and legislative history was finally allowed to be admitted as evidence of legislative intent

---

38   Ruth Sulllivan, *Sullivan on the Construction of Statutes*, 5th ed (Markham, ON: LexisNexis Canada, 2008) at 594 [Sullivan, *Construction*, 5th].

39   *Ibid.*

40   *Millar v Taylor* (1769), 98 ER 201 [*Millar*].

41   *Pepper (Inspector of Taxes) v Hart*, [1993] AC 593 (HL) [*Pepper*].

in Canadian courts. The move away from adhering to this rule was more evolutionary[42] in Canada than it was in the United Kingdom. It all began in 1976 when the Supreme Court's Chief Justice Bora Laskin consulted a variety of extrinsic sources, including legislative history, when determining the constitutionality of the *Anti-Inflation Act*. A number of subsequent constitutional cases confirmed this approach. After the *Charter of Rights and Freedoms* came into force in 1984, a number of cases referred to legislative history as a means of interpreting a variety of *Charter* provisions. And, finally, in 1998, Iaccobuci J explicitly articulated the value of using legislative history, *Hansard* in particular, as a means of statutory interpretation when considering the meaning of a statute in a non-constitutional case.[43]

1) The Battle of the Booksellers: *Millar v Taylor*

The story starts in England in the 1730s and spans a period of thirty years. These years were known to some as the "battle of the booksellers,"[44] and the case of *Millar v Taylor*[45] was the culmination of many years of litigation, all hinging on the meaning of certain provisions of the 1710 *Statute of Anne* or *Copyright Act 1710*. Under the *Statute of Anne*, the term of copyright on books published before April 1710 expired after a period of twenty-one years and those published after 1710 expired after a period of fourteen years, if and only if the title was registered with the Company of Stationers.[46]

Despite having a clearly defined term of copyright in the *Statute of Anne*, London booksellers claimed that copyright was a common law right that pre-existed the statute and thus could not be limited by legislation. There were a number of Scottish printers who insisted, on the other hand, that when the term of copyright expired these works

---

42 Stéphane Beaulac, "Parliamentary Debates in Statutory Interpretation: A Question of Admissibility or of Weight?" (1998) 43 *McGill Law Journal* 287 [Beaulac, "Debates"].

43 Sullivan, *Construction*, 6th, above note 3.

44 Thomas B Morris Jr, "The Origins of the *Statute of Anne*" (1961–62) 12 *Copyright Law Symposium* 222.

45 *Millar*, above note 40.

46 *Statute of Anne*, 1710 (UK), 8 Anne, c 19.

were in the public domain and could be reprinted at will. At first the Scottish printers produced inexpensive and unauthorized (according to the Londoners) versions of English books to sell only in the Scottish market and overseas. The issue came to a head, however, when Alexander Donaldson opened a bookshop in London, taking on the London booksellers directly by selling cheap reprints for 30 to 50 percent less than the usual London prices.

The London booksellers had no alternative but to respond forcefully to this incursion into their territory and the battle was on in earnest. Andrew Millar, a London bookseller, took up the fight. He had purchased the rights to publish James Thomson's *The Seasons* in 1729, and when the copyright term expired, a competing bookseller named Robert Taylor began selling reprints of the work. Taking up the argument that copyright was a common law right and could not be limited by statute and with no less a luminary advocate than William Blackstone, Millar took Taylor on in the courts. Sadly, Millar's health was failing, and he died before the final decision was made, but nevertheless the court found in Millar's favour and the common law right of copyright in perpetuity was confirmed.[47]

That decision didn't last for long, and in 1774 the common law right to copyright in perpetuity was extinguished by the Court of Appeal. What did last, though, was the far-reaching and unintended consequence of the judge's decision that resulted in the exclusionary rule.

So, the question begs to be asked, and I am sure you are wondering, how did a copyright dispute influence statutory interpretation in such a significant and far-reaching way?

2) Birth of the Exclusionary Rule

The answer lies in Taylor's lawyer's argument that, during the process of the passage of the bill, there were a number of amendments at the committee stage, the preamble was changed, and even the title of the bill was changed, and that "[Parliament] intended to take away

---

47   *Millar*, above note 40.

or declare there was no property [in copyright] at the common law."[48] Justice Willes would have none of that and responded to Taylor's lawyer's argument with the following:

> The sense and the meaning of an Act of Parliament must be collected from what it says when passed into a law; and not from the history of changes it underwent in the house where it took its rise. [49]

And that simple statement became the exclusionary rule with its profound influence on statutory interpretation for two centuries.

So, what was Willes J's reasoning for this ruling? As he stated in explanation, "[t]hat history is not known to the other house or to the Sovereign."[50] His fundamental reasoning was practical; there was no legal or reliable record of the debates at the time and so there really was no way of telling what Parliament meant when it made those changes to the bill.

I. THE BILLS OF RIGHTS AND PARLIAMENTARY PRIVILEGE

It makes sense here to digress a bit and talk about the history of the publication of Parliamentary Debates in the United Kingdom. Until 1771 publication of debates was considered to be a breach of parliamentary privilege. Parliamentary privilege had been encoded in the 1688 Bill of Rights,[51] which stated, "That the Freedome of Speech and Debates or Proceedings in Parlyament ought not to be impeached or questioned in any Court or Place out of Parlyament." Or, as stated in modern English, "That the freedom of speech and debates or proceedings in Parliament ought not to be impeached or questioned in any court or place out of Parliament."[52] In fact, in 1738, Parliament passed an official resolution forbidding publication of parliamentary debates in newspapers or any other publication:

---

48 *Ibid* at 217.
49 *Ibid.*
50 *Ibid.*
51 *Bill of Rights* (UK) 1688, 1 Will and Mar, c 2.
52 *Ibid*, art 9.

That it is a high indignity to, and Breach of Privilege of the House, for
any Person to presume to give, in written or printed Newspapers, any
Accounts or Minutes of the Debates or other Proceedings thereof,
or and Committee thereof—That upon discovery … the House will
proceed against the offenders with utmost Severity.[53]

1) Public Interest in Parliament

But public interest in what was happening in Parliament was very
strong. Some reporters circumvented this resolution by reporting
parliamentary proceedings as the debates of fictional organizations
with names like The *Proceedings of the Lower Room of the Robin Hood Society*,[54] but others risked prosecution by openly publishing the proceedings. The issue finally came to a head in 1771 when Brass Crosby, the
Lord Mayor of London and Chief Magistrate who was also a radical
politician, supported the campaign against the suppression of the
publication of parliamentary proceedings. Crosby was brought in
front of Parliament for failing to prosecute John Miller, the printer
of the *London Evening Post* (not the same Millar as above), for publishing reports of various parliamentary proceedings. Crosby was handed
over to the Tower of London to await trial, but when he came to trial
no judge would hear his case and he was released.

The issue of parliamentary privilege was seen as representative of
the conflict between the common people and the elites. During the
House of Commons debate as to whether Crosby should be sent to the
Tower, MP Richard Whitworth claimed "that this issue was the most
important crisis that the house had ever seen …. The people strug-
gling for the laws of the land and their liberties at large, and the representatives of those same people, from who they derive their whole
authority contending for that assumed power of unlimited indefinite

---

53   UK, *Journal of the House of Commons*, vol 23 at 148 (13 April 1738), online: https://
     books.google.ca/books?id=kBJDAAAAcAAJ&dq=journals%20of%20the%20
     house%20of%20commons%20vols%2023&pg=PA148#v=onepage&q&f=false.
54   Commonwealth *Hansard* Editors Association, "Story of Hansard," online: www.
     web.archive.org/web/20060505084502/www.commonwealth-hansard.org/chea_
     story.asp.

privilege and jurisdiction."[55] He foresaw the destruction of the country, "the commons fighting on one hand for its privileges and the people, the law of the land, on the other."[56] The 1770s were revolutionary times, the American Revolution was just a few years away and the French followed shortly thereafter, so this radical language was not surprising given the tenor of the times.

2) Parliamentary Proceedings Allowed to Be Published

As you can see from Whitworth's rhetoric, the publication of parliamentary debates was considered to be an important requirement for a democratic society. And democracy won the day; after Crosby was released from the Tower, no further attempts were made to block the publication of parliamentary proceedings.[57] Apocryphally, the expression "as bold as brass" is said to be inspired by Brass Crosby's actions.

Once the publication ban was lifted, reports of parliamentary proceedings were often published in newspapers. At the beginning, reporters were banned from taking notes and had to produce their reports from memory. This prohibition ended in 1783 in the House of Commons and soon after in the House of Lords.[58] Early parliamentary reporters included the writers Samuel Taylor Coleridge for the *Morning Post* in the early 1800s and Charles Dickens, writing for the *Mirror of Parliament* in the early 1830s.[59]

---

55 UK, HC, *Cobbetts's Parliamentary History of England*, vol 17, col 158 (27 March 1771), online: https://books.google.ca/books/about/Cobbett_s_Parliamentary_History_of_Engla.html?id=Wpg9AAAAcAAJ&redir_esc=y.

56 *Ibid.*

57 Andrew Struan, "History of Hansard," online: *Parliamentary Discourse* https://web.archive.org/web/20150713102223/parldisc.jiscinvolve.org/wp/2011/06/03/history-of-hansard.

58 UK, Parliament, "Official Report: Living Heritage — Communicating Parliamentary Business," online: www.parliament.uk/about/living-heritage/evolutionofparliament/parliamentwork/communicating/overview/officialreport.

59 Nikki Hessell, *Literary Authors, Parliamentary Reporters: Johnson, Coleridge, Hazlitt, Dickens* (Cambridge: Cambridge University Press, 2012).

J.   HANSARD

In 1803 William Cobbett began publication of the *Parliamentary Debates* and later *Cobbett's Parliamentary Debates* as a standalone publication, but he was unable to make a financial success of it. Eventually, he sold the contract to printer Thomas Hansard and in due course the debates became known colloquially as *Hansard*. The early debates were not completely reliable as they were cobbled together from newspaper reports and other sources, and so in January 1909, the Commons took over producing *Hansard*, which was now called the "Official Report." Despite the name change, *Hansard* was still colloquially referred to as *Hansard* in the United Kingdom and in some Commonwealth countries, and in 1943 the name *Hansard* was reinstated on the title page of the Official Report.[60]

1)   *Hansard* in Canada

The history of the publication of parliamentary debates in Canada is less dramatic. Prior to Confederation, in Upper Canada, although there was some initial resistance to having the reports of the debates published, they were reported nevertheless in the newspapers of the time. These were sometimes collected and published as the "Scrapbook Hansards." Shortly after Confederation, in 1880, *Hansard* became an official publication with a team of reporters responsible for accurately recording the debates in Parliament.[61]

So, you can see that back in 1769, Willes J had a very good reason for excluding parliamentary debates as evidence of legislative intent at the time of his decision. But, the next question to be asked is, if the debates were now available with the blessing of Parliament and were in fact an official parliamentary publication, then why was the exclusionary rule upheld for so many years?

---

60   Struan, above note 57.

61   Hansard Association of Canada, "Hansard History," online: www.hansard.ca/ Hansard%20History_cont.pdf.

K.   ARGUMENTS AGAINST CONSIDERING LEGISLATIVE INTENT IN STATUTORY INTERPRETATION

The common law upheld and expanded the reasons for the exclusionary rule from 1769 to the mid-twentieth century in both the United Kingdom and Canada and in other jurisdictions: There were a number of reasons given for this over the years in both caselaw and in academic commentary.

1)   Rule of Law

Critics argue that the inclusion of legislative history could be considered contrary to rule of law principles. In particular, that "the legislator puts out a text on which citizens and their advisers rely"[62] An important principle of the rule of law is that the law should be available and clear to everyone. Sullivan writes, "the law must be set out in advance with sufficient clarity so that subjects can know what is expected of them and of others, can achieve a measure of security, and can plan for the future."[63] It follows that the text of a statute is the law and anything said about the statute, like the words in a debate, is not law.

It is hard to argue with this assertion on the surface. But language itself is not always clear. All readers bring their own assumptions and background to the text and may perceive the text differently.[64] Proponents of the older "plain meaning rule" advocated that legislative intent should only be considered in statutory interpretation if a statute is found to be ambiguous. But Driedger's "modern principle" and Sullivan's works clarify that, today, in order to determine whether a provision is ambiguous one must compare the wording of a statute to the intent and see if the former clearly expresses the latter.[65] It appears that determining the meaning of a statute, for the rule of law to prevail, may require one to look beyond the text of the statute.

---

62   Francis Bennion, "*Hansard*—Help or Hindrance? A Draftsman's View of *Pepper v Hart*" (1993) 14:3 *Statute Law Review* 149 at 155.

63   Sullivan, *Interpretation*, above note 11 at 34.

64   Sullivan, *Construction*, 5th, above note 38 at 18–19.

65   Sullivan, *Interpretation*, above note 11 at 241; *Bell ExpressVu Limited Partnership v Rex*, 2002 SCC 42.

2) Parole Evidence Rule

Similar to the rule of law principle discussed above, the parole evidence rule, first articulated by Byles J in 1859 in *Earl of Shrewsbury v Scott*, argues that since *Hansard* were transcripts of parliamentary debates, to admit them into evidence would be giving priority to spoken evidence that can be considered unreliable[66] over that of the formal "records" of the legislature, which include Acts of Parliament that are "authentic beyond all matter of contradiction."[67] As *Hansard* records are now allowed in the courts as evidence of legislative intent, the question is no longer whether they should be considered but how much weight they should be given in informing a judge's decision.[68] As Sopinka J ruled in *R v Morgentaler*, judges must exercise caution when evaluating the weight and reliability of such evidence:

> The main criticism of such evidence has been that it cannot represent the "intent" of the legislature, an incorporeal body, but that is equally true of other forms of legislative history. Provided that the court remains mindful of the limited reliability and weight of Hansard evidence, it should be admitted as relevant to both the background and the purpose of legislation.[69]

3) Parliamentary Sovereignty

Another important principle in law is parliamentary sovereignty: the idea that legislation as enacted by the elected governing body is paramount. It may appear to some that a judge who refers to *Hansard*, and the legislative intent of a statute, is going beyond the law as enacted by Parliament, and that they are making their own law, even flouting the rule of law and parliamentary sovereignty. Historically these arguments have played out in commonwealth countries, causing different

---

66   Beaulac, "Debates," above note 42.

67   William Allen Jowitt, *Dictionary of English Law*, 1st ed, (London: Sweet and Maxwell, 1959) at 1487, cited in Bennion, above note 62; *Shrewsbury v Scott* (1859), 6 CBNS 1 at 213.

68   Beaulac, "Debates," above note 42.

69   *R v Morgentaler*, [1993] 3 SCR 463 [*Morgentaler*].

rules to go in and out of favour. Today in Canada the courts have put this argument to rest by adopting the liberal, pragmatic, and purposive approach found in the modern principle.

4) Members Do Not Speak for the Legislature

Another argument in favour of the exclusionary rule is that no individual can speak for the legislature as a whole; they can only speak for themselves or the party they represent.[70] Further, the speakers might be "ill-informed"[71] or their ideas might be "distorted by partisan allegiance."[72] Generally, however, debates are focused on the words of the minister or member who is responsible for explaining and defending the government's stand on a particular issue. A bill's passage is based on each member's understanding and response to the government's position.[73]

5) Access to Justice

It has been argued that aids to interpreting statutes, like *Hansard* and other legislative documents, are not easy to find or accessible to the general public. Citizens should be able to rely on the text of a statute that is readily available rather than needing to consult with additional "less accessible texts"[74] for additional understanding of the meaning of the law. The difficulty in accessing this material leads to practical issues that need to be taken into consideration when involved in researching legislative history. Adding legislative history to the mix adds complexity, time, and cost to the process of doing legal research.[75] As one judge noted, "it would be difficult for practitioners, and by extension the public, to carry out effective and reliable research and that researching *Hansard* on a particular point of

---

70   Sullivan, *Construction*, 5th, above note 38; *Gosselin v The King* (1903), 33 SCR 255.
71   Sullivan, *Construction*, 5th, above note 38 at 597.
72   *Ibid.*
73   *Ibid* at 598.
74   *Ibid* at 597.
75   Bennion, above note 62.

interpretation requires a particular skill set and great deal of time and expense."[76] Our answer to that one, of course, is that librarians already have that skill set and law librarians, in particular, are experts in all aspects of legal research and are willing and able to help.

Furthermore, resources, training, and research guides are needed to help deepen and broaden people's understanding of researching legislative intent and working with statutes. This understanding of the process of researching legislative evolution and legislative histories would help legal researchers and members of the public to locate all the materials required to make a persuasive argument.[77] Today, parliamentary materials are becoming more accessible as each jurisdiction in Canada has placed materials on the web to aid in this research. We argue that for all citizens to have access to justice and for the rule of law to prevail there should also be an understanding of the importance of the legislative process, and how to build a legislative evolution and a legislative history. Providing free access to the resources required to research legislative evolution and history goes a long way to overcoming this concern. As Lord Griffiths J noted in *Pepper (Inspector of Taxes) v Hart*, "I cannot agree with the view that consulting Hansard will add so greatly to the cost of litigation, that on this ground alone we should refuse to do so. Modern technology greatly facilitates the recall and display of material held centrally."[78]

L. WHAT CHANGED AFTER 200 YEARS OF THE EXCLUSIONARY RULE?

1) *Pepper (Inspector of Taxes) v Hart*

In the United Kingdom, the end of the exclusionary rule came quite suddenly in 1992. In the case of *Pepper (Inspector of Taxes) v Hart*, the House of Lords, after a great deal of discussion, chose to admit the

---

76   *Beswick v Beswick*, [1967] UKHL 2.

77   Lee Akazaki, "Accidental Mentor: Tip 1984: Dig up the Past for Better Legislative Interpretation" (11 March 2013), online (blog): *Canadian Lawyer Magazine* www. canadianlawyermag.com/4563/Tip-1984-Dig-up-the-past-for-better-legislative-interpretation.html.

78   *Pepper*, above note 41 at 617–18.

use of legislative history in cases where the text of the legislation is ambiguous. Looking at the issue of parliamentary privilege under Article 9 of the *Bill of Rights*, Lord Browne-Wilkinson held that:

> the plain meaning of article 9, viewed against the historical background in which it was enacted, was to ensure that Members of Parliament were not subjected to any penalty, civil or criminal for what they said and were able, contrary to the previous assertions of the Stuart monarchy, to discuss what they, as opposed to the monarch, chose to have discussed. Relaxation of the rule will not involve the courts in criticising what is said in Parliament. The purpose of looking at Hansard will not be to construe the words used by the Minister but to give effect to the words used so long as they are clear. Far from questioning the independence of Parliament and its debates, the courts would be giving effect to what is said and done there.[79]

And in doing so effectively ended the use of the exclusionary rule in English courts.

2)   What Changed in Canada?

For the purposes of this text, we are going to concentrate on what changed in Canada. Canadian jurists and academics have supported the exclusionary rule in their rulings and writings; even as recently as 1961, in *Attorney General of Canada v The Reader's Digest Association (Canada) Ltd*,[80] when the Supreme Court cited *Millar v Taylor* and invoked the exclusionary rule in order to disallow the use of *Hansard* evidence.

The trend away from the exclusionary rule in Canada began with constitutional cases. One of the earliest was the *Inflation Act* reference of 1976,[81] in which the Supreme Court was asked to determine whether the *Anti-Inflation Act* was *ultra vires* under the *Constitution Act, 1867*. In order to determine the answer, the Court looked at white papers, bulletins of the bureau of statistics, studies by professors, a speech by

---

79   *Ibid* at 638.
80   *Attorney General of Canada v The Reader's Digest Association (Canada) Ltd*, [1961] SCR 775.
81   *Re: Anti-Inflation Act*, [1976] 2 SCR 373.

the governor of the Bank of Canada, House of Commons Debates, and Standing Committee Debates. As Laskin CJ stated, "I am of the opinion that extrinsic material, bearing on the circumstances in which the legislation was passed, may be considered by the Court in determining whether the legislation rests on a valid constitutional base."[82]

With Laskin CJ having opened the door to the use of extrinsic evidence it was only a matter of time before other judges began to step through it. Finally, with the *Morgentaler* case of 1993, Sopinka J explicitly stated that "Hansard evidence ... should be admitted as relevant to both the background and the purpose of legislation."[83]

Since the passage of the *Charter of Rights and Freedoms* in 1984, there have been a number of cases that have used legislative history and other extrinsic aids in interpreting the meaning of legislation within the context of the *Charter* as well as to interpret the language of the *Charter* itself.[84]

3)   *Rizzo and Rizzo Shoes*

In 1998, the use of the exclusionary rule ended, not just for *Charter* and constitutional cases but for ordinary statutory interpretation as well. It all started with a bankruptcy. Rizzo and Rizzo Shoes was a chain of shoe stores in Ontario that filed for bankruptcy and closed in 1989. All the employees were terminated immediately and paid the wages, commissions, and vacation pay due to them as of the date of the bankruptcy by the trustee. The employees argued that they were owed appropriate termination pay in addition to the pay they received. The trustees argued that since bankruptcy was not the same as dismissal, the employees were not entitled to any sort of severance under the *Employment Standards Act*. This case wound its way slowly through the courts until it eventually reached the Supreme Court of Canada.

---

82   *Ibid* at 391.
83   *Morgentaler*, above note 69 at 484.
84   Sullivan, *Construction*, 5th, above note 38 at 688–89.

M. THE MODERN PRINCIPLE IN THE SUPREME COURT OF CANADA

Justice Iacobucci, in finding for the employees, looked very closely at the termination provisions of the *Employment Standards Act*.[85] In his decision, Iacobucci J noted:

> At the heart of this conflict is an issue of statutory interpretation. Consistent with the findings of the Court of Appeal, the plain meaning of the words of the provisions here in question appears to restrict the obligation to pay termination and severance pay to those employers who have actively terminated the employment of their employees. At first blush, bankruptcy does not fit comfortably into this interpretation. However, with respect, I believe this analysis is incomplete.[86]

He then went on to quote Driedger's modern principle:

> Today there is only one principle or approach, namely, the words of an Act are to be read in their entire context and in their grammatical and ordinary sense harmoniously with the scheme of the Act, the object of the Act, and *the intention of Parliament*.[87]

He subsequently examined statements made by the Minister of Labour recorded in Ontario's *Hansard*, specifically on the termination provisions of the *Employment Standards Act*, citing Sopinka J in the *Morgentaler*[88] case as his justification for doing so. And thus, the exclusionary rule was put to bed forever.

Justice Iacobucci's use of *Hansard* evidence in *Rizzo & Rizzo Shoes* has subsequently been described as a "model"[89] use that should serve

---

85 *Employment Standards Act*, RSO 1970, c 147, s 13(2); *Employment Standards Act*, 1974, SO 1974, c 112, s 40(7); *Employment Standards Act*, RSO 1980, c 137, ss 7(5) [rep & sub 1986, c 51, s 2], 40(1) [rep & sub 1987, c 30, s 4(1)], 40(7), 40a(1) [rep & sub *ibid*, s 5(1)]; *Employment Standards Amendment Act*, 1981, SO 1981, c 22, s 2.

86 *Rizzo & Rizzo Shoes Ltd (Re)*, [1998] 1 SCR 27 at para 20 [*Rizzo*].

87 Driedger, above note 30, cited in *Rizzo*, above note 86 at para 21 [emphasis added].

88 *Morgentaler*, above note 69.

89 Graham Steele, "'The Frailties of Hansard Evidence Are Many': The Use of House of Assembly Debates in Nova Scotia Courts, 2004–2017" (2015) 9 *Journal of Parliamentary and Political Law* 499 at 499 [Steele, "Frailties"].

as an exemplar for the use of *Hansard* evidence in the courts. In this model:

- Only the sponsoring minister [who can be assumed to be speaking for parliament] is cited.
- The quotations are brief.
- The quotations support an interpretation reached by other means.[90]

N. USE OF LEGISLATIVE INTENT IN CANADIAN COURTS TODAY

Rizzo & Rizzo Shoes is not the end of the story in Canada. The use of legislative evolution and legislative history in the Canadian courts as a means to establish legislative intent is a relatively recent phenomenon and consequently is a growing area of legal research.

When we think of materials that go into a legislative history we think primarily of bills, debates (*Hansard*), committee materials, and regulatory impact analysis statements. These documents form the core of a legislative history. To find them, the researcher must begin by tracing the evolution of the statute back from its current formulation to its first iteration and every iteration in between. After the evolution is laid out, the researcher then builds a legislative history by identifying all materials that went into its making. While the materials named have been clearly accepted as sources of legislative history, the complete list of sources is still in flux as the courts still have yet to clarify the limits of use of each source;[91] lawyers are pushing the boundaries for more aids to be accepted.

To demonstrate how Canadian courts are treating the use of these extrinsic aids, we can look at two studies on the use of *Hansard* (parliamentary debates) in the Supreme Court of Canada. Not long after *Rizzo & Rizzo Shoes* was decided, one of Canada's leading authorities in statutory interpretation, Stephane Beaulac, analyzed how *Hansard*

---

90 *Ibid* at 507–8.
91 Beaulac, "Debates," above note 42.

was used in Supreme Court of Canada cases in 1999.[92] He found that while *Hansard* was used in judicial decisions, the courts were not consistent in their application, and that some aspects of the use of *Hansard* to ascertain legislative intent remained unsettled at that time. Beaulac also contends that the use of *Hansard* in court is no longer a question of admissibility but a question of weight.[93]

Fast forward to 2010. John James Magyar repeated this study of judges' use of *Hansard* as an aid in determining legislative intent in the Supreme Court of Canada.[94] This study found that *Hansard* is no longer regarded as a second-class interpretive tool, and that *Hansard* was used as an interpretive aid even in the absence of ambiguity.

O. CAVEATS TO USING *HANSARD* AS EVIDENCE OF LEGISLATIVE INTENT

Despite the courts' current acceptance of *Hansard* as evidence of legislative intent, researchers should be aware that its use can still be problematic. Recently, former Nova Scotia parliamentarian Graham Steele published a "systematic analysis"[95] of the use of *Hansard* in the Nova Scotia courts between 2004 and 2014 in which he located cases where the judges' interpretation of *Hansard* "goes off in tangents that are interesting, though at times problematic."[96] In one Nova Scotia case, for example, the judge quotes an Ontario appeal case, in which the judge allowed "quotes from testimony from the Justice Minister and one of the minister's senior aides."[97] Steele finds it hard to fathom that an "unelected aide"[98] could be considered to speak for the intention of Parliament even though his statements were recorded in the committee

---

92   Stephane Beaulac, "Recent Developments at the Supreme Court of Canada on the Use of Parliamentary Debates" (2000) 63 *Saskatchewan Law Journal* 581.

93   Beaulac, "Debates," above note 42.

94   Magyar, above note 32; John James Magyar, *Hansard as an Aid to Statutory Interpretation in Canadian Courts from 1999–2010* (LLM Thesis, University of Western Ontario Faculty of Law, 2011) [unpublished].

95   Steele, "Frailties," above note 89 at 499.

96   *Ibid* at 509.

97   *Ibid* at 510, citing *R v Johnson* (2011), 268 CCC (3d) 423 (Ont Ct J).

98   Steele, "Frailties," above note 89 at 510.

Hansards. Even more questionable: the use of statements made by members of the opposition as evidence of legislative intent was allowed in the case of *Hartling v Nova Scotia (Attorney General).*[99] In this particular case the members of the opposition were supporting the minority government but nevertheless could not be considered to be speaking to the intention of Parliament.[100] When researching *Hansard* for evidence of legislative intent it is important to evaluate who is speaking and whether they can truly be speaking for the intention of Parliament.

P. SHOEHORNING: LEGISLATIVE HISTORY MATERIALS BEYOND *HANSARD*

Magyar's study found that in 2010, litigators were making greater effort to dig into the knowledge available to them. In a technique Magyar called "shoehorning,"[101] he describes how Canadian lawyers are using *Hansard* as a shoehorn to bring in more extrinsic aids to assist with determining legislative intent for the purposes of statutory interpretation. When a speech in Parliament discusses a particular report that is then reported in *Hansard*, this report is seen to have a more substantial link to the argument. This phenomenon speaks to *Hansard* itself having more weight as an aid to interpreting legislative intent, as well as the expanding horizons of what may be considered a part of legislative history. Magyar found that in 2010 the Supreme Court of Canada had evolved and matured in the way that it accepted *Hansard* as an interpretive tool. This study shows how it has become more important to know how to research legislative intent in Canada.

Q. USE OF LEGISLATIVE HISTORY MATERIAL IN FOREIGN COURTS

Britain, Australia, and the United States have carved their own path when it comes to using legislative history material as an aid to

---

99　*Ibid*, citing *Hartling v Nova Scotia (Attorney General)* (2009), 314 DLR (4th) 114 (NSCA).
100　*Ibid.*
101　Magyar, above note 32 at 379.

statutory interpretation.[102] As noted above, Britain's landmark case *Pepper (Inspector of Taxes) v Hart* outlined the circumstances for admitting *Hansard* as an aid to interpreting legislative intent in the United Kingdom.

Australia has legislated a purposive approach to statutory interpretation in their federal and state *Interpretation Acts*. As an example, in the federal *Interpretation Act 1901 (Cth)*, sections 15AA and 15AB[103] were amended to specify that particular types of extrinsic aids (*Hansard* at second reading, Law Reform Commission, and royal commissions, for instance) may be used to confirm the ordinary meaning of the text or to determine the meaning when the ordinary meaning of a particular provision would lead to ambiguous or absurd results.[104] Despite these constraints on the use of extrinsic aids in statutory interpretation, Australian law and government libraries recognize the importance of access to government and parliamentary information for legal specialists and the general public alike.[105]

In the United States, the first use of legislative history for statutory interpretation appears to be in 1860.[106] After that, the use of legislative history increased to such an extent that after the 1950s it became the "touchstone of federal statutory interpretation."[107] Materials for locating legislative intent, including links to legislation, the Congressional Record, and committee reports, are available on the congress.gov website[108] and on legal research databases such as LexisNexis and Westlaw, which compile specific topical legislative histories for the legal researcher. The United States Department of Justice library makes

---

102 *Ibid* at 364.

103 *Interpretation Act 1901* (Cth).

104 Gregory P Jones, "Extrinsic Aids in the Law and Australian Libraries" (1990) 21:2 *Australian Academic & Research Libraries* 107 at 112.

105 *Ibid* at 113.

106 *Dubuque & Pacific Railroad Co v Litchfield*, 64 US (23 How) 66 (1859), cited in Beaulac, "Debates," above note 42.

107 John F Manning, "Textualism and Legislative Intent" (2005) 91 *Virginia Law Review* 419.

108 Online: www.congress.gov.

their internally created legislative histories available on their website for general public use.[109]

In recent years, Justice Scalia of the Supreme Court of the United States had seriously criticized the use of legislative history as a way to interpret legislative intent[110] and urged caution regarding the unrestricted use of legislative history. But, as legislative history continues to be widely accepted in the United States, Canadian researchers can use the American experience as an example of the types of materials used and research aids that are possible in a legislative history.

One additional note that illustrates and amplifies the concept of "shoehorning" in the United States: On 6 March 2017, US President Donald Trump signed Executive Order 13780, "Protecting the Nation from Foreign Terrorist Entry into the United States,"[111] which was immediately challenged by the state of Hawaii as unconstitutional on a variety of grounds, including that it violated the First Amendment, which states in part, "Congress shall make no law respecting an establishment of religion, or prohibiting the free exercise thereof."[112] As part of the state's argument, Attorney General Douglas S Chin cited President Trump's campaign promises, statements to the press, and statements made during presidential debates asserting that if he was elected he would impose a "Muslim ban" that would effectively prevent individuals from Muslim countries from entering the United States. This is a very new and interesting interpretation of the idea of legislative intent, and there has been very little analysis or academic study of the idea that election rhetoric can or should be used as an indication of legislative intent as it "may never have been done

---

109　US Department of Justice, "Legislative Histories," online: www.justice.gov/jmd/ ls/legislative-histories.

110　Stephanie Wald, "The Use of Legislative History in Statutory Interpretation Cases in the 1992 U.S. Supreme Court Term; Scalia Rails But Legislative History Remains on Track" (1993) 23 *Southwestern Law Review* 47; Antonin Scalia, "Common Law Courts in a Civil Law System: The Role of United States Federal Courts in Interpreting the Constitution and Laws" (Lecture delivered at the Tanner Lectures on Human Values, Princeton University, 8–9 March 1995), online: tannerlectures.utah.edu/_documents/a-to-z/s/scalia97.pdf.

111　*Executive Order No 13780*, 82 Fed Reg 13209 (9 March 2017).

112　US Const amend I.

before."[113] US District Judge Derrick J Watson accepted this evidence of intent. As he stated:

> The Federal Defendants' arguments, advanced from the very inception of this action, make sense from this perspective — where the "historical context and 'the specific sequence of events leading up to'" the adoption of the challenged Executive Order are as full of religious animus, invective, and obvious pretext as is the record here, it is no wonder that the Government urges the Court to altogether ignore that history and context .... The Court, however, declines to do so.[114]

President Trump subsequently appealed this case to the US Supreme Court in 2018.[115] The admissibility of the types of statements listed above was not challenged by the Supreme Court justices. Justice Sotomayor, in fact, cites a number of President Trump's tweets in her dissenting opinion. She justified their use with the note "According to the White House, President Trump's statements on Twitter are 'official statements.'"[116]

R. RESEARCHING LEGISLATIVE INTENT IN CANADA

Although we know that Canadian courts will accept legislative evolution and legislative history as evidence of legislative intent for the purposes of statutory interpretation, there is a need for further study, as well as for more guidance and resources on the process of researching legislative intent.

As statutory interpretation takes centre stage in the courtroom, law schools are beginning to offer courses on statutory interpretation. This is a relatively recent phenomenon: "North American law schools

---

113 Jeffrey Toobin, "The Courts and President Trump's Words" *The New Yorker* (17 March 2017), online: www.newyorker.com/news/daily-comment/the-courts-and-president-trumps-words.

114 *Hawai'i v Trump*, 245 F Supp 3d 1227 at 1236 (D Hawaii 2017).

115 *Trump v Hawaii*, No 17–965, slip op (USSC 26 June 2018), Sotomayer J dissenting at 9, online: www.supremecourt.gov/opinions/17pdf/17-965_h315.pdf.

116 *Ibid* at 9, n 1.

initially responded to the post-war transformation of our legal system from the common law to an age of statutes by ignoring it."[117] As little as twenty years ago, Canadian law schools still viewed statutes "as intruders upon the purity of the Common law."[118] Slowly, this appears to be changing and Canadian law schools are now offering upper-year courses in statutory interpretation.

Statutes are at the root of the democratic process and they should be open to scrutiny and understanding by everyone in Canada; there is an expectation today that the public can access all the information surrounding a statute. If researching legislative intent is accepted by the courts, then all appropriate resources should be made available to everyone.

1) LEGIS*info*

The Parliament of Canada's website LEGIS*info*[119] does just this, and it is an ideal source for researching legislative intent. It has all of the federal materials surrounding the enactment of a bill: bill status and links to debates and committee, and then it takes the extra step of providing background materials—press releases, reports, legislative summaries and background documents, and even links to previous versions of bills. It is a portal geared towards anyone researching legislative intent, public or specialist alike. The site is clear and cleanly designed. It provides a single point of entry for everything about the history of a statute. The most obvious drawback is that it only starts comprehensively in 2001 and it does not cover historical material in this detail. Still, LEGIS*info* can be described as Canada's best resource for researching federal legislative intent and a standard that other Canadian jurisdictions would do well to follow.[120]

---

117   Ross, above note 1 at 67.

118   Paul Mitchell, "Just Do It! Eskridge's Critical Pragmatic Theory of Statutory Interpretation" (Book review of *Dynamic Statutory Interpretation* by William Eskridge) (1996) 41 *McGill Law Journal* 713 at 713.

119   Parliament of Canada, LEGIS*info*, online: www.parl.gc.ca/legisinfo/ AboutLegisInfo.aspx?Language=E&Mode=1.

120   Neil A Campbell, "Legal Research and the Exclusionary Rule" (2011) 36:4 *Canadian Law Library Review* 158 at 165.

2) Process of Researching Legislative Intent

Until all legislative history material in Canada is displayed as it is in LEGIS*info*, legal researchers will need assistance in determining what the sources for researching legislative intent are and where to find them. In the chapters that follow we will describe the places and process for researching legislative intent in Canada.

The concept of legislative history is fluid and broad and will continue to evolve. It will be interesting to see what the future will hold and how judges will continue to interpret and apply the leading cases on the issue.

chapter two

Understanding Statutes: The Process of a Bill

A. PARLIAMENT AND LEGISLATURES

Canada is a parliamentary democracy.[1] The power to create laws is outlined in the Constitution[2] and is shared by the federal Parliament of Canada, ten provincial legislatures, and three territorial governments. Representative members of Parliament (MPs), elected at the federal level, appointed federal senators, and members of provincial or territorial legislatures[3] create the laws for their respective jurisdictions.

---

1   Parliament of Canada, House of Commons, Compendium of Procedure, "Parliamentary Framework," online: www.parl.gc.ca/About/House/Compendium/webcontent/c_g_parliamentaryframework-e.htm.

2   *Constitution Act, 1867* (UK), 30 & 31 Victoria, c 3, reprinted in RSC 1985, Appendix II, No 5.

3   Legislative Assembly of British Columbia, Members of the Legislative Assembly (MLA); Legislative Assembly of Alberta, Members of the Legislative Assembly (MLA); Legislative Assembly of Saskatchewan, Members of the Legislative Assembly (MLA); Legislative Assembly of Manitoba, Members of the Legislative Assembly (MLA); Legislative Assembly of Ontario, Members of Provincial Parliament (MPP); Quebec National Assembly, Members of the National Assembly (MNA); Legislative Assembly of New Brunswick, Members of the Legislative Assembly (MLA); Legislative Assembly of Nova Scotia, Members of the Legislative Assembly (MLA); Legislative Assembly of Prince Edward Island, Members of the Legislative Assembly (MLA); Newfoundland and Labrador House of Assembly, Members of the House of Assembly (MHA); Yukon Legislative Assembly, Members of the Legislative Assembly (MLA); Legislative Assembly of

As a constitutional monarchy, the Queen (through her representatives the Governor General and provincial Lieutenant Governors) is the formal head of state and exercises formal executive authority by being referenced in most actions of government, giving royal assent to acts of Parliament, and summoning and dissolving Parliaments.[4] Parliament and legislatures are regulated by the Constitution and they have their own written rules, known as standing orders or rules to conduct their business.[5] They also follow the tradition, conventions, and customs of the Westminster style of Parliament.

B. PARLIAMENTARY CALENDAR

The parliamentary calendar begins with the opening of a Parliament after an election. Parliament opens when the Governor General summons the Parliament (or the Lieutenant Governor summons the legislature) with a series of proclamations; the process includes the swearing in of new members and the election of a Speaker. Parliaments have been numbered sequentially since Confederation and each parliament contains approximately one to seven sessions. Each session is opened with the Speech from the Throne, read by the Queen's representative, which generally sets out the government's policy views and indicates the topics of legislation that the government wants to bring forward in the coming session.

A Parliament is divided into sessions. A session contains various breaks or adjournments when the House is not in session. The House governs its own adjournments and sittings, but the House must go to the Crown to prorogue (terminate) a session or dissolve and end a Parliament.

---

the Northwest Territories, Members of the Legislative Assembly (MLA); Legislative Assembly of Nunavut, Members of the Legislative Assembly (MLA).

4   Eugene A Forsey, *How Canadians Govern Themselves* (Ottawa: Government of Canada, 1980), online: *Parliament of Canada* https://lop.parl.ca/About/Parliament/SenatorEugeneForsey/book/preface-e.html.

5   Parliament of Canada, House of Commons, "Standing Orders of the House of Commons," online: www.parl.gc.ca/about/house/standingorders/toc-e.htm; Parliament of Canada, Senate of Canada, "Rules of the Senate," online: https://sencanada.ca/en/about/procedural-references/rules/.

Prorogation is the natural end to a session in Parliament and causes the members to be released from their duties of the House. It also ends all business of Parliament; bills and motions that have not passed are said to have "died on the order paper"; committees end their business and may not meet until a new session begins. Prorogation provides for a fresh start for business in a new session. However, Cabinet and members may choose to reintroduce bills that "died" in the previous session at the start of the next session[6] and the House may also choose to pass motions authorizing committees to meet notwithstanding prorogation.[7]

Dissolution ends a Parliament and sets the next general election in motion. Dissolution is a prerogative of the Crown, normally on the advice of the prime minister or premier. The dissolution process requires governments to issue a series of proclamations that release members and senators from their duties, to issue writs for a general election, and to set the date for the next Parliament. At dissolution, all business of the Parliament ends.[8]

C. THE LEGISLATIVE PROCESS

Making law is arguably the most important work of Parliaments and legislatures. Acts of Parliament, sometimes called "Acts" and more commonly known as statutes, lay out the broad principles of the law that affect citizens' rights and benefits in their respective jurisdictions. All statutes must be approved by Parliament to become law; this activity is known as the legislative process. After a statute has been given royal assent and proclaimed, and under the authority of a statute, administrative regulations and statutory instruments may be created by the responsible ministry or government body.

The standing orders for each Parliament or legislature regulate the proceedings and describe the process of making laws in that

---

6   Marc Bosc & André Gagnon, "House of Commons Procedure and Practice, Third Edition, 2017," online: www.ourcommons.ca/About/ProcedureAndPractice 3rdEdition/index-e.html..

7   *Ibid.*

8   *Ibid.*

jurisdiction; this process in Canada is based on the British model (also known as the Westminster model). The federal Parliament is bicameral, meaning legislation has two Houses to pass through (The House of Commons of Canada and The Senate of Canada). Today, provincial legislatures have one House and are known as unicameral legislatures.

Both levels of government have a similar process of legislation. Here we will follow the process of two bills, the federal *Ending the Long-gun Registry Act* (Bill C-19)[9] and the provincial Ontario *Safe Streets Act, 1999* (Bill 8),[10] which will demonstrate the similarities and differences of the respective jurisdictions and their legislative processes as well as the documents produced in the process.

A bill is a proposed law that goes through stages known as readings for debate and study, before becoming an Act of Parliament. The statute that emerges at the end of the process may have some differences from the original bill that was introduced.

The legislative process produces documents that may help to reveal the intention of the legislature, the problem that the members are trying to correct, and the reasons for the creation of the legislation. Understanding how a Parliament operates, and its unique terminology, helps a researcher locate these important materials.

A bill requires three readings by the House in a provincial legislature or three readings by both the House of Commons and the Senate in the federal Parliament and royal assent before it can become law. A "reading" today is simply a stage in the process of legislation but the name comes from the pre-printing era when bills were actually read aloud in Parliament, so that members knew what they were voting on. Today, the process does not require the text to be read aloud.

9　Bill C-19, *An Act to amend the Criminal Code and the Firearms Act*, 1st Sess, 42st Parl, 2011 (first reading 25 October 2011), online: www.parl.gc.ca/HousePublications/Publication.aspx?Language=E&Mode=1&DocId=5193892.

10　Bill 8, *Safe Streets Act, 1999*, 1st Sess, 37th Leg, Ontario, 1999 (first reading 2 November 1999), online: www.ola.org/en/legislative-business/bills/parliament-37/session-1/bill-8.

1) Federal

a) Pre-legislative Stages

Prior to the formal legislative process of a bill in Parliament, all bills begin as a policy idea. Some sources of policy ideas originate in the public domain, such as the Speech from the Throne, budgets, political campaign platforms, Royal Commission recommendations, proposals from ministers, stakeholders, academics, or public policy organizations. While some of these sources are public documents, most at this stage are confidential within Cabinet.

Those documents and reports that lead to a policy idea and bill that are in the public domain can be accessed by many means. For example, Bill C-19 (*An Act to amend the Criminal Code and the Firearms Act*) was first introduced in concept in just a few lines in the Speech from the Throne:

> Canada's rural communities are rich in history and culture, and generations of rural Canadians have worked hard and played by the rules. They should not be the target of unfair laws. Our Government will act on its promise to introduce legislation to end the wasteful and ineffective long-gun registry.[11]

Other sources of pre-legislative stage information include studies and articles such as those found on the LEGIS*info* bills page under the "About this Bill" heading. For Bill C-19, reports by think tanks like the Fraser Institute, academic articles like those in the *Canadian Journal of Criminology and Criminal Justice,* and news articles such as one in the *Hill Times* are suggested as further background reading to understand the political and social context of this bill.[12]

---

11   Governor General, Speech from the Throne, "Here for All Canadians: Stability. Prosperity. Security" (3 June 2011), online: http://publications.gc.ca/site/archivee-archived.html?url=http://publications.gc.ca/collections/collection_2011/gg/SO1-1-2011-eng.pdf.

12   Gary A Mauser, "Hubris in the North : The Canadian Firearms Registry"(5 July 2007), online: *The Fraser Institute* www.fraserinstitute.org/studies/hubris-in-the-north-canadian-firearms-registry; Thomas Gabor, "The Federal Gun Registry: An Urgent Need for Independent, Non-partisan Research" (2003) 45:4 *Canadian Journal of Criminology and Criminal Justice* 489; Tim Naumetz, "Income Tax Files

Bills introduced previously, including government and private members' public bills, are other sources of legislation policy ideas. The idea of ending Canada's long-gun registry appears to have come up in 2006 with the introduction of a predecessor bill, Bill C-21, *An Act to amend the Criminal Code and the Firearms Act (non-registration of firearms that are neither prohibited nor restricted).*[13] The Library of Parliament's *Legislative Summary of Bill C-19*[14] identifies a series of reports (from 2003–10) on firearms control in Canada and a lengthy history of debate about the firearms regulation going way back to 1892. The reports and articles as well as the Library of Parliament's *Legislative Summary* itself are potentially useful pre-legislative sources of information when building a legislative history.

Once the idea is submitted to Cabinet, the policy may undergo public or intergovernmental consultation, which may or may not be made available to the public.[15]

Can Replace Gun Sale Records, Says Tory MP Hoeppner" *Hill Times* (5 December 2011) online: www.hilltimes.com/wp-content/themes/hilltimes-master/ secure_files/pdfs/2011/120511_ht.pdf.

13   Bill C-21, *An Act to amend the Criminal Code and the Firearms Act (non-registration of firearms that are neither prohibited nor restricted)*, 1st Sess, 39th Parl, 2006 (first reading 19 June 2006), online: www.parl.gc.ca/content/hoc/Bills/391/Government/ C-21/C-21_1/C-21_1.PDF.

14   Tanya Dupuis, Cynthia Kirkby, & Robin MacKay, "Legislative Summary of Bill C-19: An Act to amend the *Criminal Code* and the *Firearms Act*," Publication Number 41-1-C19E (2011), online: *Library of Parliament Legal and Legislative Affairs Division* http://publications.gc.ca/collections/collection_2011/bdp-lop/ls/41-1- c19-eng.pdf [Dupuis et al, "Legislative Summary"].

15   Privy Council Office, "Guide to Making Federal Acts and Regulations," 2d ed (2001) Part 2 Making Acts, online: www.canada.ca/en/privy-council/services/ publications/guide-making-federal-acts-regulations.html#pt2; Privy Council Office, "The Federal Law-Making Process and Associated Support Activities" [Privy Council, "Law Making"], online: www.canada.ca/content/dam/pco-bcp/ images/pco/fed-eng.jpg; Andre Barnes & Erin Virgint, "The Legislative Process: From Government Policy to Proclamation" (2015), online: *Library of Parliament, Legal and Social Affairs Division* http://publications.gc.ca/collections/collection_ 2016/bdp-lop/eb/YM32-5-2015-52-eng.pdf.

b) Memorandum to Cabinet

An important document developed in the pre-legislative stage is the Memorandum to Cabinet (MC), which is a minister's vehicle for explaining the legislative proposal to Cabinet. The MC is a cornerstone of the drafting process,[16] as it outlines the issue to be addressed, together with ministerial recommendations for implementing a legislative solution.

During the pre-legislative stage, the MC is drafted, consulted on within government, and considered and approved by internal Cabinet committees. The Cabinet issues its own internal committee report on the MC and decides whether it should be drafted into a bill. If approved, the Cabinet committee decision on the MC leads to the drafting of a bill for Parliament. All Cabinet materials in this process are confidential.

c) Bill Drafted

A final government bill is drafted by the Department of Justice in cooperation with the departmental legal units. Support materials are created alongside the bill, including speeches, press releases, backgrounders, and clause-by-clause analysis, all in preparation for the bill's introduction and first reading in Parliament. Many of these documents will become public as soon as the bill is introduced in Parliament.[17]

d) Parliament and Session

Bills musts be introduced when Parliament is in session. In the first session of the 41st Parliament, sixty-four House of Commons government bills were introduced and fifty of those progressed to royal assent and became law.

e) Bill Name and Number

Of those sixty-four bills introduced in the 41st Parliament, Session 1, *An Act to amend the Criminal Code and the Firearms Act* (Bill C-19) was

---

16   Privy Council, "Law Making," above note 15, ch 2.2.

17   *Ibid*, ch 2.3.

introduced as the nineteenth bill in the House of Commons, so it was given the number C-19. The letter C denotes that the bill originated in the House of Commons of Canada (Senate bills are marked with S and the number: e.g., S-5). Numbers 1–200 denote that the bill was introduced by the government and numbers 201–1000 mean the bill was introduced by a private member, not a minister.

Bills are usually given a short title for easy reference. For example, Bill C-19 is known as *Ending the Long-gun Registry Act.*

D. TYPES OF BILLS

A bill is a proposed law. Generally, there are three types of bills: government public bills, private members' public bills, and private bills. A bill may be a new initiative and a new enactment or something to amend existing law. A bill contains the government's policy or an idea written in legislative language. Bill C-19 is a public government bill that, if passed, will amend or change the *Criminal Code* and the *Firearms Act* with respect to the long-gun registry.

1) Public Bills — Government Bills

There are two types of public bills. Government bills are introduced by a minister and generally set out the government policy and have general application to the entire jurisdiction. Bill C-19, *An Act to amend the Criminal Code and the Firearms Act*, is a government public bill and sets out the government's intended policy with respect to the firearms registry.

2) Public Bills — Private Members' Bills

Private members' bills are proposed legislation introduced by a private member (any member that is not a minister) and so do not represent the government's policy. Bill C-288, *National Flag of Canada Act* (SC 2012, c 12) is a private member's bill that encourages all Canadian to display the national flag, even those living in apartments and condominiums.

3) Private Bills

Private bills are of limited effect and do not impact the public at large. They are usually specific to a place or organization, like a municipality, university, or company. Private members' bills are often confused with private bills. A private member's bill can affect the public, whereas a private bill is of limited effect. One example of a private bill is the *Canadian Council of the Girl Guides Association Act*, SC 1917 c 77.

E. DRAFTING CHARACTERISTICS[18]

Bills are often referred to by their drafting characteristics. Drafting characteristics are not official kinds of bills, but these terms indicate something about the bill's purpose or character, and researchers, members, or the government may refer to bills using these terms:

1) New Legislation

A bill introducing new legislation will generally be a new policy idea, but it could also be introduced to implement a task force, commission, or recommendation, or it may deal with an emergency situation, such as back-to-work legislation to end a strike.

2) Amending Legislation

According to the "House of Commons Procedure and Practice,"[19] there are different kinds of bills that are designed to amend existing acts:

a) Major Revisions of Existing Acts

A bill to revise an existing Act in its entirety in order to update it, or because it contains a sunset clause that indicates it must be revised after a certain time period.

---

18   For more information on House of Commons drafting characteristics, see Bosc & Gagnon, above note 6.

19   *Ibid.*

b) Amendments to Existing Acts

A bill that amends existing Acts either substantively with new policy ideas or for housekeeping measures.

c) Statute Law Amendment Bills

A bill that will eliminate errors or inconsistencies in existing Acts.[20]

3) Pro Forma Bills

A pro forma bill is generally introduced by the prime minister at the start of each session to affirm the right of the House to conduct its own proceedings and to legislate. This is a tradition in most Commonwealth Parliaments, and in Canada the bill does not go to second reading or get printed. In the House of Commons, this pro forma bill is called *An Act respecting the Administration of Oaths of Office* and is number C-1.

4) Budget Bills

A budget bill may or may not contain the term budget in its title and is referred to as such because it contains the government's budget policy implementation. Only ministers can introduce budget or money bills. A "budget bill" may spread the budget policy implementation over one bill or over several bills over the course of a session. Budget bills can include:

a) Appropriation Bills

"An initiative introduced in the House in response to the adoption of Main or Supplementary Estimates or Interim Supply. These bills are also governed by specific provisions of the Standing Orders. Only a Minister may introduce an appropriation bill."[21]

---

20 *Ibid*. Parliament of Canada, "Forms of Bills," online: www.ourcommons.ca/ About/ProcedureAndPractice3rdEdition/Ch_16_3-e.html.

21 *Ibid*.

b) Ways and Means Bills

"An initiative based on Ways and Means motions, the purpose of which is to create a new income or other tax, to continue a tax which is expiring, to increase a tax or to extend the scope of a tax. These bills are governed by specific provisions of the Standing Orders. Only a Minister may introduce a Ways and Means bill."[22]

c) Borrowing Authority Bills

"An initiative to seek authority to raise money when public revenues are not adequate to cover government expenditures."[23]

5) Draft Bills

A draft bill may be produced and studied before it is introduced for first reading in Parliament. Occasionally, the draft bill is sent to committee and studied. Changes can be made before a final version is produced and introduced to Parliament.

6) Omnibus Bills

An omnibus bill is described as an initiative to amend, repeal, and/or enact several pieces of legislation in one bill. The various proposals that an omnibus bill contains are often related to one policy decision that touches several program areas spread across many Acts. The many legislative changes it contains are spread across several schedules, or in separate parts. While omnibus bills are commonly used, and according to the Journals they have been used in Canada since 1888,[24] they are often criticized by members and by the public for their length and complexity.[25]

---

22   Ibid.

23   Ibid.

24   House of Commons Journals (26 March 1888) at 135–36.

25   Omnibus bills can be time-consuming to track and trace because they are large and complex. For more about omnibus bills, see: Louis Massicotte, "Omnibus Bills in Theory and Practice" (2013) 36:1 Canadian Parliamentary Review, online: www.revparl.ca/english/issue.asp?param=214&art=1517, and Bosc & Gagnon, above note 6. Michel Bedard, "Omnibus Bills: Frequently Asked Questions"

F. OVERVIEW: THE PROCESS OF A BILL

Pre-legislative stages
ℰ Policy proposal is considered in Cabinet committee
ℰ Memorandum to Cabinet is drafted
ℰ If approved by Cabinet, legislation is drafted and introduced in Parliament

Parliament
ℰ First Reading
  · Bill is introduced in the House or Senate
  · Bill is printed
ℰ Second Reading
  · Principle of the bill is debated in the same House as it was introduced
  · House may decide to refer the bill to committee for further study
ℰ Consideration in Committee
  · Bill is referred to a committee and examined by committee members
  · Committee may
    » call witnesses to provide information on the bill
    » receive written submission from the public on the bill
    » examine a bill clause by clause
ℰ Report Stage
  · Bill is reported back to the House by the committee
  · Report is a copy of the bill
ℰ Third Reading
  · Final debate and vote on bill as amended
  · Bill is sent to other House for consideration (House of Commons or Senate)

Royal Assent
ℰ Bill is sent to the Queen's representative, the Governor General, for assent

---

(1 October 2012), online: *Library of Parliament Research Publications* https:// lop.parl.ca/sites/PublicWebsite/default/en_CA/ResearchPublications/201279E.

- The Governor General grants royal assent by signature or traditional ceremony
- A bill with royal assent is law and assigned a statute chapter number

Coming into Force
- A statute can come into force in four ways:
  - On royal assent
  - On a date named in the statute (usually found at the end of the statute)
  - On proclamation by the Governor General, which is printed in the *Canada Gazette*
  - A combination of any of the above in force methods

G. BILL STAGES AND DOCUMENTATION — FEDERAL BILL C-19

As a bill moves through stages in Parliament, documents are produced that provide a trail of the bill's progress: The Order Paper and Notice Paper, Status of Business, Journals, *Hansard*. Other external texts such as the bill summary, news releases, and backgrounds also provide aids to tracking the progress of a bill.

1) Order Paper and Notice Paper

For a bill, or any other large agenda item to be introduced in the House, a notice must be added to the Order Paper and Notice Paper (a two-part document that contains the daily House agenda and notice of business). The member or minister must give written notice to the Clerk of the House that a bill is to be introduced forty-eight hours in advance. A notice is then added to the Notice Paper, to ensure that other members are not taken by surprise. A day after the bill is on the Notice Paper it will move to the Order Paper and stay there until the member or minister is ready to introduce it.

Bill C-19, *An Act to amend the Criminal Code and the Firearms Act*, appeared in the Order Paper and Notice Paper on 24 October 2011. Here is what the entry in the Order Paper and Notice Paper looks like for that date:

October 21, 2011 — The Minister of Public Safety — Bill entitled "An Act to amend the Criminal Code and the Firearms Act".[26]

2) Introduction and First Reading

A series of motions are voted on to move the bill through the different stages of first, second, and third reading. The only way to make changes to a bill is through an amendment to a motion on the bill that is passed by the House.

At first reading a bill is printed for members. A first reading version contains a bill summary at the start of the bill. This summary is not part of the bill, but a service to help members and the public understand what the bill is about. Here is an example of a bill summary for Bill C-19:

SUMMARY

This enactment amends the *Criminal Code* and the *Firearms Act* to remove the requirement to register firearms that are neither prohibited nor restricted. It also provides for the destruction of existing records, held in the Canadian Firearms Registry and under the control of chief firearms officers, that relate to the registration of such firearms.[27]

Bill C-19, a public government bill, was introduced at first reading in the House of Commons of Canada by the Minister of Public Safety, the Hon Vic Toews on 25 October 2011. At the time of introduction, the bill is prepared and printed for members to study and reference. In some cases, a committee is charged with preparing a bill before it is given first reading. Bill C-19 followed the traditional route of being prepared and introduced by a minister.

There are a number of publications from Parliament that will provide important details on the introduction and passage of a bill,

---

26   Parliament of Canada, "House Publications" (24 October 2011) Order Paper and Notice Paper, No 35, online: *House of Commons of Canada* www.ourcommons.ca/DocumentViewer/en/41-1/house/sitting-35/order-notice/page-4.

27   Bill C-19, above note 9.

including reading dates, who introduced and spoke about the bill, and what was said about the bill.

a) Status of Business

The Status of Business is a publication that indicates the bill sponsor, bill reading dates, committee names, and consideration of bill dates, as well as the final statute numbers for each bill. Current sessions and back issues for the Status of Business at prorogation and dissolution since 1994 are available online.[28] The Status of Business has bill information in two parts: government orders and private members' business. It also includes the status of motions, written questions, committee business, other business, and an index. Earlier versions of this publication are available in print. For pre-internet and print research, the print version of the Status of Business contains very useful legislative intent research information.

This is what the Status of Business looked like at the end of the session for Bill C-19:

> C-19—The Minister of Public Safety—An Act to amend the Criminal Code and the Firearms Act
>
> Introduced and read the first time—October 25, 2011
>
> Debated at second reading—October 26, 27, 28 and November 1, 2011
>
> Time allocation at second reading stage—Notice—October 26, 2011; adopted—October 27, 2011
>
> Read the second time and referred to the Standing Committee on Public Safety and National Security—November 1, 2011
>
> Reported without amendment (Sessional Paper No. 8510-411-24)—November 30, 2011

---

28   The Status of House Business at Prorogation, Friday 13 September 2013, indicates significant dates on the passage of Bill C-19. Parliament of Canada, "Status of House Business" (13 September 2013), online: www.parl.gc.ca/HousePublications/Publication.aspx?Pub=status&Language=E&Mode=1&Parl=41&Ses=1&File=1#DOC--477F1477BD70424A93E12E2299A73993.

Debated at report stage—February 6 and 7, 2012

Time allocation at report stage and third reading stage—Notice—
February 6, 2012; adopted—February 7, 2012

Concurred in at report stage—February 7, 2012

Debated at third reading—February 13 and 15, 2012

Read the third time and passed—February 15, 2012

Passed by the Senate—April 4, 2012

Written declaration; Royal Assent (Chapter No. 6)—April 5, 2012[29]

b) The Journals

The Journals are the official record of the House drawn from the notes
of the Clerk and table officers. Journals are like minutes of the day and
they form a record of transactions, decisions, and dates. The House of
Commons of Canada produces daily Journals online. In the past, the
daily Journals were called Votes and Proceedings, and were then bound
into sessional volumes called Journals of the House of Commons. An
index of bills provides an official source of reading and committee discussion dates for a bill. Journals can be accessed on Parliament websites. Each reading of Bill C-19 is captured in the Journals on the date it
was read and in the index.

Here is what is written in the Journals at first reading for Bill C-19:

Journals

Pursuant to Standing Orders 68(2) and 69(1), on motion of Mr. Toews
(Minister of Public Safety), seconded by Mr. O'Connor (Minister of
State), Bill C-19, An Act to amend the Criminal Code and the Firearms Act, was introduced, read the first time, ordered to be printed
and ordered for a second reading at the next sitting of the House.[30]

---

29 *Ibid*, Part I.
30 Parliament of Canada, "House Publications" (25 October 2011) *House of Commons
    Journals*, 41-1, No 36 at "Introduction of Government Bills," online: www.parl.gc.ca/
    HousePublications/Publication.aspx?Language=E&Mode=1&Parl=41&Ses=
    1&DocId=5193181.

c) *Hansard*

Hansard is essentially the verbatim transcript of the proceedings in the House and records what all the members say. Although it may be edited "in order to make the meaning more precise and accurate; ... no words or phrases may be inserted to effect material changes in the meaning of what was actually said in the House."[31] *Hansard* also produces an index organized by bill number, topic, or speaker. If a researcher is trying to find debate on a bill, the index will be the best place to start in order find the date and the actual debate. The first reading of Bill C-19 is in the House *Hansard* under the time of the legislative day called Routine Proceedings:

Official Reports (Hansard)

ROUTINE PROCEEDINGS

Ending the Long-gun Registry Act

Hon. Vic Toews (Minister of Public Safety, CPC)

moved for leave to introduce Bill C-19, An Act to amend the Criminal Code and the Firearms Act. (Motions deemed adopted, bill read the first time and printed)[32]

The topic of the Canadian Firearms Registry is also briefly discussed later in the day during the parts of the legislative day known as Member's Statements and Oral Questions. While there could be a substantial speech at first reading, it is more likely that there will be a brief introduction to the bill only. Bill C-19 is typical in that very brief statements were made at first reading and the substantial debate is found during second reading of the bill.

---

31   Alistair Fraser, WF Dawson, & John A Holtby, *Beauchesne's Parliamentary Rules & Forms*, 6th ed (Toronto: Carswell, 1989) at 19.

32   Parliament of Canada, "House Publications" (25 October 2011) *House of Commons Debates*, 41-1, No 36 at "Routine Proceedings," online: www.parl.gc.ca/ HousePublications/Publication.aspx?Pub=Hansard&Doc=36&Parl=41&Ses=1 &Language=E&Mode=1.

d) News Release and Backgrounder

At first reading, the government often issues a press release and a bill background document to the public about the first reading of a bill, particularly if the bill concerns a change that was promised earlier during election campaigns, the budget, or the Speech from the Throne. The news release can be issued by the prime minister or minister's office and/or the responsible ministry. A news release and background document issued by the government is not a parliamentary document. In this case, Public Safety Canada issued a news release and backgrounder about the first reading of Bill C-19. The title of the press release is available on the bill's LEGIS*info* page under "departmental information" and this release is now archived on the ministry website.[33]

Opposition parties may also choose to issue a press release with their party's perspective on the bill.[34] Links to these may be found at "party press releases" under "further reading" on LEGIS*info*. Older links may no longer work, but the titles can be searched for archived versions.

e) Legislative Summary

Around the time of first reading, but potentially later or earlier, the Library of Parliament may produce a Legislative Summary related to a new bill:

> Legislative Summaries explain the purpose and history of bills, analyze their key clauses, and, where available, include media reaction and comments from interest groups. They are updated as needed to reflect amendments made during the legislative process.[35]

---

33 Public Safety Canada, News Release, "Harper Government Introduces the *Ending the Long-Gun Registry Act*" (25 October 2011), online: www.publicsafety.gc.ca/cnt/nws/nws-rlss/2011/20111025-1-en.aspx; Public Safety Canada, News Release, "Abolishing the Long-Gun Registry: Proposed Reforms to the *Firearms Act* and *Criminal Code*" (25 October 2011), online: www.publicsafety.gc.ca/cnt/nws/nws-rlss/2011/20111025-2-en.aspx.

34 New Democratic Party, News Release, "Federal Government Must Keep Gun Registry Data" (5 April 2012) online: www.ndp.ca/news/federal-government-must-keep-gun-registry-data.

35 Parliament of Canada, Library of Parliament, "Research Publications: Legislative Summaries," online: https://lop.parl.ca/sites/PublicWebsite/default/en_CA/ResearchPublications/LegislativeSummaries.

The Legislative Summary for Bill C-19 is extensive and detailed, providing a rich history of firearm legislation and the firearms registry in Canada.[36]

3) Second Reading and Reference to a Committee

The next day, at second reading, Bill C-19 was debated in principle. This is the most substantial debate on the bill. Second reading debate on Bill C-19 lasted four sitting days with major speeches by all three of the party leaders, and others, on the principle and object of the bill. The House of Commons of Canada standing orders dictate the length of time that members may speak, except for the sponsoring minister and Leader of the Opposition who have no time limit stipulated.

The extract from *Hansard* below is the beginning of the minister's speech at second reading:

Official Reports (Hansard)

Government Orders

Ending the Long-gun Registry Act

Second Reading

Hon. Vic Toews (Minister of Public Safety, CPC) moved that Bill C-19, An Act to amend the Criminal Code and the Firearms Act, be read the second time and referred to a committee.

He said: "Madam Speaker, I am pleased to rise today to begin debate on Bill C-19, Ending the Long-gun Registry Act.

This is a great day for Conservatives across Canada. It marks the beginning of the end for a nearly 17-year-old legacy of waste thrust upon Canadians by the previous Liberal government. I know I speak for many of my colleagues when I say that this has been a very long time in coming. For years, many of us have stood in this place even when we were on the other side and took a stand for law-abiding hunters, farmers and sports shooters.

---

36   Dupuis et al, "Legislative Summary," above note 14.

We repeated time and again that the long-gun registry was wasteful. It was ineffective. It did nothing to keep guns out of the hands of criminals. Yet still the parties that now form the opposition stood against us and against the law-abiding Canadians for whom we were standing . . . ."[37]

a) Motions and Amendments

During the second reading debate, notice was also given for a time allocation motion on the second reading debate of Bill C-19. This motion, which passed, would ensure that the second reading debate was completed in a specific number of days, in this case three more days, bringing the total sitting days of second reading debate on this bill to four days.

At second reading there are three kinds of amendments that could be proposed: the hoist amendment, the reasoned amendment, and the referral of subject matter of the bill to committee. The hoist amendment can be moved at second reading, and it would have the effect of postponing the debate on the bill, possibly indefinitely, and may have the effect of withdrawing the bill. A hoist amendment was not proposed on Bill C-19. The second kind of amendment that can be moved at second reading is the reasoned amendment to the motion on second reading debate, which gives specific reasons for not supporting the bill and suggests that the House decline to pass it. A reasoned amendment with specific reasons for opposing Bill C-19 was proposed by Mr Jack Harris (St John's East, NDP):

> That the motion be amended by deleting all of the words after the word "That" and substituting the following:
>
> this House declines to give second reading to Bill C-19, An Act to amend the Criminal Code and the Firearms Act, because it:
> a)   destroys existing data that is of public safety value for provinces that wish to establish their own system of long-gun registration, which may lead to significant and entirely unnecessary expenditure of public funds;

---

37   *House of Commons Debates*, 41-1, No 37 (26 October 2011) at 2534 (Hon Vic Toews).

   b)   fails to respond to the specific request from the Canadian Association of Chiefs of Police for use of existing data in the interest of public safety; and

   c)   fails to strike a balance between the legitimate concerns of rural and Aboriginal Canadians and the need for police to have appropriate tools to enhance public safety.[38]

Second reading debate on Bill C-19 continued and was interrupted on the fourth day of debate by the Speaker to carry out the time allocation order. The Speaker asked all the questions necessary to end second reading, which includes the vote on the motion for second reading, referring Bill C-19 to the Standing Committee on Public Safety and National Security, and the reasoned amendment motion proposed by Mr Harris, above. The reasoned amendment motion by Mr Harris lost the vote, but the second reading and referral to committee motion passed.

b) Committee Stage

During the committee stage a smaller group of members from all political parties have an opportunity to examine the bill in detail and propose amendments to the text of the bill. The members also have a chance to hear from witnesses and interested parties on the substance of the bill and ask them questions about the bill. The members then go through clause-by-clause consideration of the bill. A bill may be referred to committee before second reading, but most commonly it is referred to committee after second reading. Bills are usually referred to standing committees, but they could also be referred to legislative committees, special committees, the Committee of the Whole (money bills must go through the Committee of the Whole), or joint committees of the House and Senate.

Bill C-19 was referred to the Standing Committee on Public Safety and National Security on 1 November 2011 and the first committee meeting to consider the bill was on 22 November 2011. Since Bill C-19 is a recent bill, the committee Minutes of Proceedings and Evidence (transcripts) are available on the Parliament of Canada website. The

---

38   *House of Commons Debates*, 41-1, No 38 (27 October 2011) at 2562 (Hon Jack Harris).

Minutes of Proceedings contain the attendance, the motions, and votes, and are valuable for researchers because they contain the text of proposed bill amendments. The Evidence contains the full text transcripts of the proceedings and are often consulted for witness testimony and the detailed clause-by-clause consideration. Evidence is the official name of the committee transcript, but it is still sometimes called the transcripts of proceedings or referred to as "committee *Hansard*."

Once the bill is adopted by the committee, it is reported back to the House with or without amendments. The "report" is usually the bill itself. Bill C-19 is reported to the House without amendment. The committee minutes are tabled in the House:

Report:

41st Parliament, 1st Session
The Standing Committee on Public Safety and National Security has the honour to present its

FIRST REPORT

In accordance with its Order of Reference of Tuesday, November 1, 2011, your Committee has considered Bill C-19, An Act to amend the Criminal Code and the Firearms Act, and agreed on Tuesday, November 29, 2011, to report it without amendment.

A copy of the relevant *Minutes of Proceedings* (Meetings Nos 11 to 15) is tabled.

Respectfully submitted,
KEVIN SORENSON
Chair

c) Report Stage

At the report stage in the House the Speaker may select motions for amendment proposed by members to be considered by the House. Members at the report stage for Bill C-19 considered ten motions for amending (deleting) specific clauses in the bill. These amendments were debated at length for two days, but in the end did not pass. At the end of the report stage, on 7 February 2012, a vote was held on the motion for concurrence on Bill C-19 and the bill moved on to third reading.

4) Third Reading

On 13 February 2012, the House considered the motion that Bill C-19, *An Act to amend the Criminal Code and the Firearms Act*, be read the third time and passed. Generally, the third reading stage of a bill is considered a formality, but it could include proposed amendments similar to those at second reading, as well as lengthy debate on the final form of the bill. The motion for third reading of Bill C-19 saw two days of debate and passed on 15 February 2012, and then it was sent to the Senate for consideration.

5) Senate

In the Senate, the bill follows a similar process of three readings and committee study. The Senate passed first reading of Bill C-19 on 16 February 2012. The second reading required two days in March and then it was referred to the Standing Senate Committee on Legal and Constitutional Affairs. The committee considered the bill and reported it back without amendment. After three days of third reading debate, Bill C-19 was passed by the Senate on 4 March 2012. As the bill progresses through the Senate, messages may be passed between the House of Commons and Senate and printed in the Journals. If the Senate chose to amend the bill it would go back to the House for consideration.

The Senate can also be the originator of bills, in which case the three readings happen in the Senate first and then the House of Commons. Bills that originate in the Senate can be distinguished by their number, which will begin with an "S" (e.g., Bill S-2).

The Senate can also choose to study a bill as it makes its way through the House of Commons. This pre-study allows a Senate committee to examine the principle of a House of Commons bill that has passed first reading but which has not yet received third reading in the House. The Senate can only study the principle or subject matter and the bill must still be referred to the Senate by the House once the three readings in the House have been completed.[39]

6) Royal Assent

Royal assent is the final stage for a bill to complete before it can become an Act of Parliament. Today a bill is usually given royal assent through a written procedure where the Clerk brings the bill to the Governor General and requests royal assent. The traditional formal royal assent ceremony also occurs a couple of times a year, preserving the tradition of the two Houses of Parliament coming together in the Senate chamber to witness the royal assent by the Crown.

After royal assent, an Act of Parliament may come into force immediately as law, or it may, in whole or in part, require a proclamation to come into force on a particular date or dates. It can also come into force on a prospective fixed date, a retroactive fixed date, or the Act of Parliament may come into force by any combination of these methods. If an Act or part of an Act is not declared in force within ten years of royal assent, then it is repealed, unless the House adopts a resolution that it not be repealed.[40]

After royal assent, the new Act is given a statute number (*An Act to amend the Criminal Code and the Firearms Act*, SC 2012, c 6) and published in the *Canada Gazette*, Part III, as well as made available on the Justice Laws Canada website.[41]

---

39 Senate, "Senate Procedure in Practice," (2015), online: www.publications.gc.ca/collections/collection_2015/sen/Y9-20-2015-eng.pdf.

40 *Statutes Repeal Act*, SC 2008, c 20.

41 *Canada Gazette*, Part III, online from 1998: www.gazette.gc.ca/rp-pr/publications-eng.html#a3 and archived at www.collectionscanada.gc.ca/canada-gazette/index-e.html; Canada, *Annual Statutes*, online from 2001: https://laws.justice.gc.ca/eng/AnnualStatutes/index.html.

H. PROVINCIAL PROCESS OF LEGISLATION (ONTARIO)

1) Types of Bills

a) Public Bills — Government Bills

Using Ontario as an example, there are three types of provincial public bills. Government bills are proposed laws introduced by a minister. Public bills may be a new initiative and a new enactment or amend an existing law. A public government bill contains the government's policy written in legislative language. Bill 8, *Safe Streets Act, 1999*,[42] the provincial bill described below is a government public bill.

b) Public Bills — Private Members' Public Bills

The second type of public bill is a private member's public bill, which is introduced by a private member, that is, any member who is not the Speaker or a Cabinet minister. These bills may be on any topic of interest to the private member, within the provincial jurisdiction, but they may not impose a tax. While private members' public bills do not have the government backing, many do receive royal assent and many others, which might not become law, will still influence public opinion, government policy, or government initiatives.

Bill 77, *Hawkins Gignac Act (Carbon Monoxide Safety), 2013*[43] is an example of a private member's public bill that was given royal assent and made into law. This bill amended the *Fire Protection and Prevention Act* respective to carbon monoxide detectors and declared the week of November 1 as Carbon Monoxide Awareness Week. An example of a private member's public bill that did not receive royal assent is Bill 54, *Fire Protection and Prevention Amendment Act (Retrofitting of Retirement Homes with Automatic Sprinklers), 2012*.[44] Although this private member's public bill did not receive royal assent, in 2013 the government

---

42   Above note 10.

43   Bill 77, *Hawkins Gignac Act (Carbon Monoxide Safety)*, 2013, 2nd Sess, 40th Leg, Ontario, 2013 (first reading 29 May 2013), online: www.ola.org/en/legislative-business/bills/parliament-40/session-2/bill-77.

44   Bill 54, *Fire Protection and Prevention Amendment Act (Retrofitting of Retirement Homes with Automatic Sprinklers)*, 2012, 1st Sess, 40th Leg, 2012, Ontario (first reading 26 March 2012) online: www.ola.org/en/legislative-business/bills/parliament-40/session-1/bill-54.

changed regulations[45] to order that all retirement homes must retro-fit automatic sprinkler systems within five years, demonstrating the possible effect on public policy that private members' public bills may have even if they don't pass into law.

c) Public Bills — Committee Bills

In 1999 the Ontario Standing Orders were amended to allow a lesser-known and the third kind of public bill to be introduced, called a committee bill. Committee bills are introduced by the chair of a standing committee. There are only a few examples of committee bills in Ontario, one of them being Bill 110, *Professional Foresters Act, 2000*, which originated in the Standing Committee on General Government.

d) Private Bills

Private bills, if passed, are of limited effect and allow a specific group or organization an exemption from the general law or provide something specific to the group or organization. Private bills would not affect the public at large. They are usually specific to a place or organization, such as a municipality, university, or company. Private bills must be introduced by a private member and they are given a number preceded by a "Pr," like Bill Pr11, *Royal Conservatory of Music Act, 2013*.[46]

2) Bill Characteristics

Like the federal bill drafting characteristic types, provincial bills may also be referred to as the unofficial kinds of bill "types," like new legislation, amending legislation, major revision, pro forma, omnibus, budget bill, and ways and means. These unofficial types of bills describe the bill's intention or contents, but they are not official kinds

---

45 Ontario *Fire Code*, O Reg 213/07 under the *Fire Protection and Prevention Act, 1997*, SO 1997, c 4 was amended by O Reg 150/13 to require retirement homes to be retrofitted with sprinklers.

46 Bill Pr11, *Royal Conservatory of Music Act, 2013*, 2nd Sess, 40th Leg, Ontario, 2013 (first reading 26 February 2013), online: www.ola.org/en/legislative-business/bills/parliament-40/session-2/bill-pr11.

of bills. For more information, see the federal list of bill characteristics, Section E, above.

3) Bill Stages and Documentation — Ontario Bill 8, *Safe Streets Act, 1999*

a) Legislature and Session

The 37th Ontario legislature is a period of roughly four calendar years. It is important to know the legislature (also called Parliament) and session number when looking up a bill number, since each legislature starts a new sequential numbering of bills. Like its federal counterpart, the provincial parliamentary cycle includes sessional sitting days, adjournments, prorogations to terminate sessions, and a dissolution to end a legislature.

b) Pre-legislative Stages

Provinces have a similar confidential Cabinet process to the federal government for developing policy ideas and producing draft bills. Policy ideas can come from public sources, like the Speech from the Throne, budgets, royal commission recommendations, ministers, stakeholder, or academic recommendations and other places. The proposed policy must be approved in Cabinet for a bill to be drafted. Internal Cabinet committees approve and recommend the policies that go forward. Ontario ministers use a Memorandum of Cabinet, a confidential document, to propose, consult, and finalize the policy idea and send it to legislative counsel for drafting into a bill. In the 1999 Speech from the Throne, the then-Ontario Premier Ernie Eves announced initiatives to make Ontario safer from crime.[47]

Bills are drafted by Ontario legislative counsel, a part of the Ministry of the Attorney General, in consultation with the member or minister who is introducing the bill.

---

47   Lieutenant Governor of Ontario, "Speech from the Throne" (22 April 1999), online: www.ontla.on.ca/library/repository/ser/10028625//1999-363.pdf.

c) First Reading

Like the federal Parliament, provinces have an Order and Notice Paper that sets out their daily agenda. Rules vary as to what needs to be in the Notice Paper section in advance of the Order Paper and when bill information is to be added. In Ontario, Bill 8 appears in the Orders and Notices after second reading and labeled as Printed on November 3, 1999.[48] However, the Votes and Proceedings (when collected and bound the Votes and Proceedings are the Journals) are the official recording of Bill 8's introduction on 2 November 1999:

> Introduction of Bills
>
> The following Bills were introduced and read the first time:
> Bill 8, An Act to promote safety in Ontario by prohibiting aggressive solicitation, solicitation of persons in certain places and disposal of dangerous things in certain places, and to amend the Highway Traffic Act to regulate certain activities on roadways. Hon. Mr. Flaherty.[49]

In the first session of the 37th Legislature, the *Safe Streets Act* was introduced as the eighth bill, so it was given the number 8. Knowing that it is Bill 8 of the 1st session, 37th Legislature distinguishes it from other Bill 8s of other legislatures. It was introduced on 2 November 1999 as *An Act to promote safety in Ontario by prohibiting aggressive solicitation, solicitation of persons in certain places and disposal of dangerous things in certain places, and to amend the Highway Traffic Act to regulate certain activities on roadways.* Bills are often given very long titles like this but contain a provision for a short title for the convenience of the reader. The last section of the bill notes: "The short title of this Act is the *Safe Streets Act, 1999.*"

Bill 8 is printed with an explanatory note inside the front cover. The explanatory note does not form part of the law, but helps to explain its purpose:

---

48   Ontario, Legislative Assembly, Orders and Notices Paper, 37-1, No 9 (3 November 1999) online: www.ola.org/en/legislative-business/house-documents/parliament-37/session-1/1999-11-03/orders-notices.

49   Ontario, Legislative Assembly, *Votes and Proceedings*, 37-1 (2 November 1999), online: www.ola.org/en/legislative-business/house-documents/parliament-37/session-1/1999-11-02/hansard#P62_14003.

EXPLANATORY NOTE

The Bill prohibits soliciting in an aggressive manner as well as soliciting persons who are in certain places. The places listed are generally places from which a person cannot easily depart or from which a person would not wish to depart until he or she has achieved his or her purpose.

The Bill prohibits disposing of needles, syringes, used condoms and broken glass in an outdoor public place unless reasonable precautions are taken to do so in a manner that will not endanger human health or safety.

The Bill amends the Highway Traffic Act to prohibit a person on a roadway from stopping, attempting to stop or approaching a motor vehicle for the purpose of offering, selling or providing any commodity or service to the driver or any other person in the motor vehicle. An exception is created to permit the offer, sale or provision of commodities and services in an emergency.

The Bill specifies the maximum penalties to which a person is liable on a first conviction and a subsequent conviction of each of the new offences. The Bill also specifies the circumstances in which a police officer may arrest without warrant a person who is believed to have committed one of the new offences[50]

i) Status of Business, Journals, and *Hansard*

Provinces have the same types of documents as the federal Parliament does for tracking the status of a bill, its reading dates, and what was said about the bill: Status of Business, Journals, and *Hansard*.

The first reading of Bill 8 was noted in the Journals, which are the official record of House proceedings from the notes of the Clerks-at-the-Table. Along with the first reading of a government public bill, Ontario bills may be tabled with a compendium, which could include things like ministry statements, backgrounder, press releases, a consolidation of the text of statutes that will be amended (if any), and

---

50   Bill 8, *An Act to promote safety in Ontario by prohibiting aggressive solicitation, solicitation of persons in certain places and disposal of dangerous things in certain places, and to amend the Highway Traffic Act to regulate certain activities on the roadways*, 1st Sess, 37th Leg, Ontario, 1999.

a clause-by-clause analysis. Every bill is different and may include more or fewer of these items in the compendium. These items are public but generally only available at the legislative library.

The standing orders contain provisions for the introduction of bills during the part of the legislative day called routine proceedings. The introduction of a bill is known as first reading. The bill is printed at first reading for the convenience of members and posted on the Legislative Assembly of Ontario website within about twenty-four hours. Bill 8 was introduced in the legislature by the Honourable Jim Flaherty, the Minister of the Attorney General:

INTRODUCTION OF BILLS

SAFE STREETS ACT, 1999 / LOI DE 1999 SUR LA SÉCURITÉ DANS LES RUES

Mr Flaherty moved first reading of the following bill:

Bill 8, An Act to promote safety in Ontario by prohibiting aggressive solicitation, solicitation of persons in certain places and disposal of dangerous things in certain places, and to amend the Highway Traffic Act to regulate certain activities on roadways / Projet de loi 8, Loi visant à promouvoir la sécurité en Ontario en interdisant la sollicitation agressive, la sollicitation de personnes dans certains lieux et le rejet de choses dangereuses dans certains lieux, et modifiant le Code de la route afin de réglementer certaines activités sur la chaussée.

The Speaker (Hon Gary Carr): Is it the pleasure of the House that the motion carry? Carried.[51]

Later, during the time for minister's statements, the minister usually makes a statement about the bill. Here is the minister's statement on Bill 8:

SAFE STREETS ACT

Hon Jim Flaherty (Attorney General, minister responsible for native affairs): Our government believes in keeping the promises it makes

---

51   Legislative Assembly of Ontario, *Hansard*, 1st Sess, 37th Parl, 2 November 1999, online: www.ola.org/en/legislative-business/house-documents/parliament-37/ session-1/1999-11-02/hansard#P63_14047.

to the people of Ontario. In the Blueprint, we made a commitment to take action about behaviour that jeopardizes the safe use of the streets.

Last month in the speech from the throne, we reiterated our intention to introduce legislation empowering police to crack down on squeegeeing and aggressive forms of solicitation experienced by many people in Ontario through panhandlers. This is one element of our broad effort to make our towns and cities safer places to live and raise families.

Our government believes that all people in Ontario have the right to drive on the roads, walk down the street or go to public places without being or feeling intimidated. They must be able to carry out their daily activities without fear. When they are not able to do so, it is time for government to act. It is time for government to exercise its responsibility to maintain and protect the ability of Ontario residents to use their streets, sidewalks and parks in a safe and secure manner.

Earlier today, I introduced the Safe Streets Act. The bill, if passed, would regulate conduct that interferes with the safe use of public spaces. It is legislation that responds to the real-life concerns Ontarians have about problems they encounter, such as squeegee-ing, aggressive solicitation, soliciting in captive audience situations, and the disposal of dangerous objects in parks, schoolyards and other public places.[52]

d) Second Reading

Second reading debate for government bills is held during the part of the legislative day called Orders of the Day, Monday to Thursday, and the timing and rules of debate are set out in the standing orders. Private members' public bills are debated on Thursdays during private members' public business. Bill 8 started the second reading stage in the legislature on 15 November 1999:

---

52 *Ibid.*

ORDERS OF THE DAY
SAFE STREETS ACT, 1999 / LOI DE 1999 SUR LA SÉCURITÉ DANS
LES RUES
Mr Flaherty moved second reading of the following bill:

Bill 8, An Act to promote safety in Ontario by prohibiting aggressive
solicitation, solicitation of persons in certain places and disposal
of dangerous things in certain places, and to amend the Highway
Traffic Act to regulate certain activities on roadways.[53]

At second reading, members speak on the principle of the bill and
this is often the best place in the debates to find minister's statements
as to the purpose of the bill:

Today we proceed with the debate on second reading of Bill 8, the
Safe Streets Act, 1999. When the people of Ontario talk about the
quality of life in their communities, certain things come to mind.
Key among these things is the ability to use their streets and their
public places without being impeded and without being concerned
for their own safety and security. Yet, for the past few years, the
experience of many people in large and small urban areas of Ontario
has been different. Motorists driving on downtown streets now
sometimes find their way blocked by people with squeegees, sometimes cleaning windshields without permission and sometimes
being abusive when they don't receive payment. Shoppers, including the elderly, sometimes find they can't get into their favourite
department store without being blocked by people who are aggres-
sively soliciting . . . .

The introduction of the Safe Streets Act is action in response
to the concerns we've heard from the people of Ontario. They have
asked us to act on the problems of squeegeeing and aggressive
solicitation, which have interfered with their safe passage in public
places. They have asked us to act to keep their neighborhoods free
from carelessly-disposed-of dangerous objects.

---

53 Legislative Assembly of Ontario, *Hansard*, 1st Sess, 37th Parl, 15 November 1999,
    online: www.ola.org/en/legislative-business/house-documents/parliament-37/
    session-1/1999-11-15/hansard.

Our government is exercising its responsibility and taking leadership to maintain and protect the ability of Ontario residents to use their streets, sidewalks and parks in a safe and secure manner. I urge the members of the opposition to support the right of the people of Ontario to have access to public places without interference and intimidation.[54]

Bill 8 was debated at second reading again on 16, 17, and 18 November. A time allocation motion was passed on November 18, requiring members to vote on the second reading motion the next day. It was then referred to the Standing Committee on Justice and Social Policy:

The Deputy Speaker (Mr Bert Johnson): Pursuant to the order of the House dated November 18, 1999, I'm now required to put the question on second reading of Bill 8. Mr Flaherty has moved second reading of Bill 8. Is it the pleasure of the House that the motion carry? Carried.

Pursuant to the order of the House dated November 18, 1999, this bill is referred to the standing committee on justice and social policy.[55]

e) Committee Stage

The provincial legislative committee system is a smaller version of the federal committee system. Standing committees of legislatures are permanent and provided for in the standing orders of the legislature, roughly corresponding to government departments. Standing committees usually examine bills but they also do other important work, considering estimates and appointments, for example. Provincial legislatures also have a type of ad hoc committee, called a select or special committee, that is formed for a particular purpose and disbanded after their work is completed.

Since committees are formed with a smaller group of members, they are more flexible and more informal. They hear from witnesses, debate the bill, and, finally, often consider each clause of the bill

---

54   Ibid.
55   Legislative Assembly of Ontario, Hansard, 1st Sess, 37th Parl, 18 November 1999, online: www.ola.org/en/legislative-business/house-documents/parliament-37/session-1/1999-11-18/hansard#P733_218814.

before voting on it and reporting back to the legislature. It is important to note that not every committee will consider a bill clause by
clause, and those that do this work may not provide a detailed analysis of every clause in a bill.

The committee may choose to travel to hear from witnesses. Witnesses are often experts and interest groups who will explain things
and offer opinions on the bill. On 29 November 1999 the Standing
Committee on Justice and Social Policy heard from groups including the Canadian Civil Liberties Association, the Centre for Equal-
ity Rights in Accommodation, Mennonite Central Committee, Low
Income Families Together, the Toronto Police Services, and others.
On 20 November 1999 the Committee continued to discuss Bill 8.

Witnesses may also submit written comments on the bill. In
Ontario, these are called exhibits or witness submissions. For Bill 8
there are nine exhibits: seven exhibits are from interest groups, one
exhibit is a report from the Legislative Research Service called "Recent
Statistics for Homelessness and Panhandling," and one exhibit is
from the Ministry of the Attorney General, which includes a first
reading copy of Bill 8, a compendium, a clause-by-clause analysis, the
Highway Traffic Act, and the Bill 8 Media Kit. The clause-by-clause consideration is usually held during the final days of the committee work.

f)   Reported to the House

On 1 December 1999 the Standing Committee on Social Policy reported
Bill 8, without amendment, back to the House. The motion to adopt
the report, which is simply the text of the bill, in the legislature was
carried, and Bill 8 is ordered for third reading.

g)   Third Reading

The third and final reading of Bill 8, *Safe Streets Act* happened on
7 December and 8 December 1999. December 7 saw lengthy debate
from all three political parties and a motion for deferral of the third
reading vote was carried. On December 8, in the part of the day for
deferred votes, a "vote on division" for Bill 8 was held. A vote on division means that the Speaker counts individual members' votes and
that the individual votes are recorded. Bill 8, *Safe Streets Act* passed

third reading motion with forty-nine members voting for it (ayes) and thirty-six members voting against it (nays).

h) Royal Assent

Provinces also require that royal assent be given to bills before they become an Act of the Legislature. Royal assent was given by the Lieutenant Governor of Ontario, on behalf of the Queen, to five bills, including Bill 8, on 19 December 1999. Royal assent is recorded in the Journals and *Hansard*.

I. WHERE TO FIND BILLS

Online, full-text versions of current Canadian bills can be found on the Parliament of Canada and provincial and territorial legislatures' websites. Generally, the Parliament and legislature bills are available for all three readings from the early 2000s to the present day, although some jurisdictions do not provide all readings, and early coverage of the full text varies.

TABLE 2.1: WHERE TO FIND BILLS

Jurisdiction	Bill Website	Dates of Full Text Availability
Federal Parliament of Canada: House of Commons of Canada	LEGIS*info* www.parl.ca/LEGISINFO	1994–current For bills from 1994–2000 LEGIS*info* provides full text where available.
Federal Parliament of Canada: Senate of Canada	LEGIS*info* www.parl.ca/LEGISINFO	1994–current For bills from 1994–2000 LEGIS*info* provides full text where available.
Alberta	Legislative Assembly of Alberta www.assembly.ab.ca	1906–current Early reference to bills may not contain full text.

Jurisdiction	Bill Website	Dates of Full Text Availability
British Columbia	Legislative Assembly of British Columbia www.leg.bc.ca	1992–current
Manitoba	Legislative Assembly of Manitoba www.gov.mb.ca/legislature	1999–current
New Brunswick	Legislative Assembly of New Brunswick www.gnb.ca/legis	2000–current
Newfoundland and Labrador	House of Assembly of Newfoundland and Labrador www.assembly.nl.ca	2000–current
Northwest Territories	Legislative Assembly of Northwest Territories www.assembly.gov.nt.ca	2008–current
Nunavut	Legislative Assembly of Nunavut www.assembly.nu.ca	Current only
Nova Scotia	Nova Scotia Legislature www.nslegislature.ca	1995–current
Ontario	Legislative Assembly of Ontario www.ola.org	1995–current
Prince Edward Island	Legislative Assembly of Prince Edward Island www.assembly.pe.ca	1997–current Early bills may not contain full text.
Quebec	National Assembly of Quebec www.assnat.qc.ca/en/index.html	1994–current
Saskatchewan	Legislative Assembly of Saskatchewan www.legassembly.sk.ca	2008–current
	Freelaw www.publications.gov.sk.ca/freelaw	1997–current
	Law Society of Saskatchewan Bills database https://library.lawsociety.sk.ca/databasespub/saskbills2002.htm	1993–current
Yukon	Yukon Legislative Assembly www.legassembly.gov.yk.ca	2004–current

For historical bills or bills that are not online, a researcher will have to look for print collections of bills. Here are some locations to find Canadian bills in print:

- Library and Archives Canada
- Legislative libraries (see Appendix 2)
- Provincial archives (see Appendix 2)
- University libraries
- Public libraries

A researcher may also find digitized versions of the text of federal or provincial bills on these resources:

- Internet Archive: https://archive.org
- Early Canadiana Online: www.eco.canadiana.ca
- British North America Legislative Database 1758–1867: https://bnald.lib.unb.ca

chapter three
Intrinsic Aids to Statutory Interpretation

A. INTRINSIC AIDS TO STATUTORY INTERPRETATION

As noted in Chapter 1, researchers should be aware that indications of legislative intent may be found in *intrinsic aids*. These appear in the text of the statute or regulation and might include titles, preambles, marginal notes, headings, punctuation, and schedules.[1] Judges will look at these intrinsic aids first for indications of legislative intent before they consider other extrinsic sources such as legislative history or legislative evolution, according to the hierarchy for statutory interpretation established by Driedger's modern principle.

In order to ascertain which part of a statute can be considered as evidence of meaning and which parts are tangential to that meaning, it is often a good idea to look at the interpretation Act or equivalent for the jurisdiction of the statute that you are researching.

In Ontario, for example, section 68 of the *Legislation Act*[2] specifies that

> 68 (1) A preamble to a new Act is part of that Act and may be used to help explain its purpose.

---

1   Pierre-André Côté, *The Interpretation of Legislation in Canada*, 4th ed (Toronto: Carswell: 2011).
2   *Legislation Act*, SO 2006, c 21, Schedule F, s 68.

(2) A preamble to an Act that amends one or more other Acts is part of the amending Act and may be used to help explain the purpose of the amendments.

While section 70 defines those parts of a statute that can only be used for reference rather than evidence of intent:

Reference aids

70 Tables of contents, marginal notes, information included to provide legislative history, headnotes and headings are inserted in an Act or regulation for convenience of reference only and do not form part of it.[3]

Although in this instance the statute specifies only that the preamble can be used, there are other parts of the statutes that can also be used.

1) Preambles

Preambles are an optional element in a statute that appear in the text of the legislation after the title and before the numbered provisions;[4] they are usually identified as such by a heading. A preamble will set out the "purposes and policies"[5] of a statute. The role of a preamble might be to persuade readers as to the value of the statute, to explain why that statute was enacted, to establish its goals, or to provide a hint to judges about how that statute should be interpreted.[6]

There are numerous examples in caselaw where judges have used the preamble to guide their interpretation, although there has been some disagreement as to how much weight it should be given. At present it seems that the prevailing sentiment is that a preamble should be given as much weight as "seems appropriate in the

---

3   *Ibid*, s 70.

4   Ruth Sullivan, *Sullivan on the Construction of Statutes*, 6th ed (Markham, ON: LexisNexis, 2014) [Sullivan, *Construction*, 6th].

5   Kent Roach, "The Uses and Audiences of Preambles in Legislation" (2001) 47 *McGill Law Journal* 129 at 135.

6   *Ibid*.

circumstances,"[7] in other words, "to clarify what is obscure"[8] if the meaning of the enactment is not clear.

2) Titles

According to parliamentary procedure, bills are required to "be given a title indicating the [entire] purpose and scope of the proposed act"[9] and the provisions of the Act should not exceed the scope as identified by the title.[10] Short titles are provided for easy reference to the statute and are not bound by the same requirements. Despite that difference, the courts have looked at both long and short titles as evidence of legislative intent.[11] As with preambles, the weight of the title as a mechanism for ascertaining legislative intent depends on the circumstances.[12] In places where the meaning of the statute is ambiguous, the courts have deemed it appropriate to use the title as a guide, but not if the wording of the text is clear.

3) Headings

Although headings are often specifically excluded as a source of statutory interpretation by the various interpretation Acts, some judges have nonetheless used headings to contextualize the structure and meaning of a statute.[13] While some headings can be considered merely labels,[14] others do create a hierarchical structure that can be useful in interpreting the meaning of a statute.[15] The use of a heading as a tool for interpretation, like the other intrinsic sources, depends on the clarity of the wording of the statute.

---

7   Sullivan, *Construction*, 6th, above note 4 at 453.

8   *Fraser, Viger & Co, Ltd c Lachine (Cité)* (1918), 28 BR 181 at 184, cited in Côté, above note 1 at 66.

9   Sullivan, *Construction*, 6th, above note 4 at 440.

10 *Ibid.*

11 Côté, above note 1.

12 Sullivan, *Construction*, 6th, above note 4 at 446.

13 *Ibid.*

14 Côté, above note 1.

15 Sullivan, *Construction*, 6th, above note 4.

4) Marginal Notes

As with headings, many interpretation Acts define marginal notes as reference aids rather than as integral parts of a statute. And, as with headings, the courts, including the Supreme Court of Canada in *R v Wigglesworth*,[16] have chosen to use marginal notes as interpretation aids. The courts have, however, been very specific that they should receive only "minimal weight."[17]

5) Punctuation

Given the recent American case in which the Oxford comma (or at least the absence of one in Maine's overtime law) ended up costing the Oakhurst Dairy a substantial amount of money,[18] it is surprising that punctuation is not given more weight in Canadian statutory interpretation than it has been. Having said that, punctuation has been used to "resolve ambiguity,"[19] but it is not generally given a great deal of weight. Misplaced punctuation does not "override the meaning suggested by the provision as a whole."[20]

6) Schedules

Schedules are usually materials in a statute that are an addendum to the body of the statute. A schedule could contain "lists, tables, charts and maps"[21] as well as other documents. Despite being part of a statute, a schedule does not have the force of law unless it is "incorporated into the act by either expressly or by implication."[22] If the text

---

16   *Ibid.*
17   Ruth Sullivan, *Statutory Interpretation*, 3d ed (Toronto: Irwin Law, 2016) at 169. [Sullivan, *Interpretation*].
18   AJ Wittingham, "An Oxford Comma Changed This Court Case Completely" (16 March 2017), online: *CNN* www.cnn.com/2017/03/15/health/oxford-comma-maine-court-case-trnd/index.html.
19   Sullivan, *Interpretation*, above note 17 at 170.
20   *Smart Hardware Co v Town of Melfort* (1917), 32 DLR 552 (Sask SC), cited in Côté, above note 1 at 76.
21   Sullivan, *Interpretation*, above note 17 at 171.
22   *Ibid.*

of the Act refers to the schedule, then it can be considered incorporated. The courts have used schedules that have not been incorporated as evidence of legislative intent, but as an extrinsic rather than an intrinsic aid to interpretation.

7)   Lessons for the Researcher

While the text of the statute will provide all the intrinsic aids mentioned here, there might still be research to be done. You might be called on to locate cases in which the use of one type of aid or another was justified by the courts, especially if your argument hinges on the use of that aid. The cases cited in this section provide access to the leading cases, but you will have to ensure that your caselaw research is up to date.

chapter four

Extrinsic Aids to Statutory Interpretation: Legislative Debates

A. EXTRINSIC AIDS

Extrinsic aids are generally defined as any source beyond the actual text of a statute or regulation that can be used to aid statutory interpretation.[1] Legislative evolution and legislative history are the two types of extrinsic aids to statutory interpretation that are the focus of this guide. While legislative evolution is restricted to the text of a bill or statute and changes to that bill or statute, legislative history casts a much wider net and can include the many kinds of extrinsic aids, documents, and records, for example, that surround the bill's evolution.

B. LEGISLATIVE DEBATES (*HANSARD*)

A critical component of compiling a legislative history is locating what has been said about a bill in Parliament. Records of what was said about a bill, when it was introduced, why it was amended, and its different stages are captured in various official House documents, including the official reports of proceedings, also called *Hansard* or referred

---

1   Ruth Sullivan, *Sullivan on the Construction of Statutes*, 6th ed (Markham, ON: LexisNexis Canada, 2014) at 657.

to as the parliamentary debates. For the courts, lawyers, and researchers, these records offer understanding of the intention of Parliament.

Hansard is central to the development, research, and story of legislative intent. While what was said about a bill will never replace the actual words of the bill, the surrounding debate can provide important insight into the bill's intent. The work of researching *Hansard* as part of a legislative history and the use of the modern principle of statutory interpretation was validated in Canada by the *Rizzo and Rizzo Shoes* case. Today, *Hansard* is the most important extrinsic aid to understanding legislative intent and should always be checked when putting together a legislative history; but it wasn't always this way.

Hansard has its own history, evolving from being a small private publication produced by a fledgling independent printer to becoming an official parliamentary publication. *Hansard* also has a history with the courts; originally it was not admissible as evidence of legislative intent under the exclusionary rule but now it has become standard practice for courts to accept *Hansard* as evidence of legislative intent.

A brief look at the history of *Hansard*, and *Hansard* as aid to statutory interpretation, will demonstrate its central role in researching legislative intent. In 1803, William Cobbett began publication of the *Parliamentary Debates*, later *Cobbett's Parliamentary Debates*, as a standalone publication, published separately from the newspapers of the day. Eventually, he sold the contract to printer Thomas Hansard and in due course the debates became popularly known as *Hansard*. The early debates were not completely reliable as they were cobbled together from newspaper reports and other sources, and so in January 1909, the Commons took over producing *Hansard*, which was now called the "Official Report." Despite the name change, *Hansard* was still colloquially called *Hansard* in the United Kingdom and in some Commonwealth countries, and in 1943 the name *Hansard* was reinstated on the title page of the Official Report.[2]

---

2   Andrew Struan, *History of Hansard*, online: *Parliamentary Discourse* https://
     web.archive.org/web/20150713102223/parldisc.jiscinvolve.org/wp/2011/06/03/
     history-of-hansard.

C. *HANSARD* IN CANADA

The history of the publication of parliamentary debates in Canada is less dramatic. Prior to Confederation, in Upper Canada, although there was some initial resistance to having the reports of the debates published, they were reported nevertheless in the newspapers of the time. These were sometimes collected and published as the "Scrapbook Hansards." Shortly after Confederation, in 1880, *Hansard* became an official publication with a team of reporters responsible for accurately recording the debates in Parliament.[3]

D. FROM THE EXCLUSIONARY RULE TO THE MODERN PRINCIPLE

Legislative intent was barred from consideration by the courts in England for over 200 years. The exclusionary rule, like other rules of interpretation, is not explicitly set out in a statute but rather was a common law principle established and upheld by caselaw. Under the exclusionary rule, "the legislative history of an enactment was not permissible to assist in interpretation"[4] and "could not be used as direct evidence of legislative intent."[5] This principle was followed by the courts in the United Kingdom from its first articulation in 1769[6] until 1992.

In Millar *v* Taylor, Willes J first articulated the exclusionary rule:

> The sense and the meaning of an Act of Parliament must be collected from what it says when passed into law; and not from the history of changes it underwent in the house where it took its rise.[7]

And that simple statement became the exclusionary rule, with its profound influence on statutory interpretation, for two centuries.

---

3   *Hansard History*, online: *Hansard Association of Canada* www.hansard.ca/ Hansard%20History_cont.pdf.
4   Ruth Sullivan, *Sullivan on the Construction of Statutes*, 5th ed (Markham, ON: LexisNexis Canada) 2008 at 594 [Sullivan, *Construction*, 5th].
5   *Ibid*.
6   *Millar v Taylor* (1769), 98 ER 201.
7   *Ibid* at 217.

So, what was Willes J's reasoning for this ruling? As he stated in explanation, "[t]hat history is not known to the other house, or to the Sovereign."[8] His fundamental reasoning was practical; there was no legal or reliable record of the debates at the time and so there really was no way of telling what Parliament meant when it made those changes to the bill.

In the United Kingdom, the end of the exclusionary rule came quite suddenly, in 1992, in the case of *Pepper v Hart*.[9] The House of Lords, after a great deal of discussion, chose to admit the use of legislative history in cases where the text of the legislation was ambiguous.

The trend away from the exclusionary rule in Canada began with constitutional cases, such as the *Inflation Act* reference of 1976.[10] In the *R v Morgentaler* case of 1993, Sopinka J explicitly stated that *Hansard* evidence should be admitted as relevant to both the background and the purpose of legislation.[11] Since the passage of the *Charter of Rights and Freedoms* in 1984, there have been a number of cases that have used legislative history and other extrinsic aids in interpreting the meaning of legislation within the context of the *Charter*, as well as to interpret the language of the *Charter* itself.[12]

E. THE MODERN PRINCIPLE IN THE SUPREME COURT OF CANADA

In 1998, the exclusionary rule was put to bed forever—not just for *Charter* and constitutional cases but for ordinary statutory interpretation as well—in *Rizzo and Rizzo Shoes Ltd (Re)* at the Supreme Court of Canada. Justice Iacobucci, in finding for the employees, looked very closely at the termination provisions of the *Employment Standards Act*.[13] In his decision, Iacobucci J noted:

---

8   *Ibid.*

9   *Pepper (Inspector of Taxes) v Hart*, [1993] AC 593 (HL).

10 *Re: Anti-Inflation Act*, [1976] 2 SCR 373.

11 *R v Morgentaler*, [1993] 3 SCR 463 at 464 [*Morgentaler*].

12 Sullivan, *Construction*, 5th, above note 4 at 688–89.

13 *Employment Standards Act*, RSO 1970, c 147, s 13(2); *Employment Standards Act*, 1974, SO 1974, c 112, s 40(7); *Employment Standards Act*, RSO 1980, c 137, ss 7(5) [rep &

At the heart of this conflict is an issue of statutory interpretation. Consistent with the findings of the Court of Appeal, the plain meaning of the words of the provisions here in question appears to restrict the obligation to pay termination and severance pay to those employers who have actively terminated the employment of their employees. At first blush, bankruptcy does not fit comfortably into this interpretation. However, with respect, I believe this analysis is incomplete.[14]

He then went on to quote Driedger's modern principle:

Today there is only one principle or approach, namely, the words of an Act are to be read in their entire context and in their grammatical and ordinary sense harmoniously with the scheme of the Act, the object of the Act, and *the intention of Parliament.*[15]

He subsequently examined statements made by the minister of labour recorded in Ontario's *Hansard*, specifically on the termination provisions of the *Employment Standards Act*, citing Sopinka J in the *Morgentaler*[16] cases as his justification for doing so. And thus the exclusionary rule was ended forever.

Justice Iacobucci's use of *Hansard* evidence in *Rizzo* has subsequently been described as a "model"[17] use that should be used as an exemplar for the use of *Hansard* evidence in the courts. In this model:

＊ Only the sponsoring minister [who can be assumed to be speaking for parliament] is cited.
＊ The quotations are brief.

---

sub 1986, c 51, s 2], 40(1) [rep & sub 1987, c 30, s 4(1)], 40(7), 40a(1) [rep & sub *ibid*, s 5(1)]; *Employment Standards Amendment Act, 1981*, SO 1981, c 22, s 2.

14　*Rizzo & Rizzo Shoes Ltd (Re)*, [1998] 1 SCR 27 at para 20 [*Rizzo*].

15　Elmer Dreidger, *The Construction of Statutes*, 2d ed (Toronto: Butterworths, 1983) at 87, cited in *Rizzo*, above note 14 at para 21 [emphasis added].

16　*Morgentaler*, above note 11.

17　Graham Steele, "'The Frailties of Hansard Evidence Are Many': The Use of House of Assembly Debates in Nova Scotia Courts, 2004–2017" (2015) 9 *Journal of Public Policy, Administration and the Law* 499 at 499.

☞ The quotations support and interpretation reached by other means.[18]

F. *HANSARD* IN COURTS TODAY

There is evidence in recent years that courts are using *Hansard* as an important extrinsic aid in legislative intent, not only in referring to the debates themselves, but because *Hansard* is allowed to be used to bring into evidence and give weight to other extrinsic aides, a practice known as shoehorning.[19] *Hansard* often provides a rich description of the bill's legislative intent through speeches in Parliament, at second reading, or in committee transcripts (sometimes called committee *Hansard*) at the committee stage. The speeches may refer to other important extrinsic aids that, when put together, point to legislative intent.

G. FINDING OFFICIAL TRANSCRIPTS OF LEGISLATIVE DEBATES (*HANSARD*)

Hansard is published in each jurisdiction on every day that there is a sitting of the Parliament or legislature. Each jurisdiction has their own *Hansard* department that transcribes and publishes "substantially verbatim"[20] transcripts of what was said by members. *Hansard* can be found in print and online. Various tools, like indexes, a table of contents, and online search are usually available to provide access to the debates by speaker, date, or topic. Other tools and documents can supplement and point to important parts of the transcripts. For

---

18 *Ibid* at 507–8.

19 John James Magyar, "Evolution of Hansard Use at the Supreme Court of Canada: A Comparative Study in Statutory Interpretation" (2012) 33:3 *Statute Law Review* 363; John James Magyar, *Hansard as an Aid to Statutory Interpretation in Canadian Courts from 1999–2010* (LLM Thesis, University of Western Ontario Faculty of Law, 2011) [unpublished].

20 Ian Church, *Official Report (Hansard) House of Commons Centenary Volume 1909–2009, An Anthology of Historic and Memorable House of Commons Speeches to Celebrate the First 100 Years* (London: House of Commons, 2009).

instance, a jurisdiction's Journals (a compilation of the daily Votes and Proceedings) provide the official record of bill reading dates.

More researchers are relying on online access to *Hansard*, but sometimes only the print copies of *Hansard* exist. The good news is that there are ongoing digitization projects that are putting older *Hansard* volumes online in a way that is accessible and useable.

Before the official transcripts of proceedings began publishing, often a jurisdiction would patch a version of *Hansard* together from newspapers or journals or other reports. These gave a picture of the debates and parliamentary proceedings through the various sources. These publications are called things like "scrapbook Hansard" or "newspaper Hansard."

Hansard's terms of reference were set by a House of Commons Select Committee in 1893, which defined it as being a report:

> which, though not strictly verbatim, is substantially the verbatim report with repetitions and redundancies omitted and with obvious mistakes (including grammatical mistakes) corrected, but which, on the other hand, leaves out nothing that adds to the meaning of the speech or illustrates the argument.[21]

According to *Beauchesne's Parliamentary Rules & Forms*,

> Hansard is not a verbatim transcript of the debates of the House. It is a transcript *in extenso* [at full length]. In the case of repetition or for a number of other reasons, such as more specific identification, it is acceptable to make changes so that anyone reading Hansard will get the meaning of what is said. Those who edit Hansard have an obligation to make a sentence more readable since there is a difference between the spoken and the written word.[22]

---

21   *Ibid* at xvi.

22   Arthur Beauchesne et al, *Beauchesne's Parliamentary Rules & Forms*, 6th ed (Toronto: Carswell, 1989) at 19.

H. WHERE TO FIND *HANSARD*

Print copies of *Hansard* can be found in Parliamentary libraries, legislative libraries, archives (see Appendix 2), as well as university and public libraries in Canada.

TABLE 4.1: WHERE TO FIND *HANSARD*

CANADA	
Print	
Official Report of Proceedings (*Hansard*)	**Dates**
House of Commons Debates (*Hansard*)	1875–current
Debates of the Senate (*Hansard*)	1871–current
Web	
Official Report of Proceedings (*Hansard*)	**Dates**
House of Commons Debates (*Hansard*) Parliament of Canada: www.ourcommons.ca/DocumentViewer/en/house/latest/hansard	1994–current
House of Commons Debates (*Hansard*) Canadian Parliamentary Historical Resources: http://parl.canadiana.ca	1867–1993
Debates of the Senate Parliament of Canada: www.parl.gc.ca	1996–current
Debates of the Senate Canadian Parliamentary Historical Resources: http://parl.canadiana.ca	1871–1995
Other	
Other Reports of Proceedings[23]	**Dates**
Reconstituted debates of the House of Commons Canadian Parliamentary Historical Resources: http://parl.canadiana.ca	1867–1874
Reconstituted debates of the Senate Canadian Parliamentary Historical Resources: http://parl.canadiana.ca	1867–1870
Debates of the Senate—French translation Canadian Parliamentary Historical Resources: http://parl.canadiana.ca	1871–1874
House of Commons *Hansard* and Senate *Hansard* Searchable open dataset: www.lipad.ca	1901–current

---

23   "Scrapbook Hansard" and older transcripts.

ALBERTA

Print

Official Report of Proceedings (*Hansard*)	Dates
Alberta *Hansard*	1972–current

Web

Official Report of Proceedings (*Hansard*)	Dates
Alberta *Hansard* Legislative Assembly of Alberta: www.assembly.ab.ca	1972–current
Hansard text, indexes and search: www.assembly.ab.ca/net/index. aspx?p=adr_home&adr=adr_hansard	

Other

Other Reports of Proceedings	Dates
Scrapbook Hansard (historical collection of newspaper clippings and a few speech transcripts) https://librarysearch.assembly.ab.ca/client/en_CA/scrapbookhansard	1906–1971

BRITISH COLUMBIA

Print

Official Report of Proceedings (*Hansard*)	Dates
Official Report of Debates	1970–current

Web

Official Report of Proceedings (*Hansard*)	Dates
Official Report of Debates Legislative Assembly of British Columbia: www.leg.bc.ca	1970–current
Hansard text, indexes and search: www.leg.bc.ca/documents-data	

Other

Other Reports of Proceedings	Dates
Press clippings: British Columbia Legislative Assembly sessional clipping books	1890–1977
Compiled by the Legislative Library of British Columbia: www.leg.bc.ca/learn-about-us/legislative-library	
Press clippings: British Columbia Legislative Assembly sessional clipping books	1890–1977
Compiled by the Legislative Library of British Columbia: www.leg.bc.ca/learn-about-us/legislative-library	

MANITOBA

Print	
Official Report of Proceedings (*Hansard*)	**Dates**
Debates and Proceedings	1958–current
Web	
Official Report of Proceedings (*Hansard*)	**Dates**
Debates and Proceedings	1958–current
Legislative Assembly of Manitoba: www.gov.mb.ca/legislature	
Other	
Other Reports of Proceedings	**Dates**
Press clippings: *Hansard* scrapbooks: from newspaper legislative accounts, 1885–1984. Legislative Library of Manitoba: www.gov.mb.ca/chc/leg-lib	1885–1984
Legislative Reporting in Early Manitoba Newspapers	1873–1886
Published accounts of Manitoba Legislative Assembly and Legislative Council activities from 1873–1886 from the *Winnipeg Free Press* and *Daily Times* newspapers. www.gov.mb.ca/chc/leg-lib/elr.html	

NEW BRUNSWICK

Print	
Official Report of Proceedings (*Hansard*)	**Dates**
Journal of Debates (*Hansard*) Bound edition: 1980–1996.	1980–1996
Since that period, available on loose-leaf format, and electronic since 2002. Available on request at the New Brunswick Legislative Library	
Web	
Official Report of Proceedings (*Hansard*)	**Dates**
Journal of Debates (*Hansard*)	Not available online
The Journals and some speeches and related documents are available at: Legislative Assembly of New Brunswick www.gnb.ca/legis	1980–current
Other	
Other Reports of Proceedings	**Dates**
Older debates are called: Synoptic Reports Available in print	1837–1979

NEWFOUNDLAND AND LABRADOR

Print

Official Report of Proceedings (*Hansard*)	Dates
Hansard	1975–current

Web

Official Report of Proceedings (*Hansard*)	Dates
Hansard House of Assembly of Newfoundland and Labrador www.assembly.nl.ca	1980–current
Hansard Indexes www.assembly.nl.ca/HouseBusiness/Hansard/Index	1998–current

Other

Other Reports of Proceedings	Dates
Historical *Hansard* House of Assembly Debates and Legislative Council Debates: www.assembly.nl.ca/HouseBusiness/Hansard/Historical	1932–1933

NORTHWEST TERRITORIES

Print

Official Report of Proceedings (*Hansard*)	Dates
Hansard	1951–current

Web

Official Report of Proceedings (*Hansard*)	Dates
Hansard Legislative Assembly of Northwest Territories: www.assembly.gov.nt.ca	2000–current
Hansard search: www.assembly.gov.nt.ca/documents-proceedings/hansard/search	2003–current

NOVA SCOTIA

Print

Official Report of Proceedings (*Hansard*)	Dates
Debates and Proceedings	1851–current

Web

Official Report of Proceedings (*Hansard*)	Dates
Hansard (Debates) Nova Scotia Legislature: https://nslegislature.ca	1855–current
Debates and Proceedings of the House of Assembly of the Province of Nova Scotia Early Canadiana Online: http://eco.canadiana.ca/view/oocihm.9_01339	1855–1867

Other

Other Reports of Proceedings	Dates
Official report of the debates and proceedings of the Legislative Council (*Note*: The Legislative Council was abolished in 1928) Nova Scotia Legislative Library	1858–1861, 1875–1922
Journal and proceedings of His Majesty's Council of the Province of Nova-Scotia 1836–1928 Nova Scotia Legislative Library	1836-1928
Journal and proceedings of His Majesty's Council of the Province of Nova-Scotia Early Canadiana Online: http://eco.canadiana.ca/view/oocihm.9_00947	1830-1928
Journals and votes of the House of Assembly for the Province of Nova Scotia Early Canadiana Online: http://eco.canadiana.ca/view/oocihm.9_00946	1767-1867
Journals for the years 1758–1760 are in manuscript form only.	1758–1830 (manuscript)

NUNAVUT

Print

Official Report of Proceedings (*Hansard*)	Dates
Hansard Official Report	1999–current

Web

Official Report of Proceedings (*Hansard*)	Dates
Hansard Official Report Legislative Assembly of Nunavut: http://assembly.nu.ca	1999–current
The Blues (draft *Hansard*): http://assembly.nu.ca/hansard	current

ONTARIO

Print

Official Report of Proceedings (*Hansard*)	Dates
Official Report of Debates (*Hansard*)	1944–current

Web

Official Report of Proceedings (*Hansard*)	Dates
Official Report of Debates (*Hansard*) Legislative Assembly of Ontario: www.ola.org	1975–current
Hansard Indexes by Subject and Speaker for each session www.ola.org/en/legislative-business/house-hansard-index	2007–current
Advanced *Hansard* Search: http://hansardindex.ontla.on.ca	1975–current
Official Reports of Debates (*Hansard*) Internet Archive — Canadian Government Publications: https://archive.org/	1945–1980

Other

Other Reports of Proceedings	Dates
Scrapbook *Hansard* (historical collection of newspaper clippings on the topic of Ontario's legislative debates) in Microform at the Ontario Legislative Library	1867–1994
Ontario Scrapbook *Hansard* 1867–1944: Indexes for 1878, 1881, 1882, 1895, 1900, 1904, 1905, 1906, 1907	1867-1941
Legislative Library of Ontario: Indexed Press clippings ("Newspaper *Hansard*")	1841-1953

PRINCE EDWARD ISLAND

Print

Official Report of Proceedings (*Hansard*)	Dates
Hansard (Daily Debates)	1996–current

Web

Official Report of Proceedings (*Hansard*)	Dates
Hansard (Daily Debates) Legislative Assembly of Prince Edward Island: www.assembly.pe.ca	1996–current

QUEBEC

Print

Official Report of Proceedings (*Hansard*)	Dates
Hansard (Daily Debates)	1964–current

Web

Official Report of Proceedings (*Hansard*)	Dates
Hansard (Daily Debates) www.bibliotheque.assnat.qc.ca/fr/6964-recherche-%E2%80%93-debats-de-l-assemblee-nationale-1867	1964–current

Other

Other Reports of Proceedings	Dates
Débats reconstitués www.bibliotheque.assnat.qc.ca/fr/6964-recherche-%E2%80%93-debats-de-l-assemblee-nationale-1867	1867–1963

SASKATCHEWAN

Print

Official Report of Proceedings (*Hansard*)	Dates
Debates and Proceedings, Official Report	1947–current

Web

Official Report of Proceedings (*Hansard*)	Dates
Debates and Proceedings, Official Report Legislative Assembly of Saskatchewan: www.legassembly.sk.ca	1947–current (most complete from 1998–current)

Other

Other Reports of Proceedings	Dates
Scrapbook *Hansard*. Microfilmed copies at the Legislative Library. Original scrapbooks are located at the Saskatchewan Archives.	1888–1950

YUKON

Print

Official Report of Proceedings (*Hansard*)	Dates
Hansard	1978–current

Web

Official Report of Proceedings (*Hansard*)	Dates
Yukon Legislative Assembly: http://legassembly.gov.yk.ca	2006–current
Hansard Index: www.legassembly.gov.yk.ca/house/hansard.html	1978–current
Hansard Search: www.legassembly.gov.yk.ca/house/hansard.html	1978–current
Blues (preliminary transcripts, unedited *Hansard*): http://legassembly.gov.yk.ca/house/blues.html	Current

chapter five

Extrinsic Aids to Statutory Interpretation: Committees

A. INTRODUCTION

A Parliament or legislature uses various kinds of committees (a smaller group of members) to do specific and more detailed work than a large Parliament can accomplish. Committees are an integral part of the legislative process. They consider, modify, and debate bills, hear public input on bills and issues, and do clause-by-clause analysis of a bill. Committees also examine departmental spending (estimates), consider papers tabled in the House, order-in-council appointments, and deal with other important matters as assigned by legislation or the House.

Committees are smaller and more flexible than the House. Provincial legislative committees could have seven to eight members and federal committees could have as many as fifteen. The committee membership is usually a reflection of the party standings in the House with a similar proportional party standing in the committees. Customs and the Parliament's standing orders dictate how the committees are made up in each jurisdiction.

In addition, since they are extensions of the House and allow direct input from citizens, committees are a great illustration of democracy at work. Citizens can submit documents to the committee in the form of reports that are called "briefs" federally and provincially are sometimes known as "exhibits" or "witness submissions." Citizens can also appear as witnesses before the committee to answer questions from members and state their views. Committees have the power to send for persons and documents to complete their work. Committees sometimes travel and hold meetings throughout a jurisdiction to gather input.

There are two kinds of committees in the parliamentary committee system: permanent committees and special committees. Generally, each jurisdiction has permanent committees that are assigned, via standing orders, to consider business related to particular policy areas or ministries. Federally and in Ontario, these permanent committees are called standing committees, but committee names differ across the provinces. Special committees are formed for a specific purpose by the House or legislature and are dissolved once they complete their report. Federally today these committees are called special committees. In Ontario they are called select committees and are formed to examine and report on specific matters only.

B.　WHY DO WE RESEARCH COMMITTEES?

Committee materials are an important type of extrinsic aid that helps to reveal the intention of Parliament. They are a rich source of legislative history as it is in committee that members of Parliament will discuss a bill in detail and possibly amend it. In addition, experts provide the committee with their opinions on the subject matter of the proposed legislation. These opinions and the committee members' responses and any reasons for the amendments are all recorded in the committee records.

Committee reports are often used as evidence of legislative intent. In *Nemeth v Canada*, for example, Cromwell J explicitly stated that the use of both the 1998 *Minutes and Proceedings* and the *Sixteenth Report* of the Standing Committee on Justice and Human Rights was admissible, given the usual caveats about how much weight this evidence should be allowed:

> 46 These suspension provisions were added to the *IRPA* as consequential amendments when the *EA* was enacted in 1999. Their purpose was explained by Departmental officials testifying before

Parliamentary committees. Resort to this material is appropriate where, as here, it is relevant and reliable and provided it is used with caution and not given undue weight.[1]

Another example of the use of committee materials by the courts can be found in the 2005 Supreme Court of Canada case *Hilewitz v Canada (Minister of Citizenship and Immigration); De Jong v Canada (Minister of Citizenship and Immigration)*.[2] The Court deliberated whether immigration applicants' financial resources should be considered when determining if the admission of children with disabilities might reasonably be expected to cause excessive demands on the social services of the Canadian government.[3]

In reviewing the intent behind the *Immigration Act*,[4] section 19(1)(a)(ii), the justices referred to, and quoted, the minutes and evidence from the 1977 *Standing Committee on Labour Manpower and Immigration* in their decision. The Court used these committee materials as direct evidence of the meaning of the legislative provision in question and attached considerable weight to the views of the sponsoring department as revealed in the committee proceedings.

Justice Abella, after referring to portions of the committee transcript and to a brief submitted to the committee, concluded that "this review of the legislative history indicates a legislative intention to shift from an approach based on categorical exclusion to one calling for individualized assessments."[5] The committee materials informed the justices' understanding of legislative intent behind the *Immigration Act*, section 19(1)(a)(ii).

In addition, Ruth Sullivan writes, if the remarks of a particular expert witness in committee can be linked to an understanding of the text, then some weight can be given to the expert testimony in committee.[6]

---

1   *Nemeth v Canada (Justice)*, 2010 SCC 56 at para 46.

2   *Hilewitz v Canada (Minister of Citizenship and Immigration); De Jong v Canada (Minister of Citizenship and Immigration)*, 2005 SCC 57 [*Hilewitz*].

3   Ruth Sullivan, *Statutory Interpretation*, 3d ed (Toronto: Irwin Law, 2016) at 268 [Sullivan, *Interpretation*].

4   RSC 1985, c I-2.

5   *Hilewitz*, above note 2 at para 53.

6   Sullivan, *Interpretation*, above note 3.

C. TRANSCRIPTS OF THE COMMITTEE PROCEEDINGS

The materials that help a researcher put together legislative history could include the transcripts of the committee proceedings. They may be referred to as "committee *Hansards*" and at the federal level they are called "evidence of proceedings." The evidence contains the verbatim record of the proceedings, including discussion of the bill by members and witnesses.

D. MINUTES

Committees also keep minutes of their proceedings. Minutes are often overlooked as a source of committee information. The minutes may contain the full text of a proposed amendment to a bill. While the committee transcript will provide the discussion surrounding the amendment, they don't usually contain the amendment itself.

E. WITNESS BRIEFS

Committees put out a notice to invite interested parties to make submissions on an issue or bill. The committee can also call for witnesses to answer questions about the bill. The witnesses speaking to a bill are usually policy experts, stakeholders, or interest groups. Their testimony is recorded in the transcript and they may submit a report as well. These witness reports, filed with the committee materials, are called "briefs" (federally) or "exhibits" (in Ontario) and are often referred to as "witness submissions" or "submissions."

F. CLAUSE BY CLAUSE

Near the end of the committee proceedings the members will often, but not always, go over the bill clause by clause and vote on a motion to pass the sections as amended or unamended. This discussion will be part of the committee transcript. Researchers should note that section numbers in the bill are often different from the section numbers in the statute. In these cases, it may take some detective work to discover the corresponding bill section number of interest. Generally, there are no concordances relating bill numbers to statute numbers but reading the bill and identifying content that is in the statute will help determine the sections of interest.

During clause-by-clause committee work there could be discussion about the clauses, but often they are just passed without discussion. Clauses are often passed in large groups at this point (i.e., the motion to pass clause 1-10 is voted on with no further detail about the individual sections). It is often more fruitful to read the earlier stages of committee work and look for discussion by topic rather than by clause.

G. COMMITTEE REPORT

The committee members may produce a report on their work, or for committees considering bills, the report is most likely a copy of the amended bill, along with the minutes and evidence of the meetings considering the bill. The House *Hansard* transcripts and Journals indicate that the bill was "reported to the house" as part of the "report stage" in the legislative process. Committees assigned to study a particular topic or policy issue will often produce a written report that is more like a layperson's understanding of a written report, with an introduction, arguments, recommendations, and a conclusion. These committee reports are also tabled in the House.

H. FEDERAL COMMITTEES

The federal committee system is the largest in Canada with both the House of Commons and the Senate of Canada using committees to study bills and other matters. The Senate established its first committee on the second day of the first Parliament in 1867.

1) Standing Committees

Standing committees are permanent throughout a Parliament and receive their mandates in three different ways: from the Standing Orders, by an Order of Reference from the House, or through legislation. Committees can only conduct the business stated in the Orders of Reference and cannot exceed the scope of those mandates or Orders of Reference.

Standing committees conduct most, but not all, of the examination of bills, so most often a researcher will be looking at standing committee materials for information that could be used as evidence of legislative intent for federal bills. The House regularly refers bills to standing committees, but these committees deal with other matters regularly as well: reports tabled in the House, estimates, order-in council appointments, and the failure of the government to respond to petitions or written questions.[7]

Committees are empowered by the House to conduct their business as they see fit by examining the matters that the House refers to them, reporting to the House, requiring the attendance of persons or the production of documents, publishing their findings, and other powers. Committees must stay within the scope of their mandate, but they can request additional powers from the House.

The standing orders provide for the number and names of standing committees. The current House of Commons of Canada and Senate Standing Committees can be found on the Parliament of Canada's website.

2) Legislative Committees

A legislative committee is created solely to study a particular bill at committee stage in the legislative process. This type of committee may also be used to prepare a bill. Once the work of a legislative committee is complete the committee is dissolved, unlike standing committees, which exist for the life of the Parliament.[8]

3) Special Committees

A special committee is an ad hoc type of federal committee, appointed by the House or Senate to carry out a specific mandate, inquiry, or task

---

7   Parliament of Canada, House of Commons, "Committees Practical Guide,"
     online: www.parl.gc.ca/About/House/PracticalGuides/Committees/CmtesPG__
     Pg02-e.htm [*Committees Practical Guide*].

8   *Ibid.*

in a limited time frame and report back. A special committee ceases to exist after its final report or at prorogation.

4) Joint Committees

Joint committees are made up of both senators and members of the House of Commons. They have a proportionate number of members from each House, reflecting their relative sizes. Such committees may be established through the procedural rules of each House (a standing joint committee) or by a motion adopted by each House (a special joint committee).

While joint committees may consider legislation, they traditionally deal with issues of a non-legislative nature of common interest to both Houses. Once senators have been appointed to serve on a joint committee, a message is sent to the House of Commons indicating the names of the Senate members. Similarly, once the House of Commons membership is determined, a message is sent from the House to the Senate. Joint committees have a Senate chair and a House of Commons chair who alternately or jointly preside over meetings.

There are two standing joint committees: Scrutiny of Regulations and Library of Parliament.

5) Subcommittees

Subcommittees are established by the main committee and may exist either as long as that committee exists or until their task is completed. Subcommittees report to the main committee and are not authorized to report directly to the House of Commons. The composition of a subcommittee is not always proportional to the party representation in the main committee. A standing committee may appoint members to a subcommittee not only from its own ranks, but also from the list of associate members.[9]

---

9   *Ibid.*

I. TRANSCRIPTS, EVIDENCE, AND MINUTES

A federal committee's proceedings are the printed, edited transcripts, available in both English and French, of the testimony received by the committee. The transcripts are known as "evidence" of the committee. While separate issues are often prepared for each meeting of a committee, in some cases a number of meetings may be contained in one issue. Also, a single issue of evidence will sometimes deal with more than one order of reference or topic. Minutes are also kept by the committees and contain the official record of decisions, proposed amendments, and votes. Minutes are often helpful for researching legislative intent but are not usually a main source of information.

J. BRIEFS

A brief is a written submission from a stakeholder that provides opinions, comments, and recommendations on an issue or bill being studied by a parliamentary committee. Briefs can be well-reasoned opinion or argument that may prove useful to legislative intent research. It is important to be aware of how much weight was given to the report in the committee *Hansard* to see how much it influenced or supported the proposed legislation.

Briefs submitted to committees become part of their public archives. As a result, they may be provided to the public, possibly on the committee website. In addition, a copy of every brief is retained by Library and Archives Canada as part of the records of the committee.

When a committee presents a report to the House of Commons, a list of the names of the organizations and individuals who have submitted briefs will appear as an appendix to the report.[10]

K. WHERE TO FIND FEDERAL COMMITTEE MATERIALS

When compiling a legislative history, the best place to access committee materials is where it is connected to the bill of interest. LEGIS*info* is the

---

10   Parliament of Canada, House of Commons, "Guide for Submitting Briefs to the House of Commons Committees," online: www.parl.gc.ca/About/House/WitnessesGuides/guide-brief-e.htm.

best resource for this kind of research, as it keeps all committee material alongside the bill going back to 1994. The Parliament of Canada website has other tools to access committee materials by subject, speaker, and keyword, search for witnesses, and find reports. Historical federal committee materials are digitized on the Canadian Parliamentary Historical Resources website (http://parl.canadiana.gc.ca) and available in print in libraries. Witness submissions to committees are kept at the Archives of Canada in print form. Some current submissions may be found online.

1) LEGIS*info* (1994–present)

The best place to find federal committee materials related to a particular bill since 1994 is LEGIS*info*. Links to House and Senate meeting minutes and the committee report as presented in the House and Senate are provided.

As mentioned earlier, LEGIS*info* compiles committee information with other bill information on the bill's page. Here the researcher can see the bill's committee name, meeting dates, minutes, transcripts (evidence), reports, date and transcript of the report to the House or Senate, and the progress of the bill through the committee system. Committee links from LEGIS*info* go to the committee websites where the documents and often video and witness information will reside.

Briefs (submitted by witnesses to a committee) might be found in the LEGIS*info* "Further Resources" links about the bill, but a complete collection of exhibits is available at the Archives of Canada.

🦅 LEGIS*info*

www.parl.gc.ca/LEGISinfo/Home.aspx?ParliamentSession=42-1

2) Parliament of Canada Publication Search

The Parliament of Canada Publication Search tool can be used to find House of Commons committee evidence from the 1st Session of the 37th Parliament and onward (September 2001–present). Committee evidence is available five to ten days after the meeting.

Use the "Committee" tab on the Publication Search tool to view committee information, with the most current information located at the top. Searching can be further narrowed by keyword, parliament and session, committee name, topic, person speaking, province, caucus, and participation type (member or witness/appearance). The search results can be exported by CSV, XML, or a search RSS can be set up. This tool also includes a search for *Hansard* and Journals, and all publications can be searched together.

 Publication Search
www.parl.gc.ca/Parliamentarians/en/PublicationSearch?PubType=40017

3) All Committees' Work — House of Commons Committee Materials

To search committee materials from 1994 to the present, go to the committees home page and select either the Parliament/Session from the sliding timeline tool or the particular committee. Next, locate the particular committee and session and view reports and evidence of the committee. The years 1994–97 are linked to their location on an archival site.

 House of Commons All Committees' Work
www.parl.gc.ca/Committees/en/Work

4) Witness Search (1997–present)

Use the Witness Search to find witness testimony across all House of Commons standing committees from the 36 Parliament, 1st Session to the current (22 September 1997–present). Search by witness and/or organization name. Further filters of Parliament/Session, Committee, Study/Activity, and/or Date can help narrow down the search.

 House of Commons Witness Search
www.parl.gc.ca/Committees/en/WitnessSearch

5) Substantive Reports of Committees (1867–present)

The PARLINFO section of the Parliament of Canada website contains a search and browse tool for reports of the House, Senate, and joint committees. It provides information on Legislative, Select, Sessional,

Special, Standing, and Subcommittee Reports since 1867. The reports deal with bills, special subjects, and committee administration. Links are provided to the full text of reports where available (generally full text reports from 1998–present).

    ❧ Substantive Committee Reports: House, Senate, and Joint Committees

    https://lop.parl.ca/sites/ParlInfo/default/en_CA/Parliament/procedure/committeeReports

6) Senate Committee Reports (1994–present)

Legislative and Special Study Senate Committee (Standing, Special, and Joint) reports are available on the Senate website in this one-stop shop. Use the drop-down menu to select the Parliament and Session, then select the committee and browse for the report of interest.

    ❧ Senate Committee Reports

    https://sencanada.ca/en/Committees/reports

7) Major Legislative and Special Study Reports by Senate Committees (1961–2012)

This site provides full-text access to selected Senate reports compiled from the Journals of the Senate and the Library of Parliament information. These reports are identified and made available because, as it is noted on the site, Senate committee reports are "highly praised for their thoroughness and insight and have been valuable contributions to public policy development in Canada."[11] These reports may also be found on the specific committees' websites or in public, university, and legislative libraries.

---

11   Parliament of Canada, Senate, "Major Legislative and Special Study Reports by Senate Committees" (2017) Preface, online: https://sencanada.ca/en/committees/about/directorate/#PREFACE.

❦ Major Legislative and Special Study Reports by Senate
   Committees
   https://sencanada.ca/en/committees/about/directorate

8) Individual Committee Websites

Each committee of the House of Commons of Canada often has full
materials available for the current committees, including upcoming
business, transcripts, video or audio proceedings, news releases, mandates, minutes, and witness briefs.

9) Print Resources

a) Journals

The Journals of the House of Commons and the Journals of the Senate
are the official record of house business and can be used to find committee names and dates of the consideration of bills.

Occasionally in the past, committee reports were printed full text
in the Journals.

b) *Hansard*

Hansard indexes can be used as a tool to provide access to committee
names and dates of bill consideration, although Journals are the official record of bill status dates. *Hansard* generally provides access to
bill information by topic and speaker in the index.

Occasionally in the past, committee reports were printed full text
in *Hansard*.

c) Libraries

University, public, and legislative libraries can provide access to historical committee materials.

Committee transcripts minutes and reports are at the Library of
Parliament and on parliamentary websites, and selected materials are
at other parliamentary, university, and even public libraries.

Federal exhibits (witness submissions to committees) are not normally part of the committee materials provided online or contained with

the reports, but they can be found at the Archives of Canada (Library and Archives Canada). See Appendix 2 for library and archives listings.

10) Canadian Parliamentary Historical Resources Portal

This federal portal provides access to historical digitized committee transcripts and reports in English and French. Contents of the portal can be browsed by date and it is searchable by keyword.

- ☞ English
  - House of Commons of Canada committee materials: 3rd Parliament to 34th Parliament
  - Senate of Canada committee materials: 6th Parliament to 34th Parliament
- ☞ French
  - House of Commons of Canada committee materials: 1st Parliament to 34th Parliament
  - Senate of Canada committee materials: 20th Parliament to 34th Parliament

- ☞ Canadian Parliamentary Historical Resources Portal: http://parl.canadiana.ca.

L. PROVINCIAL AND TERRITORIAL COMMITTEES

1) Provincial and Territorial Legislatures' Websites

Research for bill committee information should start with locating the correct jurisdiction's legislature and session number and then bill number. For modern committee materials (1990s onward), look to the individual provincial or territorial legislature's websites.

Most provincial or territorial legislatures add the committee name and the dates that a committee considered a bill to their bill status pages. Some legislatures also link the committee transcripts to the meeting dates on their individual bill pages. It is best when researching legislative intent to start by looking at the specific legislature's bill website. In some cases, the transcripts of the committee meetings may not be linked from the bill's page, and in those cases the researcher will need to go to the committee page and locate the transcripts and reports by date.

A legislature's website will usually provide access to committee transcripts and reports. Some will also provide access to exhibits (witness submissions). Committee minutes and video/audio are less likely to be available online at the provincial level, but some jurisdictions are now providing access to these materials online.

Each jurisdiction is unique and should be examined individually by the researcher. Here is an overview of navigating provincial legislature committee materials on the legislature's website:

Alberta

The Legislative Assembly of Alberta have standing, special standing, legislative policy, and select special committees. They also have, and appear to use frequently, the Committee of the Whole.

The "documents and records" area of the Legislative Assembly of Alberta website contains links to committee websites, membership lists for current committees, committee indexes (2007–current), and committee search (1991–current). There is a "simple search" and an "advanced search" option.

The best place to find the dates of committee consideration of bills is on the website in the bill and amendments section, under "bill status report." Browse by legislature and session and select the bill of interest to see the dates of committee consideration and links to the transcripts.

The committee indexes can also be consulted for the bill name and there are links to the bill consideration in committee transcripts. Alberta's committee reports can be found on individual committee websites.

  ε Legislative Assembly of Alberta documents and records website for committees, committee transcripts, indexes, and reports: www.assembly.ab.ca/net/index.aspx?p=adr_home

  ε Legislative Assembly of Alberta bill status report website: www.assembly.ab.ca/net/index.aspx?p=bills_statusarchive

British Columbia

The Legislative Assembly of British Columbia uses select, standing, and special committees. They also use the Committee of the Whole.

From the parliamentary committee area of the Assembly website, each committee website details the committee membership, terms of reference, advertisements, meeting notices, reports, media releases, minutes transcripts, and related sites as available from 1992–current. (Most committee materials start later, in 2001.)

In British Columbia, some committees even have video recording links and witness submissions available.

Find committee consideration of bill dates with links to the text of transcripts on the "list of bills with *Hansard* debates" table in the bills area of the website.

A link to previous committees has committee materials by committee name and legislature session from 1992.

❦ Legislative Assembly of British Columbia committees' website:
www.leg.bc.ca/parliamentary-business/committees

Manitoba

The Legislative Assembly of Manitoba uses standing or special committees.

Committee materials can be accessed two ways on the Manitoba Assembly website. For current committee materials it is best to use the status of bills document for the committee dates of a particular bill. Historical committee materials are accessed through the *Hansard* area of the website.

"Bill status" is a link under the bills area of the Legislative Assembly of Manitoba website. The status of bills document will list the dates of first, second, and third reading of current bills and the dates that current bills were in committee.

Transcripts of the committee debates start online in 1987 under "legislative business."

Indexes to the standing and special committee debates start in 1999. Note that committee name abbreviations are used in the indexes to refer to committees.

Standing committee reports are available on the Legislative Assembly of Manitoba website from 1999 to current in the committees' area.

🕸 Legislative Assembly of Manitoba website

Hansard: http://gov.mb.ca/legislature/hansard/hansard.html

Committees: http://gov.mb.ca/legislature/committees/index.html

New Brunswick

The Legislative Assembly of New Brunswick uses standing and select committees and the Committee of the Whole.

There is no committee *Hansard* on the New Brunswick Assembly website. Materials must be accessed in a print collection. Check university, pubic, and law libraries for access to the print materials.

Standing and select committee reports are available on the Legislative Assembly of New Brunswick website from 1999–current.

🕸 Legislative Assembly of New Brunswick committee reports website:
www.gnb.ca/legis/business/committees/reports-e.asp

Newfoundland and Labrador

The Newfoundland and Labrador House of Assembly has permanent standing committees and ad hoc select committees.

The "Progress of Bills" area of the Assembly website indicates the committee dates for a bill. Go to the "Committees" area of the website to retrieve the relevant transcripts.

Transcripts and reports are available by committee from about 2008–current on the Assembly website under "Committees." Audio recording are available from about 2015–current with the transcripts.

🕸 Newfoundland and Labrador House of Assembly committees' website
www.assembly.nl.ca/Committees

🕸 Newfoundland and Labrador House of Assembly progress of bills website
www.assembly.nl.ca/HouseBusiness/Bills

Northwest Territories

The Legislative Assembly of the Northwest Territories has permanent standing committees, ad hoc special committees, as well as the Committee of the Whole.

Committee transcripts are not available on the Legislative Assembly website but reports and committee news releases are available from 2008–current. Check the "Status of Bills" document in the bills area of the website to find out when a bill was sent to a committee.

> ❦ Legislative Assembly of Northwest Territories committees' website:
> www.assembly.gov.nt.ca/committees-18th-assembly

Nova Scotia

The Nova Scotia Legislature has permanent standing committees and ad hoc select committees or special committees, as well as the Committee of the Whole.

The bills area of the legislature website indicates the committee meeting dates. Committee meeting transcripts can be accessed in the committee area of the website from 1996 to current. In the case of the law amendments committee, witness submissions are available online.

> ❦ Nova Scotia Legislature committees' website:
> https://nslegislature.ca/legislative-business/committees

Nunavut

The Legislative Assembly of Nunavut has permanent standing committees and ad hoc special committees.

The "Standing and Special Committees" area of the Assembly website contains transcripts and reports under "committee documents" from 2014 to current.

> ❦ Legislative Assembly of Nunavut standing and special committees' website:
> https://assembly.nu.ca/standing-and-special-committees

Ontario

The Legislative Assembly of Ontario uses permanent standing and ad hoc select committees, and while used less today, it is still possible for Ontario to use the Committee of the Whole.

Use the bills area of the Assembly website to browse and find the bill of interest. The bill webpage includes links to the committee debate under the "debate" tab.

Committee transcripts and reports can be accessed from the committees' area of the website. Committee documents can be browsed by committee name and date from 1990 to current.

Ontario also has a speaker and subject index on the website for all standing and special committees from 2007 to current.

❦ Legislative Assembly of Ontario committees' website:
www.ola.org/en/legislative-business/committees

Prince Edward Island

The Legislative Assembly of PEI uses permanent standing and ad hoc select committees as well as the Committee of the Whole.

The bills area of the website will indicate the committee consideration dates. Specific committee transcripts can be retrieved from the committees' area of the website.

Committee transcripts are organized by year (2004–current) and committee name. Audio recordings are also available for more recent committees.

❦ Legislative Assembly of PEI committees' website:
www.assembly.pe.ca/legcommittees

Quebec

The National Assembly of Quebec uses standing committees, which include nine sectorial committees. Select committees and Committee of the Whole are also used.

Use the bills area of the website to find committee transcripts links under "stages in the consideration of bill #."

Each committee has its own website that provides access to the *Journal des débats* (*Hansard*) going back as far as 1963 to current. Committee reports and discussion papers can be searched from about 1996 to current. Briefs submitted to committees by witnesses are also searchable and available in full text, 2003 to current.

Video and audio recordings of clause-by-clause committee considerations are available from 2009 to current. Video and audio recordings of committee consultations and public hearings are available 2001–present.

Committees can be searched or browsed on their own or as part of the larger parliamentary proceedings search. Searches can be narrowed by session, type of proceedings, type of documents, and keywords.

⌲ National Assembly of Quebec committees' website:
www.assnat.qc.ca/en/abc-assemblee/travail-commission.html

Saskatchewan

The Legislative Assembly of Saskatchewan uses permanent standing committees and ad hoc special committees.

Find committee dates for consideration of a bill on the bill page of the Assembly website. Go to the committees' area to search for the committee name and the date of interest to read transcripts.

The Saskatchewan committees' area of the website includes access to transcripts, reports, notices, video, and minutes.

⌲ Legislative Assembly of Saskatchewan committees' website:
www.legassembly.sk.ca/legislative-business/legislative-committees

Yukon

The Legislative Assembly of Yukon uses permanent standing committees and ad hoc special committees to examine business of the House.

The committees' section of the Yukon website has reports, news releases, and transcripts. The date range varies by committee but can start as early as 2007 to current.

⌲ Legislative Assembly of Yukon committees' website:
www.legassembly.gov.yk.ca/committees/index.html

M. PROVINCIAL HISTORICAL COMMITTEE MATERIALS

1) Legislative Libraries

The Legislative Library of British Columbia catalogue has links to scanned copies of committee materials from 1990 to the present. Some historical committee materials are also available in full text through the catalogue from the 1970s, and even a few materials from the 1930s.

The Legislative Library of Ontario has committee materials in print from 1960 to the present. For historical committee items that do not have indexes there are tables of contents shelved with the materials that help to access the dates of bill consideration.

In Ontario, witness exhibits lists and committee tables of contents are available full text through the legislative library catalogue. Search the bill number in the catalogue to find the exhibit list. You can view the document in print by making an appointment at the Legislative Library.

The Saskatchewan Legislative Library adds committee documents and reports to their repository.

The NWT Legislative Library archives the electronic versions of most current tabled documents and committee reports when available.

2) University Libraries and Public Libraries

University law library and government library collections can be searched for particular committee reports or transcripts. Public libraries may have larger reports of wider interest.

3) Archives

Provincial archives have government document collections that include committee materials. See Appendix 2 for library and archives listings.

4) Internet Archive

The Internet Archive may also include some particular committee reports in full text.

Use the Wayback Machine to check for archived committee websites if you know the URL.

chapter six

Extrinsic Aids to Statutory Interpretation: Other Sources

A. THE USE OF EXTRINSIC AIDS IN THE COURTS

It should be noted that the intent of a government is not the same as legislative intent, but as Sullivan notes in the *Construction of Statutes*, government policy is often the impulse and the author of legislation.[1] In 2012, Magyar noted that Canadian lawyers are looking beyond *Hansard* to locate additional resources to them to help support their argument.[2] However, *Hansard* is used to buttress the credibility of other extrinsic resources, as the courts give more weight to the government policy materials if they are specifically mentioned in the *Hansard* debates on a particular bill.

In the 2008 Supreme Court of Canada decision, *Tele-Mobile Co v Ontario*,[3] Tele-Mobile wanted an exemption under the *Criminal Code* that would result in compensation for the company for their efforts to produce data and documents to aid criminal investigations. Tele-Mobile claimed that producing data to aid police investigation constituted undue hardship and they argued that they should be compensated for this work to produce the documents for the investigative process.

---

1   Ruth Sullivan, *Sullivan on the Construction of Statutes*, 5th ed (Markham, ON: Lexis-Nexis Canada, 2008) at 614.

2   John James Magyar, "Evolution of Hansard Use at the Supreme Court of Canada: A Comparative Study in Statutory Interpretation" (2012) 33:3 *Statute Law Review* 363.

3   *Tele-Mobile Co v Ontario*, 2008 SCC 12.

During this case, the Court reviewed years of government and telecommunications industry consultation, including Department of Justice discussion papers, consultation documents, a news release, and a summary of submissions to a parliamentary committee, to shed light on the circumstances surrounding the claimed undue hardship of producing documentation in order to aid police investigations. Examining the history of government interaction with the telecommunications industry through these documents, the Court noted that the ongoing conversation between government and the telecom industry indicated that the government was aware of the compensation issues, so the Court concluded that the silence in the legislation regarding exemption and compensation for telecommunications companies was intentional.

B. EXTRINSIC AIDS TO STATUTORY INTERPRETATION — OTHER SOURCES: GOVERNMENT POLICY PAPERS

There are many techniques and documents that governments employ to state their policy or view on an issue. The issues under consideration could be anything that touches citizens' lives including crime, traffic, business, agriculture, health, etcetera. Policy papers vary from a broad overview of a topic, such as a report on health care reform, to the specific, such as a press release on fish farming methods. Documents that explain a government's policy could go by many different names. Common types of documents that describe a government's policy and/or reasons for that policy include white papers, green papers, policy papers, consultation documents, studies, sessional papers, press releases, backgrounders, ministerial speeches, pamphlets, annual reports, business briefing books, estimates, and other things. This definition should not be limited to particular documents because over time different governments choose to express their policy in different types of documents.

Policy papers are generally not official legislative documents produced through the legislative process, but they may become part of the process by being tabled in the House as sessional papers for discussion or submitted to parliamentary committees as evidence.

1) White Papers

The term "white paper" comes from Britain, when government policy papers that were too small to be bound with a hard, blue cover, which large government reports were issued in, were bound in white.[4] Today in Canada the term white paper is commonly used for official documents presented by ministers that explain the government's policy on an issue. While white papers may be approved by Cabinet and tabled in the House, they may also be subject to further changes.[5] Now there appears to be less concern with the colour of the document but the characteristics of these policy documents remain. They contain a report or document or language explaining the government's policy position on a particular issue.

White papers have long been admissible as evidence of legislative intent, even as far back as 1975 when Laskin CJ used the federal government's white paper, "Attack on Inflation," to assist in determining the intent of the 1975 *Anti-Inflation Act*:[6]

> In order to determine whether the legislation here in question was enacted to combat such an emergency, it is necessary to examine the legislation itself, but in so doing I think it not only permissible but essential to give consideration to the material which Parliament had before it at the time when the statute was enacted for the purpose of disclosing the circumstances which prompted its enactment. The most concrete source of this information is, in my opinion, the White Paper tabled in the House by the Minister of Finance and made a part of the case which was submitted on behalf of the Attorney General of Canada.[7]

---

4   Parliament of Canada, "White Papers: Introduction," online: *PARLINFO* https://web.archive.org/web/20151216094241/www.parl.gc.ca/Parlinfo/pages/WhitePapers.aspx.

5   See various definitions of white papers at Parliament of Canada, "White Papers, Appendix," online: *PARLINFO* https://web.archive.org/web/20151216152750/www.parl.gc.ca/ParlInfo/Pages/WhitePapersAppendix.aspx.

6   *Anti-Inflation Act*, SC 1974–75–76, c 75.

7   *Reference re: Anti-Inflation Act (Canada)*, [1976] 2 SCR 373 at 437–38.

2) Green Papers

The term "green paper" is also from Britain. Green papers are commonly issued by governments specifically to invite public comment and discussion on an issue prior to policy formulation.[8] Today in Canada green papers are usually called consultation or discussion documents, and while not always green or even referred to as green papers, they are identified as green because they are issued before policy formation (i.e., before the white paper).

Green papers have also been used as tools to understand the intention of a piece of legislation. In 2017, for example, the Supreme Court allowed the use of a 1985 Department of Finance green paper[9] as a means to ascertain the intent of a number of sections of the *Bank Act*:

> 104 The relevant legislative history may be used to shed light on Parliament's object and purpose in passing the 1991 amendment. As stated by McIntyre J. in *Upper Churchill Water Rights Reversion Act, 1980, Re*, [1984] 1 S.C.R. 297 (S.C.C.), in constitutional cases, "extrinsic evidence may be considered to ascertain not only the operation and effect of the impugned legislation but its true object and purpose as well" (p. 318).
>
> 105 Here the relevant legislative record begins with the 1985 Department of Finance Green Paper, The Regulation of Canadian Financial Institutions: Proposals for Discussion (pp. 84–85). While the sale of insurance by banks was not discussed in detail, the Green Paper did endorse the concept of a level playing field for all participants selling a particular product. The Senate Standing Committee responding to the Green Paper agreed, and also recommended a level playing field such that no institution would obtain a competitive advantage as a result of being subject to a different regulatory regime than its competitors (*Towards a More Competitive Financial Environment* (1986), Sixteenth Report of the Standing Committee, at p. 64).[10]

---

8   Parliament of Canada, "Green Papers: Introduction," online: *PARLINFO* https://web.archive.org/web/20151215141205/www.parl.gc.ca/ParlInfo/Pages/GreenPapers.aspx.

9   Canada, Department of Finance, *The Regulation of Financial Institutions: Proposals for Discussion* (Ottawa: Department of Finance, 1985).

10   *Western Bank v Alberta*, 2007 SCC 22 at paras 104–5.

3) Sessional Papers

Sessional papers refer collectively to reports that the House of Commons has ordered to be created and tabled in the House in order for them to carry out their business. These reports include departmental annual reports, committee reports, various government department reports, royal commissions, drafts of proposed legislation, answers to written questions, background papers, compendia, and ways and means motions.

Sessional papers are compilations of reports and miscellaneous material and, as such, are not cited as a whole in the courts. Instead, you will see individual reports from the sessional papers cited. As an example, in the 2014 case *Mohawks of the Bay of Quinte v Brant*, the court cited a report from 1867 that was included in the sessional papers as evidence of the intent of "Indian legislation":[11]

> [T]he annual report for the year ended June 30, 1876, of the Indian Branch, Department of the Interior, "Report of Minister of the Interior for the year ended 30th June, 1876" by David Mills in *Sessional Papers*, No. 11 (1877), at p. xiv, describes an important purpose and intention of Indian legislation.[12]

Sessional papers can be valuable for delving into the intent of older or historical statutes.

4) Studies

Government department and ministries will create task forces and produce independent studies on matters of policy interest. The documents and reports produced by these studies may contain reasons that led to particular legislation being introduced (see also Commissions of Inquiry, below).

---

11   *Mohawks of the Bay of Quinte v Brant*, 2014 ONCA 565 at para 68.
12   *Ibid.*

5) Press Releases, Backgrounders, and Speeches

Press releases are often issued with the introduction or passage of a bill in Parliament and can contain an explanation of the legislative intent behind the bill. Similarly, backgrounders are usually press-release length and will go into further reasons for the introduction of a bill. A minister may make a speech on a bill when it is introduced, explaining the reasons for its introduction. Speeches can be captured in a press release or in their own separate document, in libraries, and/or on the ministry website.

6) Memorandum to Cabinet

The Memorandum to Cabinet (MC) is an internal Cabinet document that explains the reasons for introducing a government bill. These documents are not usually publicly available for current bills. Historical MCs may become available at provincial archives.

Memoranda to Cabinet have also been used as evidence of legislative intent. In *Energy Probe v Canada (Attorney General)*,[13] for example, Wright J, while inquiring into the intent of the *Nuclear Liability Act*, quoted from a 1961 Memorandum to Cabinet:

> The N.L.A.'s [*Nuclear Liability Act's*] dual purpose and the government's intention is best reflected in a memorandum to Cabinet dated November 21, 1961:
>
> ... the problem to be resolved by the legislation pertains to the extraordinary and peculiar hazards deriving from the existence of nuclear reactors and related devices....
>
> [T]he intention of the proposed legislation will be to provide financial protection to the public and, at the same time, reasonable protection for the nuclear operators against catastrophic claims in the development of nuclear resources for peaceful purposes.[14]

---

13   *Energy Probe v Canada (Attorney General)* (1994), 17 OR (3d) 717 (Gen Div).
14   *Ibid* at para 28.

There are specific stipulations as to how these memoranda can be used. Section 25 of the *Access to Information Act*[15] states that

> Notwithstanding any other provision of this Act, where a request is made to a government institution for access to a record that the head of the institution is authorized to refuse to disclose under this Act by reason of information or other material contained in the record, the head of the institution shall disclose any part of the record that does not contain, and can reasonably be severed from any part that contains, any such information or material.

Cabinet material that can be severed is defined in section 69 of the *Access to Information Act* as

> 69 (1) This Act does not apply to confidences of the Queen's Privy Council for Canada, including, without restricting the generality of the foregoing,
>
> (a) memoranda the purpose of which is to present proposals or recommendations to Council;
>
> (b) discussion papers the purpose of which is to present background explanations, analyses of problems or policy options to Council for consideration by Council in making decisions;
>
> (c) agenda of Council or records recording deliberations or decisions of Council;
>
> (d) records used for or reflecting communications or discussions between ministers of the Crown on matters relating to the making of government decisions or the formulation of government policy;
>
> (e) records the purpose of which is to brief ministers of the Crown in relation to matters that are before, or are proposed to be brought before, Council or that are the subject of communications or discussions referred to in paragraph (d);
>
> (f) draft legislation; and
>
> (g) records that contain information about the contents of any record within a class of records referred to in paragraphs (a) to (f).[16]

---

15   *Access to Information Act*, RSC 1985, c A-1, s 25.

16   *Ibid*, s 69.

As Memoranda to Cabinet are not published it may be necessary for the researcher to make a freedom of information request to access that material.

C. EXPLANATORY NOTES

Back in 1975, the courts were still applying the exclusionary rule to explanatory notes. In *Highway Victims Indemnity Fund v Gagné*, Pigeon J noted:

> In his factum and at the hearing, counsel for the Fund sought to rely on the explanatory notes accompanying the bill tabled in the Legislative Assembly. These notes are parliamentary documents to which the rule of exclusion set forth in *The Attorney General of Canada v The Reader's Digest Association (Canada) Ltd* ... must be applied.[17]

But this approach began to evolve, even before the exclusionary rule met its complete demise. In 1979, for example, in *Harris c Verdun (Cité)*, Greenberg J of the Quebec Superior Court used the explanatory notes to Quebec's *Bill 67* as a guide to understanding its purpose:

> Although not binding upon the Court, the "Explanatory Notes" which appeared immediately preceeding the English text of the Act, when the same was first published by the Editeur Officiel du Québec as Bill 67 of the Second Session of the Thirty-first Legislature of the Assemblée Nationale du Québec, read as follows:
>
> > "The object of this bill is the implementation in Québec of a compensation scheme for persons suffering bodily injuries caused by an automobile, and to entrust the Régie de l'assurance automobile du Québec with the administration of a compensation fund."
>
> The Act is therefore remedial legislation, which put into place the social purpose expressed in those "Explanatory Notes."[18]

---

17   *Highway Victims Indemnity Fund v Gagné*, [1977] 1 SCR 785 at para 11.
18   *Harris v Verdun (Cité)*, [1979] CS 690 at paras 12–13.

Justice Cromwell confirmed this approach in the Supreme Court, quoting the fifth edition of *Sullivan on the Construction of Statutes*:

> While explanatory notes are less authoritative than legislated statements of purpose, they nonetheless provide some insight to legislative purpose.[19]

He thereby firmly entrenched the use of explanatory notes as a means to determine legislative intent in the Canadian courts.

D. DOCUMENTS PREPARED BY THE LIBRARY OF PARLIAMENT

The Library of Parliament provides parliamentarians and researchers with legislative summaries of proposed legislation. These summaries provide an in-depth analysis of the proposed legislation, its background, "including the purpose and history of the legislation, an analysis of important clauses, and comments from interest groups, the media and other sources."[20] These legislative summaries have also been used by the courts as evidence of legislative intent.

One example of this use is *Kinsel v Canada (Citizenship and Immigration)*, in which, under the heading "Purposive Analysis," Dawson JA specifically identifies a Library of Parliament Legislative Summary as a source for determining legislative purpose:

> *(iii) Purposive analysis*
> A second, more relevant statement of legislative purpose is found in the Legislative Summary [LS-591E] prepared by the Library of Parliament, Parliamentary Information and Research Service in respect of Bill C-37.[21]

19　Sullivan, *Construction*, 5th, above note 1 at 272, cited in *R v TELUS Communications Co*, 2013 SCC 16 at para 138.

20　Canada, Library of Parliament, "Publications Available for Viewing," online: www.publications.gc.ca/collections/Collection-R/LoPBdP/mat-e.html#3.

21　*Kinsel v Canada (Citizenship and Immigration)*, 2014 FCA 126 at para 71.

E. SUGGESTIONS FOR RESEARCHERS

In addition to researching treatises and texts on statutory interpretation, another method of finding out whether a specific type of extrinsic material has been used by the courts is by checking a caselaw digest or subject index. VLex Canada, for example, lists a number of legislative history sources that have been used in the exploration of legislative intent. These include:

- ❦ Legislative debates
- ❦ Draft bills
- ❦ Conference reports
- ❦ White and green papers
- ❦ Legislative committee reports and minutes
- ❦ Lobbying
- ❦ Reports of commissions and public inquiries
- ❦ Minutes of joint committees of senate and house of commons
- ❦ Cabinet minutes
- ❦ Political speeches
- ❦ Speech from the Throne
- ❦ Social and political background
- ❦ Travaux préparatoires of treaties and conventions
- ❦ Budget papers
- ❦ Ministerial comments
- ❦ Ministerial documents
- ❦ Regulatory Impact Analysis Statements
- ❦ Law reform material[22]

F. FINDING TOOLS FOR GOVERNMENT POLICY PAPERS, SESSIONAL PAPERS, AND OTHER SOURCES

1) LEGIS*info* — About This Bill

Each federal bill's LEGIS*info* page will contain links to departmental information, a legislative summary, and further reading in the bottom

---

22 VLex Canada, *MLB Topics — Statutes — Interpretation — Extrinsic Aids — Legislative history (1641–1660)*, online: https://vlex.com/MLB-key-number-system.

right-hand menu. Look under departmental information to find links to government press releases, studies, and background documents related to the particular bill. Provincial legislatures do not have a comparable background information tool to LEGIS*info*.

❦ LEGIS*info*
www.parl.gc.ca/LEGISINFO

2) Sessional Papers

Sessional papers are available in published print collections as individual papers, and many are unpublished, but still available.

Each sessional paper is assigned an identifying number in chronological order based on the date that the item was tabled. Print collections of published sessional papers for the Parliament of Canada, "Sessional Papers of the Dominion of Canada," were published between 1865 and 1925 and are available in selected libraries as well as through Early Canadiana Online 1867–1900 and the Internet Archive 1901–1925.

There are many unpublished federal sessional papers as well that are not in these collected works. A block of unpublished papers is not available at all as it was lost in the fire that destroyed the Parliament Buildings in 1915. Some historical, unpublished federal sessional papers are available in selected libraries.

Modern sessional papers can be difficult to find as many continue to go unpublished. Those that are published are often published individually and there is no recent collective source of sessional papers. For instance, in Ontario, "Sessional Papers of the Province of Ontario" are available from 1868–1948 at selected libraries and on the Internet Archive from 1968–1948. Since 1948 the Ontario sessional papers have been published individually. You may need to search the ministry, the publishing body website, or a library catalogue in order to locate individual items.

Note that sessional paper titles can be found indexed in the Journals and on legislature websites.

3) Library of Parliament Research Publications

The Library of Parliament produces non-partisan research publications that provide analysis to members of Parliament on matters of current importance, such as new bills or policy issues. A legislative summary, which outlines the purpose and history of a bill, was produced for Bill C-19. In addition to summarizing the bill, the legislative summary gives valuable background to firearms registration requirements in Canada since 1877, a history of the *Firearms Act* and Firearms Registry, as well as pointing to related reports, statistics, and government programs. The legislative summary is used by parliamentarians during the process of moving the legislation through the House, committee, and Senate. Legislative summaries are kept on the Parliament website and available through LEGIS*info* with the relevant bill.

☞ Library of Parliament Research Publications
https://lop.parl.ca/sites/PublicWebsite/default/en_CA/ResearchPublications

4) Compendia

Ontario often tables a compendium with the first reading of a bill in the House. The compendium may contain some explanation of the bill's purpose, a press release, and the full text of the Acts affected by the new bill. Compendia can be found in print at the Legislative Library of Ontario and searched for in the catalogue.

5) PARLINFO White Papers

The Parliament of Canada White Papers List offers catalogue information including title, date, author, and a brief description, as well as full text links, where available, of important federal white papers from 1939–2015. The collection can be browsed or searched by year, subject, title, department, and ministry.

☞ PARLINFO White Papers
Archived version available on the Wayback Machine
http://webarchive.bac-lac.gc.ca:8080/wayback/20151209070355/http://
www.parl.gc.ca/ParlInfo/Pages/WhitePapers.aspx

6) PARLINFO Green Papers

The Parliament of Canada green papers list offers information such as year, subject, title, department, and ministry from 1971–2010 with links to the full text where available.

☞ PARLINFO Green Papers
Archived version available on the Wayback Machine
http://webarchive.bac-lac.gc.ca:8080/wayback/20151208142540/http://
www.parl.gc.ca/ParlInfo/Pages/GreenPapers.aspx

7) PARLINFO Speeches from the Throne and Motions for Address in Reply

Speeches from the Throne from 1867 to current, including links to the text of the speech.

☞ PARLINFO Speeches from the Throne
https://lop.parl.ca/sites/ParlInfo/default/en_CA/Parliament/procedure/
throneSpeech

8) PARLINFO Budget Speeches

Historical list from 1867 to the date of federal budget speeches, with links to the full text of the speech in *Hansard*.

☞ PARLINFO Budget Speeches
https://lop.parl.ca/sites/ParlInfo/default/en_CA/Parliament/procedure/
budgets

9) Government Ministry and Department Websites

Government ministry, department, agencies, and board websites can be searched to find particular reports or other documents relevant to a legislative history. Check the publications and reports area of a particular site or try general internet searching. For historical government documents, especially from bodies that no longer exist, and if you have the URL, try the Internet Archive Wayback Machine. Without an URL, try searching libraries and GALLOP (see below).

10) GALLOP

The Government and Legislative Libraries Online Publications Portal (GALLOP) indexes full text and bibliographic government document records from nine Canadian provinces (not including PEI), one territory (Northwest Territories), and the federal Depository Service Program (DSP). GALLOP records often include a link to the full text of the government documents. Search the portal by keyword, title, and jurisdiction in the advanced search. The content provides more governmental documents and less legislative documentation, so it is a rich resource for government policy papers. It is also useful for cross-jurisdictional research, as all or selected jurisdictions can be searched together. Search results can be narrowed down after the search as well.

GALLOP is a collaboration of the Association of Parliamentary Libraries in Canada and relies on individual library collections and contributions, which are added to the portal several times a year. The scope note indicates that the "Portal scope is based on the collection policies and practices of individual APLIC libraries. Content varies with each jurisdiction. The portal is not comprehensive or exhaustive." Full details of the scope can be found on the website.

🐚 GALLOP
http://aplicportal.ola.org

11) Legislative Libraries

Provincial legislative libraries and the Library of Parliament should contain near-complete legislative documentation for bills, *Hansard*, and committees, and they are often the only place to find historical materials. In addition, they have many government documents and policy resources used by governments that could help with legislative intent research. Resources available to the public vary with jurisdiction. Most legislative libraries have their catalogues accessible to the public on their websites and include links to many digitized documents, with the notable exception of the Library of Parliament, which does not have a publicly available catalogue.

See Appendix 2 for legislative library and provincial archive contact information.

12) Library and Archives Canada

The federal Library and Archives Canada and provincial archives will have historical policy papers in their collections. Researchers can search the individual archives for the jurisdiction they are concerned with.

Library and Archives Canada, through the Government of Canada Web Archive, provides access to archived web pages of the federal government. Access these older versions of government department websites by institution or URL.

  ❧ Government of Canada Web Archive, Library and Archives
     Canada
     www.bac-lac.gc.ca/eng/discover/archives-web-government/Pages/
     web-archives.aspx

13) News Releases

Federal government news releases can also be searched on the Government of Canada website 2002–current.

  ❧ Government of Canada News Archive Search (2002–current)
     www.canada.ca/en/news/archive-search.html

14) University Libraries

University libraries, particularly those with law and government collections, will have some important materials for researching legislative intent. Check university library catalogues online for particular materials and holdings. In addition, the library websites have excellent guides for researching legal and government resources.

15) Government Publication Checklists

Legislative libraries and governments often produce a checklist of government documents that is published each month or, in the case of the federal government, each week. This index is a title list of ministry policy papers and other types of government publications. Current checklists are online. Historical print checklists are available in libraries.

❧ Weekly Checklist of Canadian Government Publications
Online from 1995–2015
Includes print and online documents
http://epe.lac-bac.gc.ca/100/201/301/weekly_checklist/

❧ Continued by the Weekly Acquisitions List
http://epe.lac-bac.gc.ca/100/201/301/weekly_acquisition_lists/index.html
http://publications.gc.ca/site/eng/weeklyAcquisitionList/lists.html

❧ Alberta Queen's Printer Government Publication Search, 1995–current
www.qp.alberta.ca/511.cfm

❧ British Columbia Government Publications Monthly Checklist
Online from 1990–current
www.llbc.leg.bc.ca/databases/checklist

❧ Manitoba Government Monthly Publications Checklist
Online from 2006–current
Links to full text documents when available
www.gov.mb.ca/chc/leg-lib/checklist.html

❧ Newfoundland and Labrador Government Publications
Online from 1995–current
www.gov.nl.ca/publications

❧ New Brunswick Government Publications Checklist (annual)
Online from 2000–current
www1.gnb.ca/leglibbib/en/Publications.aspx/Index

❧ **Checklist of Northwest Territories Government Publications (annual)**
Online from 1994–current
www.assembly.gov.nt.ca/library/checklist

❧ **Publications of the Province of Nova Scotia Monthly Checklist**
Online from 2009–current
http://nslegislature.ca/index.php/library/publications/

❧ **Ontario Government Publications Monthly Checklist**
From 1971–1997 in print only. Ceased.

❧ **Government Documents — Our Ontario**
Historical and current publications online
http://govdocs.ourontario.ca/agencies

❧ **Publications Ontario**
www.publications.serviceontario.ca

❧ **Prince Edward Island Government Publications**
Recent publications listing
www.princeedwardisland.ca/en/publications

❧ **Digital Québec gouvernement publications**
Bibliothèque et Archives nationales du Québec (BAnQ)
http://pnq.banq.qc.ca/sdx/pnq/accueil.xsp

❧ **Checklist of Saskatchewan Government Publications**
Online from 1997–current
www.legassembly.sk.ca/library/monthly-checklist/

16) Internet Archive

The Internet Archive Canadian Libraries collection has numerous notable collections that are relevant to legislative intent research. Below are two examples of collections that may include government policy papers. To find materials, you can limit the search to a sub-collection or search the entire Internet Archive:

a) Canadian Government Publications Portal

Internet Archive Canada, with advice and assistance from government and university librarians across Canada, have digitized more than 20,000 Canadian government publications and made them freely available online. This page is meant to serve as a portal for discovering publications digitized by Internet Archive Canada, to be a reference for future digitization initiatives, and provide incentive to grow the list of titles that have been preserved and dedicated to the public domain.

Beginning in 2004, Internet Archive Canada began to digitize material from the Library and Archives of Canada. This work has continued steadily over the last decade as part of projects sponsored by: Ontario Digitization Initiative, Legislative Assembly of Ontario, Ontario Council of University Libraries, University of Ottawa, University of Alberta, and University of Toronto.[23]

> ☙ https://archive.org/details/governmentpublications

17) The Sessional Papers of the Dominion of Canada

Sessional Papers are "reports and papers that have been tabled in the House of Commons (and sometimes the Senate) and deposited with the Clerk. These papers include annual reports of government departments and boards, the Estimates, the Public Accounts, and the reports of the Royal Commissions."[24]

> ☙ Early Canadiana Online (1868–1925)
> http://eco.canadiana.ca/view/oocihm.9_08052

> ☙ Internet Archive: Sessional Papers of Canada Collection (1869–1925)
> https://archive.org/details/sessionalpaperscanada

---

23 Canadian Government Publications Portal, online: *Internet Archive* https://archive.org/details/governmentpublications.

24 Canada, "About the Sessional Papers of the Dominion of Canada," online: *Internet Archive* https://archive.org/details/sessionalpaperscanada&tab=about.

18) Wayback Machine

The Internet Archives FAQ section describes the Wayback Machine as

> a service that allows people to visit archived versions of Web sites. Visitors to the Wayback Machine can type in a URL, select a date range, and then begin surfing on an archived version of the Web. Imagine surfing circa 1999 and looking at all the Y2K hype, or revisiting an older version of your favorite Web site. The Internet Archive Wayback Machine can make all of this possible.[25]

When governments change their websites, important documents can be lost. The Wayback Machine is a handy resource that can yield impressive results for the legislative intent researcher, particularly when looking for historical policy papers. The major drawback is that you need to know the URL at the time the document was produced to start your search.

    Wayback Machine
https://archive.org/web/

G. PROVINCIAL DIGITAL COLLECTIONS

1) Digital Collection of Manitoba Government Publications

    More than 4,000 full-text PDFs of publications issued by Manitoba government departments, boards, agencies, and offices of the Legislative Assembly
    New and historic reports, studies, annual reports, bulletins, and pamphlets
    Browse by department and subject
    Search by keyword in full text and controlled metadata fields
Digital Collection of Manitoba Government Publications
www.gov.mb.ca/chc/leg-lib/dc.html

---

25   Internet Archive, "Frequently Asked Questions," online: https://archive.org/about/faqs.php#The_Wayback_Machine.

2) Our Ontario: Ontario Government Documents

Provides access to about 37,000 government documents in full text from the eArchive collection of the Ontario Legislative Library, and new documents are added quarterly. This site is a collaboration between OurDigitalWorld and the Ontario Legislative Library, with support from Scholars Portal. The site can be navigated by agency/ministry, a list of serials, or an advanced search.

> ❦ Our Ontario Government Documents
> http://govdocs.ourontario.ca/

H. OTHER

1) Policy Horizons Canada

> We are a federal government organization that conducts foresight. Our mandate is to help the Government of Canada develop future-oriented policy and programs that are more robust and resilient in the face of disruptive change on the horizon. To fulfill our mandate, we:
>
> ❦ Analyze the emerging policy landscape, the challenges that lie ahead, and the opportunities opening up.
> ❦ Engage in conversations with public servants and citizens about forward-looking research to inform their understanding and decision-making.
> ❦ Build foresight literacy and capacity across the Public Service.
>
> We produce content that may attract academic, public, and international attention, and do not publish commentary on policy decisions of the Government.[26]

Policy Horizons Canada publishes a wide range of reports, discussion papers, and policy briefs on emerging issues in society, economy, environment, governance, and technology. The publications can be browsed by most recent, type, or date.

> ❦ "About Us," online: *Policy Horizons Canada*
> https://horizons.gc.ca/en/about-us/

---

26 Policy Horizons Canada, "About Us," online: https://horizons.gc.ca/en/about-us.

2) Government of Canada Public Opinion Research Reports

Public opinion polls archived by Library and Archives Canada.

☞ Government of Canada Public Opinion Research Reports/
Rapports de recherche sur l'opinion publique publiés par le
gouvernement du Canada
http://epe.lac-bac.gc.ca/100/200/301/pwgsc-tpsgc/por-ef/index.html

I. EXTRINSIC AIDS TO STATUTORY INTERPRETATION — OTHER SOURCES: ROYAL COMMISSIONS, COMMISSIONS OF INQUIRY, AND TASK FORCES

Royal commissions are the most well known of the various types of commissions of inquiry that a government can use to inform itself about an issue of the day. A commission of inquiry is generally established by a government to do one of two things: (1) to provide advice to the government, including policy advice, usually with a broad mandate, or (2) to investigate and look into a particularly contentious event, usually with a more focused mandate.[27] Commissions of inquiry are an important part of the government, distinct from the legislature, judiciary, and executive branches of government,[28] and they have deep roots in the commonwealth system of government, with many British royal commissions still relevant to Canadian law.

Royal commissions usually investigate matters of broad national or provincial importance, and at the other end of the spectrum, task forces are usually used for more routine matters. At times, and still today, these investigations may be called public inquiries. Task forces and even departmental inquires have similar functions to a commission of inquiry. But there is not always a clearly defined line as to what makes something a royal commission, a commission of inquiry, or a task force. The commissioner and people involved are appointed to provide an impartial investigation and report back to the government.

---

27 *Inquiries Act*, RSC 1985, c I-11.
28 Ontario Law Reform Commission, *Report of Public Inquiries, Executive Summary*
(Toronto: Ontario Law Reform Commission, 1992) at 1, online: https://archive.org/
stream/esreportonpublicooonta#page/n3/mode/2up.

The government can choose to investigative an event or collect information to inform their policy direction on any issue. The federal *Inquiries Act*[29] and provincial equivalent Acts[30] provide for commissions of inquiry to be established in their respective jurisdictions.

An order in council (OIC) usually establishes the commission as a royal commission or a commission of inquiry. A task force may be established by OIC or at the request of a government department. In addition, more than eighty-seven federal Acts and other provincial Acts provide for government powers to investigate matters through task forces or departmental inquires. So while commissions of inquiry are the most well-known type of inquiry, there are many ways a government can conduct investigations.

Commissions of inquiry and royal commissions are led by a distinguished individual, often a judge, but not always. Commissions also have the power to subpoena witnesses, take evidence under oath, and request documents for review and study. However, the commission's recommendations are not binding—they cannot make a finding of guilt or liability.[31] Task forces are often led by experts in their field and similarly they cannot make a finding of guilt or liability. However, commissions of inquiry, royal commissions, and task force findings may influence public opinion and direct government policy to varying degrees.

Recent examples of royal commissions include the federal *Commission of Inquiry into the Sponsorship Program and Advertising Activities* in 2005/2006, known as the "Sponsorship Commission" and the *Commission on the Future of Healthcare in Canada* in 2002, known as the "Romanow Commission."

Commissions of inquiry produce a final report that Cabinet can choose to make public or not. Other materials like briefs, submissions, evidence, working papers, and other documents are often available

---

29 Above note 27.

30 See, for example, *Public Inquiry Act*, SBC 2007, c 9.

31 "A commission should not be permitted to express any conclusion of law regarding the civil or criminal responsibility of any individual or organization ....": Ontario Law Reform Commission, *Report of Public Inquiries, Executive Summary*, above note 28 at 5.

for research into a commission of inquiry. Library and Archives Canada is responsible for the records surrounding federal commissions of inquiry.[32] Often modern commissions of inquiry make their supporting materials available on a website, which is then housed by archives, legislative libraries, or other institutions.

1)   How Commissions of Inquiry Are Used in Court

Often it is difficult to see a direct link from a broad and sweeping commission of inquiry to resulting legislation, but commissions of inquiry can actually help shape public policy for decades.[33] For instance, a famous British royal commission led by Lord Durham after the rebellions of 1837–38 led to the passage of the *Act of Union* and the creation of a single province of Canada with equal representation in Upper and Lower Canada. After the *Act of Union*, the Province of Canada made frequent use of royal commissions, which laid the groundwork for Confederation.[34]

The Durham Commission and early confederate royal commissions are not your everyday examples of commissions that could be used as evidence of legislative intent. But there are numerous examples in caselaw where the courts have used royal commissions as evidence for the intention of Parliament, which suggests that royal commissions can indeed be used as an extrinsic aid to legislative intent.

In one example, at the Supreme Court of Canada in *R v Vasil*,[35] the Court referred to a British *Royal Commission on the Law Relating to Indictable Offences*[36] from 1879, which itself provided commentary on

---

32   Canada, Privy Council Office, "About Commissions of Inquiry: Records," online: www.canada.ca/en/privy-council/services/commissions-inquiry/about.html.

33   Barbara Lauriat, "'The Examination of Everything'—Royal Commissions in British Legal History" (2010) 31:1 *Statute Law Review* 24.

34   Thomas J Lockwood, "A History of Royal Commissions" (1967) 5:2 *Osgoode Hall Law Journal* 172, online: digitalcommons.osgoode.yorku.ca/cgi/viewcontent. cgi?article=2383&context=ohlj.

35   *R v Vasil*, [1981] 1 SCR 469.

36   Great Britain, Royal Commission Appointed to Consider the Law Relating to Indictable Offences, *Report of the Royal Commission appointed to consider the Law relating to Indictable Offences: with an Appendix containing a Draft Code embodying*

an English Draft *Criminal Code* of 1878. The Court said that the Canadian Parliament not only adopted many of the provisions in the English Draft *Code* but also the reasons as expressed in the Royal Commission Report, and the Supreme Court of Canada then used those reasons from the royal commission to interpret the section of the *Criminal Code* in question.[37]

When you read Chapter 8, you will see that during the course of that research, a royal commission on the revision of the *Criminal Code* was uncovered. The report may have been relevant to the legislative changes to the polygamy section of the *Criminal Code* that were being researched for that chapter. The report was examined but found not to have made any mention of polygamy. Still, it was worth reviewing due to the importance of royal commissions to Canadian public policy.

Originally, commission of inquiry reports were not admissible as evidence of legislative intent. In the 1983 decision *Morguard Properties Ltd v City of Winnipeg*, Estey J wrote that while useful for providing context to the issue at hand:

> It has, of course, been long settled that, in the interpretation of a statute (and here I do not concern myself with the constitutional process as, for example, in the *Re Anti-Inflation Act* judgment ... the report of a commission of enquiry such as a Royal Commission may be used in order to expose and examine the mischief, evil or condition to which the Legislature was directing its attention. However, in the interpretation of a statute, the court, according to our judicial philosophy, may not draw upon such reports and commentaries, but must confine itself to an examination of the words employed by the Legislature in the statutory provision in question and the context of that provision within the statute ....
>
> The logic is, of course, inexorable that the Legislature may well have determined not to follow the recommendations set out in the report of the Commission which had earlier been placed before the house. On the other hand, as we have seen in *Eastman Photographic*

---

the *Suggestions of the Commissioners* (London: Her Majesty's Stationery Office, 1879), online: www.lareau-legal.ca/EnglishDraftCodeONE.pdf.

37 Ruth Sullivan, *Sullivan and Driedger on the Construction of Statutes*, 4th ed (Markham, ON: LexisNexis Canada, 2002) at 485.

Materials Co. v. Comptroller-General of Patents, Designs and Trade-Marks, [1898] A.C. 571 at p. 575, Lord Halsbury stated:

> "... no more accurate source of information as to what was the evil or defect which the Act of parliament now under construction was intended to remedy could be imagined than the report of that commission."[38]

By 1998, this philosophy had changed and in *R v Mercure*,[39] La Forest J indicated that the use of legislative history that included reference to the Royal Commission on Bilingualism and Biculturalism was useful in "revealing legislative purpose":

> In my view, this case can be resolved simply by the application of the ordinary principles of statutory construction. However, all parties stressed the legislative history of the appropriate provisions and grounded some of their arguments in that history. At all events, it forms a useful backdrop for a consideration of the central issues and is of assistance in revealing legislative purpose. For much of the following historical discussion, I have relied upon Claude-Armand Sheppard, *The Law of Languages in Canada* (1971), c. I-C (a study of the Royal Commission on Bilingualism and Biculturalism).[40]

2) Tools to Find Commissions of Inquiry and Royal Commission Materials

Below is a list of finding tools for locating commission reports from the federal and provincial governments.

a) Commissions of Inquiry

The Privy Council Office provides access to archived commissions of inquiry from 1871 onward, including royal commissions. Archived reports, documents, and websites are maintained by Library and Archives Canada.

---

38   *Morguard Properties Ltd v City of Winnipeg*, [1983] 2 SCR 493 at 498–99 [*Morguard*].
39   *R v Mercure*, [1988] 1 SCR 234.
40   *Ibid* at 248.

☞ Privy Council Office: Commissions of Inquiry

www.canada.ca/en/privy-council/services/commissions-inquiry.html

b) Index to Federal Royal Commissions

Library and Archives Canada provides this site with bibliographic access to materials for more than 200 royal commissions in Canada since Confederation. Items in the index include commission reports, briefs, submissions, evidence, working papers, and other documents. Links to commission websites are included if available. The material on this site connects to the Privy Council Office Archived Commission of Inquiry website.

☞ Index to Federal Royal Commissions

www.bac-lac.gc.ca/eng/discover/royal-commissions-index/Pages/
index-federal-royal-commissions.aspx

☞ Manuscript Bibliography of Canadian Federal Royal Commissions and Commissions of Inquiry, Canada Depository and Services Program, 29 May 2013:

An extensive, multi-part manuscript of a bibliography of royal commissions and commissions of inquiry. Pages are scanned by the Depository and Services Program (DSP) and then combined into one file by Data and Government Information Centre, Queen's University.
https://qspace.library.queensu.ca/handle/1974/8068

☞ Federal and Provincial Royal Commissions, Commissions of Inquiry, and Reports

Queen's University, Q-Space: A resource at Queen's University to access federal and provincial commissions of inquiry and royal commissions online by date, author, title, and subject.
https://qspace.library.queensu.ca/handle/1974/6873

c) Early Canadiana Online

Early Official Publications in Early Canadiana Online includes some royal commission reports.

☞ Early Canadiana Online

http://eco.canadiana.ca

d) Libraries

Legislative, university, and public libraries will have selected commission of inquiry reports. Try libraries in the jurisdiction of interest, such as the British Columbia Legislative Library catalogue or the Nova Scotia Legislative Library catalogue for some full text provincial commission reports.

e) Sessional Papers

A jurisdiction's sessional papers may include commissions of inquiry, royal commissions, and task force reports.

3) Where to Find Royal Commission Reports

Alberta Royal Commissions
Alberta's royal commissions, the orders in council that established the commissions, and selected briefs, exhibits, and testimony are digitized in this tool. Browse by commissioner, place name, subject heading, publisher, and title, or use the simple or advanced search. The digital collection is maintained by the University of Alberta, organized around the reference book: *Royal Commissions and Commissions of Inquiry in the Province of Alberta 1905–1976* (Legislative Library).

> ☞ Alberta Royal Commissions
> http://royal.library.ualberta.ca

British Columbia Royal and Special Commissions: 1872–1980
The most comprehensive collection of British Columbian royal and special commissions reports with documents dating back to 1872. Browse by title, author/commission, and year. All royal and special commission reports published after 1980 are available online and can be searched in the legislative library catalogue. Also in the BC Legislative Library catalogue (online: https://llbc.ent.sirsidynix.net/client/en_GB/main) you can access three online publication checklists to see summaries of commissions of inquiries and related materials for BC commissions of inquiry.

- Marjorie C Holmes, Royal Commissions and Commissions of Inquiry under the *Public Inquiries Act* in British Columbia Checklist 1872–1942 (Victoria: Provincial Library, 1945)
- Judith Antonik Bennett, Royal Commissions and Commissions of Inquiry under the *Public Inquiries Act* in British Columbia Checklist 1943–1980 (Victoria: Legislative Library, Province of British Columbia, 1982)
- Judith Antonik Bennett Harvey, Royal Commissions and Commissions of Inquiry under the *Inquiry Act* and Significant Inquiries in British Columbia 1981–2005: A Checklist (Victoria: Legislative Library, Province of British Columbia, 2009)
- British Columbia Royal and Special Commissions: 1872–1980
  www.llbc.leg.bc.ca/commissions

New Brunswick Commissions of Enquiry: The Early Years

Browse and access fifty-seven commission reports conducted between 1784 and 1950. This site was put together by the Legislative Library, the University of New Brunswick Libraries, and the Provincial Archives of New Brunswick.

- New Brunswick Commissions of Enquiry: The Early Years
  https://lib.unb.ca/Texts/NBHistory/Commissions/index.htm

Ontario Royal Commissions

- *Royal Commissions and Commissions of Inquiry for the Provinces of Upper Canada, Canada, and Ontario, 1792 to 1991: A Checklist of Reports*
  This reference book provides bibliographic information, summaries, and locations of royal commissions and commissions of inquiry. It is available full text through the digital repository "Our Ontario."
  http://govdocs.ourontario.ca/node/11668

- Individual reports can be found in library catalogues, "Our Ontario," and in sessional paper collections.

Les commissions d'enquête au Québec depuis 1867 (In French only)
A directory of commissions of inquiry established by the Government
of Quebec since 1867 under the commissions of inquiry or certain sections of the Act. Find bibliographic information and links to online
documents if available. The directory provides an update of the following two works:

 ☞ Virginie Jamet, *Commissions et comités gouvernementaux et parle-
    mentaires du Québec 1867–1986 : liste bibliographique annotée* (Qué-
    bec: Bibliothèque de l'Assemblée nationale, 1987).
 ☞ Diane Chamberland, Claude Lajoie, *Rapports de comités, commis-
    sions et groupes de travail, 1987–1997 : liste bibliographique* (Québec:
    Assemblée nationale, 1998).
 ☞ Les commissions d'enquête au Québec depuis 1867

    www.bibliotheque.assnat.qc.ca/guides/fr/98-les-commissions-
    d-enquete-au-quebec-depuis-1867

J. EXTRINSIC AIDS TO STATUTORY INTERPRETATION — OTHER SOURCES: LAW REFORM COMMISSIONS

1) Introduction

Law reform commissions, also known as law commissions, are
independent bodies set up by government to suggest ways to improve,
update, and reform a jurisdiction's laws. Law reform commissions
are independent of governments, so they are not necessarily tied to
any political mandate. But they are still subject to the fiscal and political realities of the day—they can and have been abolished from time
to time.

Law reform commissions are advisory in nature and their advice
is not necessarily implemented. Law reform commissions in jurisdictions around the world consult and suggest ways to improve laws and
offer draft law suggestions. They offer an important and reasoned con-
tribution to debate on legislation. Law reform commission work could
also be done by part of a government ministry or by a law foundation.

Law reform commissions produce reports through research and
consultation, including input from the public and the legal profession.

The resulting reports may include the legislative evolution and a legislative history of the law in the particular area, mentions of policy papers and other applicable bills and legislation, legislation in other jurisdictions, and suggested draft legislation.

A law reform commission report is an incredible tool for legislative intent research; it may do much if not all of the important research legwork. A report may point to public speeches, *Hansard,* and other reports, and give a lot of context for the thinking behind a particular law. Even historical reports offer a window into a policy area and are valuable tools well into the future. For example, the Ontario Law Reform Commission's Report on Public Inquires[41] gives a detailed historical overview of public inquires or commissions of inquiry that includes examination of the law, the law as it relates to the Constitution, a survey of other jurisdiction's law on public inquiries, and recommendations for the future of public inquires.

Canada and each of the provinces either have or had a law commission, but there are no permanent law reform agencies in the territories.

a) Law Commission of Canada

The Law Reform Commission of Canada existed from 1971[42] to 1992,[43] and re-emerged in 1997 as the Law Commission of Canada,[44] only to be abolished in 2006.[45]

---

41 Ontario Law Reform Commission, *Report on Public Inquiries* (Toronto: Ontario Law Reform Commission, 1992), online: https://digitalcommons.osgoode. yorku.ca/library_olrc/146/.

42 *Law Reform Commission Act,* SC 1969–70, c 64.

43 "The Law Reform Commission will accordingly be wound up and any necessary continuing resources transferred to the Department of Justice." See "Bill C-63, An Act to dissolve or terminate certain corporations and other bodies," 2nd reading, *House of Commons Debates,* 34-3 No 1 (30 April 1992) at 9888–89.

44 *Law Commission of Canada Act,* SC 1996, c 9.

45 "As part of that promise, the government has eliminated funding for the Law Commission of Canada." See House of Commons, Standing Committee on Justice and Human Rights, *Evidence,* 39-1 No 6 (6 November 2006) at 1535, online: www.ourcommons.ca/DocumentViewer/en/39-1/JUST/meeting-29/evidence.

b) Alberta Law Reform Institute

The Alberta Institute of Law Research and Reform was set up through an agreement by the Law Society of Alberta and the University of Alberta in 1967.[46] An agreement in 2012 continues the renamed Alberta Law Reform Institute's objectives, which are:

> The consideration of matters of law reform with a view to proposing to the appropriate authority the means by which law of Alberta may be made more useful and effective;

and

> The preparation of proposals for law reform in Alberta, with respect to both the substantive law and the administration of justice.[47]

c) British Columbia Law Institute

The Law Reform Commission in BC started in 1969[48] and was ended in 1997 by funding cuts. At the same time, the British Columbia Law Institute incorporated with a purpose stated in its constitution to:

> promote the clarification and simplification of the law and its adaptation to modern social needs, promote improvement of the administration of justice and respect for the rule of law, and promote and carry out scholarly legal research.[49]

d) Manitoba Law Reform Commission

The Manitoba Law Reform Commission was established in 1971[50] and continues to operate.

---

46   Gavin Murphy, *Law Reform Agencies* (Ottawa: Department of Justice International Cooperation Group, 2004) at 16, online: http://publications.gc.ca/collections/Collection/J2-247-2004E.pdf [Murphy, *Agencies*].

47   Alberta Law Reform Institute, "About ALRI," online: www.alri.ualberta.ca/index.php/about-alri.

48   *Law Reform Commission Act*, SBC 1969, c 14.

49   British Columbia Law Institute, "Our History," online: www.bcli.org.

50   *Law Reform Commission Act*, SM 1970, c 95, and later the *Law Reform Commission Act*, SM 1989–90, c 25.

e) Law Reform Commission of Nova Scotia

The Law Reform Advisory Committee was created in 1969[51] and existed until the Act's repeal in 1990. The Law Reform Commission of Nova Scotia was created at that time.[52]

f) New Brunswick Legislative Services Branch

The Law Reform Branch of the New Brunswick Department of Justice was established in 1971.[53] In 1993 it was renamed the Legislative Services Branch.[54]

g) Newfoundland Law Reform Commission

The Newfoundland Law Reform Commission was created in 1971,[55] but the first commissioners were not appointed until the 1980s. In the 1992 provincial budget, the commission lost its funding.[56]

h) Law Commission of Ontario

The Ontario Law Reform Commission existed from 1964 to 1996.[57] Today, the Law Commission of Ontario, established in 2007,[58] continues to make recommendations to:

- ễ make the legal system more relevant, accessible and efficient;
- ễ simplify or clarify the law;
- ễ use technology to increase access to justice;
- ễ stimulate critical debate about law; and
- ễ promote scholarly legal research.[59]

---

51 *Law Reform Act*, SNS 1969, c 14.
52 *Law Reform Commission Act*, SNS 1990, c 17.
53 Murphy, *Agencies* above note 46 at 24.
54 The New Brunswick Legislative Services Branch existed until 2017 with a mandate that included "law reform projects."
55 *Newfoundland Law Reform Commission Act*, 1971, SN 1971, c 38.
56 Christopher Curran, "Law Reform in the Lean, Mean 90's" (Paper delivered at the Federal Law Reform Conference, Halifax, 1993) at 1.
57 *Ontario Law Reform Commission Act*, 1964, SO 1964, c 78.
58 The Law Commission of Ontario was originally established by agreement dated 6 July 2007. See Law Commission of Ontario, "About Us," online: www.lco-cdo. org/en/learn-about-us.
59 *Ibid.*

i)   Law Foundation of Prince Edward Island

Prince Edward Island established a law reform commission in 1970[60] and it was repealed in 1989. The Law Foundation of Prince Edward Island is now responsible for law reform activities; its mandate is detailed on its website:

> The Foundation has the power to establish and maintain a fund and use the proceeds thereof for the purposes of:
> - Legal education, legal research or law reform;
> - The promotion of legal aid; and
> - Aiding in the establishing, operating and maintaining of law libraries in Prince Edward Island.[61]

j)   Quebec Research Centre of Private and Comparative Law

A Civil Code Revision Office was established in 1995, and in 1992 the Quebec Law Reform Institute was created by statute[62] but was not brought into force. The Quebec Research Centre of Private and Comparative Law manages the Civil Code Revision Office materials.

k)   Saskatchewan Law Reform Commission

The Saskatchewan Law Reform Commission was established in 1971[63] and continues to operate today with a purpose "to review the law in Saskatchewan with a view to its systematic modernization and simplification."[64]

2)   How Is Law Commission Work Used in the Court?

Traditionally, law reform commission reports were used by courts to examine the mischief at which the legislation was aimed, but they were not traditionally used for direct evidence of legislative intent in

---

60   *The Law Reform Commission Act*, SPEI 1970, c 32.

61   Law Foundation of Prince Edward Island, online: www.lawfoundationpei.ca.

62   *An Act Respecting the Institut Québécois de Réforme du Droit*, SQ 1992, c 43.

63   *The Law Reform Commission Act*, SS 1971, c 21.

64   Law Reform Commission of Saskatchewan, online: www.lawreformcommission. sk.ca.

court.[65] Courts at times recognized that there was a possibility the legislature did not follow report recommendations.[66]

Today, according to Ruth Sullivan in the *Construction of Statutes*, and given the effect of *Rizzo and Rizzo Shoes* on cases of statutory interpretation, it is hard to see why a court would not use a law reform commission report for evidence of external context, direct evidence of legislative purpose, or direct evidence of the meaning of text. Often, if you compare the report to the statute, it is pretty clear if the report was followed; plus the reports often include draft legislation that matches the legislation in the jurisdiction.

For example, in *Diamond Estate v Robbins*,[67] the judge relied on a law reform commission report as an extrinsic aid to show legislative intent of the statute being considered. The case looked into a provision in the *Limitations Act* and the judge said that the

> *Limitations Act* is based on the extensively researched work of the New-foundland Law Reform Commission (Commission) and gives effect to substantially all of the recommendations of the Commission thereof. Accordingly, it is appropriate to refer to the Commission's reports as evidence of context, legislative purpose and textual meaning.[68]

3) Tools to Find Law Reform Commission Reports

Library and Archives Canada (LAC)
LAC has a collection of Law Commission of Canada publications and has archived the ceased commission's entire body of work.

> ☞ Archived Law Commission of Canada website (captured 6 December 2006)
> http://epe.lac-bac.gc.ca/100/206/301/law_commission_of_canada-ef/
> 2006-12-06/www.lcc.gc.ca/default-en.asp@lang_update=1

---

65   Sullivan, *Construction*, 5th, above note 1 at 600.
66   *Morguard*, above note 38.
67   *Diamond Estate v Robbins*, 2006 NLCA 1.
68   *Ibid* at para 62.

Alberta Law Reform Institute

Current reports can often be found on the law reform commission or agency's website. For a directory of current Canadian and international law reform commissions, consult the Alberta Law Reform Institute website.

   Alberta Law Reform Institute

Links to Other Law Reform Agencies

www.alri.ualberta.ca/index.php/help-links/links-to-other-lra

British Columbia Law Institute's Law Reform Database

The British Columbia Law Institute's Law Reform Database is a searchable database of current and historical world law reform commission reports.

The British Columbia Law Reform Institute hosts the World Law Reform database of world law reform agency publications and records. This database includes law reform publications from Canada, the Commonwealth of Nations, and the United States. Most of these publications are held within the British Columbia Law Institute's library. Where available, the records include links to current full text reports on the internet.

The World Law Reform database can be searched by words in the title, subject, keywords, jurisdiction, year, agency, document type, ISN (International Standard Number), and document number. The subject field uses subject headings from the Moys classification scheme. Keywords are taken from the text of the document and some synonyms are added.

   Law Reform Database British Columbia Law Institute

www.bcli.org/law-reform-resources/law-reform-database

Manitoba

   Manitoba Law Reform Commission

Find current consultations and archived projects, 1971–current.

www.manitobalawreform.ca/index.html

New Brunswick

🌶 **New Brunswick Office of the Attorney General Law Reform**

Access law reform notes and documents on the Attorney General website.

www2.gnb.ca/content/gnb/en/departments/jag/attorney-general/content/law_reform.html

Nova Scotia

🌶 **Law Reform Commission of Nova Scotia**

Find current, consultation, and archived discussion documents and final reports from the 1990s–current.

www.lawreform.ns.ca/reports

Ontario

🌶 **Law Commission of Ontario**

Access current and past commission projects on the website.

www.lco-cdo.org

🌶 **Ontario Law Reform Commission Database**

Archived commission reports 1967–96, put together by the Osgoode Digital Commons, Osgoode Law School, York University.

http://digitalcommons.osgoode.yorku.ca/library_olrc

Saskatchewan

🌶 **Law Reform Commission of Saskatchewan**

Current consultations and archived projects available 1974–current.

http://lawreformcommission.sk.ca

Uniform Law Conference of Canada (ULCC)

The ULCC produces suggested draft laws for provinces and keeps archive versions of older suggestions on its website. From the home page:

> The Uniform Law Conference of Canada was founded in 1918 to harmonize the laws of the provinces and territories of Canada, and where appropriate the federal laws as well. The Uniform Law Conference of Canada also makes recommendations for changes to

federal criminal legislation based on identified deficiencies, defects or gaps in the existing law, or based on problems created by judicial interpretation of existing law.[69]

☞ **Uniform Law Conference of Canada**
www.ulcc.ca/en/home

Check the internet archive and legislative and university library catalogues for scanned copies of reports in digital repositories. (See legislative library listing in Appendix 2.)

Other Sources

☞ **Internet Archive**
https://archive.org/index.php

☞ **United Kingdom Law Commission**
Find publications and reports 1995–current
www.lawcom.gov.uk

☞ **Earlier reports on law commission work**
1965–current on BAILII
www.bailii.org/ew/other/EWLC

---

69   Uniform Law Conference of Canada, online: www.ulcc.ca/en/home.

chapter seven

How to Trace the Legislative Evolution of a Statute

A. BEFORE YOU START

If you have been asked to trace the legislative evolution and history of a statute, it is not always necessary to start from scratch. Searching court websites, WestlawNext Canada, or even Google might yield an extant legislative evolution or history (or both) that you can use as a jumping-off point for your own research. You might also want to look at law reform commission reports, practitioner texts, or annotated statutes. Although you should never rely wholly on research prepared by someone else and would need to double check and update the information provided, it still might be useful to have an existing document as a guide.

B. LEGISLATIVE EVOLUTION

Ruth Sullivan's definition of legislative evolution from her treatise *Sullivan on the Construction of Statutes* has a very specific meaning:

> **Legislative evolution:** "the evolution of a legislative provision consists of successive enacted versions from inception to the version in place when the relevant facts occur."[1]

---

1   Ruth Sullivan, *Sullivan on the Construction of Statutes*, 6th ed (Markham, ON: LexisNexis, 2014) at 660.

The Supreme Court of Canada has adopted Sullivan's definition of legislative evolution in a number of cases. In *Marche v Halifax Insurance Co*, for example, Bastarache J (in his dissent) states:

> According to Professor Sullivan, "[o]ne of the most effective ways of establishing legislative purpose is to trace the evolution of legislation from its inception, through successive amendments, to its current form."[2]

1) Tracing the Evolution of a Statute

To trace evolution of a statute or section of a statute (which is also known as backdating), start by looking at the current statute and then work your way backwards to its inception. Make note of any changes to the statute and when those changes occurred. The information on when the changes took place can later be used to locate the legislative history of the statute.

2) The Source Reference

One useful tool for tracing a statute back is the source reference. For federal and Ontario statutes the source reference appears at the end of each section of the statute and provides citations to all the statutes that have amended that section, either back to the most recent statute revision or back to that section's inception, whichever is more recent. Citations for the source references follow a similar pattern to conventional citation but there are some differences. Here is an example from section 2 of the current federal *Citizenship Act*:

> (2) For the purposes of this Act,
> (a) a person is deemed to be born in Canada if the person is born on a Canadian vessel as defined in section 2 of the Canada Shipping Act, 2001, or on an aircraft registered in Canada under the Aeronautics Act and regulations made under that Act;

---

2   *Marche v Halifax Insurance Co*, 2005 SCC 6 at para 98 [*Marche*].

(b) a person who is lawfully present and entitled to permanently reside in Canada is deemed to have been lawfully admitted to Canada for permanent residence; and

(c) a person against whom a removal order has been made remains under that order

  (i) unless all rights of review by or appeal to the Immigration Appeal Division of the Immigration and Refugee Board, the Federal Court of Appeal and the Supreme Court of Canada have been exhausted with respect to the order and the final result of those reviews or appeals is that the order has no force or effect, or

  (ii) until the order has been executed.

RS, 1985, c C-29, s 2; RS, 1985, c 28 (4th Supp), s 36; 1992, c 21, s 6; 2000, c 12, s 74; 2001, c 26, s 286, c 27, s 227.1; 2002, c 8, s 183; 2008, c 14, s 1.[3]

Because the jurisdiction of the Act is implicit you do not see a reference to it in the source reference. In the above example, RS 1985, c C-29, s 2 refers to the *Revised Statutes of Canada 1985*; the annual volumes are referred to only by date, chapter number, and section; 1992, c 21, s 6, for example, is referring you to the 1992 annual volume of the Statutes of Canada, chapter 21, section 6. This same pattern applies to the provinces that include source references with their statutes.

3) Tracing the Evolution of a Recent Statute

Here is an example, using the *Civil Marriage Act*, SC 2005, c 33 s 5, *Marriage of Non-Resident Persons*, of tracing a section of a statute back to its inception when the entire statute is online.

a) Source References Method: Current Provision

Using Justice Laws Canada (http://laws.justice.gc.ca/eng) or CanLII (www.canlii.org), locate the current statute. Justice Laws Canada provides official versions of the statutes.

---

3 *Citizenship Act*, RSC 1985, c C-29, s 2.

Civil Marriage Act
SC 2005, c 33 s 5(3)
Assented to 2005-07-20

Marriage of non-resident persons

5(1) A marriage that is performed in Canada and that would be valid in Canada if the spouses were domiciled in Canada is valid for the purposes of Canadian law even though either or both of the spouses do not, at the time of the marriage, have the capacity to enter into it under the law of their respective state of domicile.

Retroactivity

(2) Subsection (1) applies retroactively to a marriage that would have been valid under the law that was applicable in the province where the marriage was performed but for the lack of capacity of either or both of the spouses to enter into it under the law of their respective state of domicile.

Order dissolving marriage

5(3) Any court order, made in Canada or elsewhere before the coming into force of this subsection, that declares the marriage to be null or that grants a divorce to the spouses dissolves the marriage, for the purposes of Canadian law, as of the day on which the order takes effect. 2005, c 33, s 5; 2013, c 30, s 3; 2015, c 29, s 5(E).

The source reference tells you that this statute was introduced in 2005. It also tells you that the statute was amended twice, once in 2013 and again in 2015.

To trace the history of the wording of a section of the statute you will need to look at the amendments as well as the original statute. One method of locating the amendments is to look at the point-in-time versions of statutes if they are available. On e-Laws, for example, point-in-time versions are available from January 2004. You can also take a similar approach on CanLII and, as an added bonus, CanLII enables you to compare the changes to a statute side by side on the screen. Although the information you see on CanLII is identical to that on the government laws websites, it is not an official version.

The best method is to locate the original amending Acts in the annual statutes (called source law on Ontario's e-Laws). The annual statutes will give you the full context of the amendments and may provide additional information that could be useful in determining legislative intent.

b) Source References Method: Amending Provisions

1) Working in reverse order, from the source references provided, the most recent amendment cited above is *The Zero Tolerance for Barbaric Cultural Practices Act*, SC 2015, c 29 s 5(E), which amends a number of statutes, including the *Civil Marriage Act*. As the most recent amendment, this statute provides the current wording of the Act.

Marriage of non-resident persons

5 (1) A marriage that is performed in Canada and that would be valid in Canada if the spouses were domiciled in Canada is valid for the purposes of Canadian law even though either or both of the spouses do not, at the time of the marriage, have the capacity to enter into it under the law of their respective state of domicile.

Retroactivity

(2) Subsection (1) applies retroactively to a marriage that would have been valid under the law that was applicable in the province where the marriage was performed but for the lack of capacity of either or both of the spouses to enter into it under the law of their respective state of domicile.

Order dissolving marriage

(3) Any court order, made in Canada or elsewhere before the coming into force of this subsection, that declares the marriage to be null or that grants a divorce to the spouses dissolves the marriage, for the purposes of Canadian law, as of the day on which the order takes effect.

2) The amendment previous to the one above occurred in 2013 in the *Civil Marriage of Non-residents Act*, SC 2013, c 30 s 3. In the annual statute, the summary at the beginning of the Act explains the purpose of the Act. The point-in-time version does not include the summary.

Summary

This enactment amends the Civil Marriage Act in order to provide that all marriages performed in Canada between non-residents, whether they are of the same sex or of the opposite sex, that would be valid in Canada if the spouses were domiciled in Canada are valid for the purposes of Canadian law even if one or both of the non-residents do not, at the time of the marriage, have the capacity to enter into it under the law of their respective state of domicile. It also establishes a new divorce process that allows a Canadian court to grant a divorce to non-resident spouses who reside in a state where a divorce cannot be granted to them because that state does not recognize the validity of their marriage.

And then section 3 provides the text of the section:

3. Section 5 of the Act and the headings before it are replaced by the following:

Marriage of non-resident persons

5 (1) A marriage that is performed in Canada and that would be valid in Canada if the spouses were domiciled in Canada is valid for the purposes of Canadian law even though either or both of the spouses do not, at the time of the marriage, have the capacity to enter into it under the law of their respective state of domicile.

Retroactivity

(2) Subsection (1) applies retroactively to a marriage that would have been valid under the law that was applicable in the province where the marriage was performed but for the lack of capacity of either or both of the spouses to enter into it under the law of their respective state of domicile.

Order dissolving marriage

(3) Any court order, made in Canada or elsewhere before the coming into force of this subsection, that declares the marriage to be null and void or that grants a divorce to the spouses dissolves the marriage, for the purposes of Canadian law, as of the day on which the order takes effect.

At first glance, the text of this provision and the previous provision seem to be identical. The wording for section 5(3) changed from "... marriage to be null *and void* or that grants a divorce" in 2013 to "... marriage to be null or that grants a divorce ..." in 2015. In some cases, although the changes are minor, they may be legally significant. What is significant in this instance is that this provision did not appear in the original statute and was added in 2013. As some same-sex spouses who had married in Canada "could not dissolve the marriage in their own country because it was not legally recognized there, and they could not do it in Canada either because they were not 'ordinarily residents' as required under Canada's *Divorce Act*."[4]

c) Looking at the Original Provision of the Statute

Finally, a look at the original statute (SC 2005, c 33, s 5) shows that the section referring to the marriage of non-resident persons does not appear in the statute.

d) Using a Finding Tool to Trace the Evolution of a Statute

Another method of tracing back the history of a section of a statute is by using a Table of Public Statutes. This is particularly useful if the statute does not include source references. Each jurisdiction provides an alphabetical table, which includes the name of the statute, the title of the minister responsible for that statute, and a list of amendments (and repeals) for each section. Some tables also include the dates that the original and amending statutes have come into force (CIF). Most jurisdictions have these tables online and some are searchable. These tables usually go back to as far as the most recent revision. The federal table, for example, includes all statutes since RSC 1985, and the table for Ontario goes back to RSO 1990.

The entry for the *Civil Marriage Act* in the Table of Public Statutes and Responsible Ministers looks like this. You can see that the entry for section 5 includes all the amending statutes listed in the source

---

4   Kim Brown, *Same-Sex Divorce for Non-residents of Canada: What Has Changed*,
       online: *Shulman Law Firm* https://shulman.ca/same-sex/divorce-canada-sex-
       non-residents-changed.

reference as well as the CIF (coming into force) information. To view the text of the amendments you will still have to look at the annual statutes.

Table of Public Statutes and Responsible Ministers
Updated to 2017, c 34 and *Canada Gazette*, Part II, Vol 151, No 26 (2017-12-27)
Civil Marriage Act—2005, c 33
(Mariage civil, Loi sur le)

Minister of Justice and Attorney General of Canada
section 2.1, added, 2015, c 29, section 4
section 2.2, added, 2015, c 29, section 4
section 2.3, added, 2015, c 29, section 4
section 5, 2013, c 30, section 3; 2015, c 29, section 5(E)
section 6, 2013, c 30, section 4
section 7, 2013, c 30, section 4
section 8, 2013, c 30, section 4
section 9, 2013, c 30, section 4
section 10, 2013, c 30, section 4
section 11, 2013, c 30, section 4
section 12, 2013, c 30, section 4
section 13, 2013, c 30, section 4
section 14, repealed, 2013, c 30, section 4
section 15, repealed, 2013, c 30, section 4
General, 2013, c 30, section 2
CIF, 2005, c 33 in force on assent 20-07-2005
CIF, 2013, c 30, sections 2 and 3 in force on assent 26-06-2013; section 4
    in force throughout Canada 14-08-2013, *see* SI/201393
CIF, 2015, c 29, sections 4 and 5 in force on assent 18-06-2015[5]

4) Tracing the Evolution of an Older Statute

a) Source References and Finding Tools: Older Statutes
While tracing the evolution of a recent statute, where all iterations are online, is not too complicated, tracing the evolution of an older

---

5   Government of Canada, *Table of Public Statutes and Responsible Ministers*, online: *Justice Laws* https://laws-lois.justice.gc.ca/eng/TablePublicStatutes/index.html.

statute will be more complex. You will need to consult print statutes or their online equivalent. You may also need to refer to a variety of finding tools in order to build a comprehensive record of the evolution of a particular statute.

b) Using a Finding Tool

Using the Tables of Public Statutes is one approach to tracing the evolution of a statute. These tables are particularly useful if the jurisdiction does not include source references. Each table includes the name of the statute, ordered alphabetically; the title of the minister responsible for that statute; and a list of amendments (and repeals) for each section. Some tables also include the dates that the original and amending statutes have come into force. Most jurisdictions have these tables online and some are searchable. These tables usually go back to as far as the most recent revision. The federal table, for example, includes all statutes since RSC 1985, and the table for Ontario goes back to RSO 1990. To trace the evolution of a statute back to previous revisions, check the Table of Public Statutes for the year before the revision. As an example, for Ontario, if you want to locate all the changes and amendments between the 1980 and 1990 revision, check the Table of Public Statutes for the year 1989 to see all the revisions to a statute that occurred between 1980 and the 1990 revision. You would then need to look at the annual volumes for each amendment indicated to see the text of each of those amendments.

c) Following the Source References

Another more direct record is to follow the source references, if they are available, backwards from one section to its previous version. Using this approach, you see the text and its changes immediately rather than using the intermediary step of a finding tool.

The following example was chosen because it illustrates how deeply you can dive into the evolution of an older statute and it provides some good examples of the roadblocks and complications you may find on the way. Take heart though, not every record of legislative evolution is this complex. We are going to look at section 293 (the polygamy section) of the current *Criminal Code* and trace it back to its inception in 1886. Although the source reference method has been used to describe this process, for jurisdictions that do not provide source references, a Table of Public Statutes (or equivalent) will provide the same roadmap for moving back in time. Look at the Table for the year or session that immediately precedes each revision to locate any changes to the statute between revisions.

The current iteration of section 293 of the *Criminal Code* from Justice Laws Canada looks like this:

Criminal Code (RSC, 1985, c C-46)

Polygamy

293 (1) Every one who

(a) practises or enters into or in any manner agrees or consents to practise or enter into

(i) any form of polygamy, or

(ii) any kind of conjugal union with more than one person at the same time, whether or not it is by law recognized as a binding form of marriage, or

(b) celebrates, assists or is a party to a rite, ceremony, contract or consent that purports to sanction a relationship mentioned in subparagraph (a)(i) or (ii), is guilty of an indictable offence and liable to imprisonment for a term not exceeding five years.

Evidence in case of polygamy

(2) Where an accused is charged with an offence under this section, no averment or proof of the method by which the alleged relationship was entered into, agreed to or consented to is necessary in the indictment or on the trial of the accused, nor is it necessary on the trial to prove that the persons who are alleged to have entered into the relationship had or intended to have sexual intercourse.
RS, c C-34, section 257.

The source reference indicates that this section has not been amended since the previous statute revision in 1970, where the *Criminal Code* appears in chapter C-34. Note the section number is different and we should be looking at section 257 rather than section 293.

Criminal Code, RSC 1970 c 34 section 257

The text of section 257 reads as follows:

257.(1) Every one who

(a) practises or enters into or in any manner agrees or consents to
practise or enter into

  (i) any form of polygamy, or

  (ii) any kind of conjugal union with more than one person at
    the same time, whether or not it is by law recognized as a
    binding form of marriage; or

(b) celebrates, assists or is a party to a rite, ceremony, contract or
consent that purports to sanction a relationship mentioned in
subparagraph (a)(i) or (ii), is guilty of an indictable offence and
is liable to imprisonment for five years.

Evidence in case of polygamy

(2) Where an accused is charged with a polygamy offence under
this section, no averment or proof of the method by which the alleged
relationship was entered into, agreed to or consented to is necessary
in the indictment or upon the trial of the accused, nor is it necessary
upon the trial to prove that the persons who are alleged to have entered
into the relationship had or intended to have sexual intercourse.

1953–54, c 51, s 243.

As you can see, the wording of the provision did not change between
the 1970 and 1985 revisions.

Criminal Code, SC 1953–54, c 51, s 243.

The next step is to look at the source reference for the 1970 revision,
which is now referring you to 1953–54, c 51, section 243. This will lead
us to the Annual Statutes for 1953–54. As a side note, statutes were
published for each session rather than annually prior to 1983 and so
you will often see reference to older statute volumes where the date
spans more than one year. Section 243 of the *Criminal Code* in the 1953–
54 sessional volume looked like this.

243.(1) Every one who

(a) practises or enters into or in any manner agrees or consents to
practise or enter into Polygamy.

(i) any form of polygamy, or

(ii) any kind of conjugal union with more than one person at the same time, whether or not it is by law recognized as a binding form of marriage; or

(b) celebrates, assists or is a party to a rite, ceremony, contract or consent that purports to sanction a relationship mentioned in subparagraph (i) or (ii) of paragraph (a), is guilty of an indictable offence and is liable to imprisonment for five years.

Evidence

(2) Where an accused is charged with an offence of polygamy under this section, no averment or proof of the method by which the alleged relationship was entered into, agreed to or consented to is necessary in the indictment or upon the trial of the accused, nor is it necessary upon the trial to prove that the persons who are alleged to have entered into the relationship had or intended to have sexual intercourse.

Once again, you can see that the wording has not changed but we seem to be at a dead end in terms of tracing the statute's evolution, since there is no source reference. The lack of a source reference could mean that we have reached the inception of this section of the statute (or the statute as a whole) or it could mean that there is an anomaly in publication that we should investigate further. The Statutes of Canada were revised in 1952 so it might be useful to look in some of the finding tools in that revision to see if we can find any hints as to whether the code existed previously.

d) Using a Finding Tool When There Is No Source Reference

The Table of History and Disposal of Acts (Illustration 7.1) that accompanies the 1952 revision is one good source to consult as it lists all the statutes that appeared in the previous revision along with a list of amendments until the current revision.

This table shows that the *Criminal Code* existed as chapter 36 of the *Revised Statutes of Canada* 1927. It indicates that chapter 36 was not consolidated into the 1952 revision and also that it was not repealed. This means that the 1927 version of the *Criminal Code* was still good law

ILLUSTRATION 7.1

TABLE OF HISTORY AND DISPOSAL OF ACTS, RSC 1952

4   *History and disposal of Acts.*

REVISED STATUTES OF CANADA, 1927.

Chap.	Title.	Disposal.
29	Trust Companies	Consolidated, except par. (a) of s. 2, repealed 1947, c. 75, s. 1; s. 3, repealed 1947, c. 75, s. 2; ss. (1) of s. 8, repealed 1950, c. 53, s. 1; par. (b) of s. 12 repealed 1947, c. 75, s. 3; par. (d) of s. 15, repealed 1947, c. 75, s. 4; s. 18, repealed 1947, c. 75, s. 5; s. 21, repealed 1950, c. 53, s. 2; s. 22, repealed 1950, c. 53, s. 3; ss. (2) of s. 26, repealed 1950, c. 53, s. 4; s. 27, repealed 1947, c. 75, s. 7; ss. (1) of s. 29, repealed 1950, c. 53, s. 5; pars. (a) (b) (f) of ss. (1) of s. 35, repealed 1947, c. 75, s. 8; ss. 36, 37, repealed 1947, c. 75, ss. 9, 10; par. (m) of s. 62, repealed 1947, c. 75, s. 11; s. 63, repealed 1947, c. 75, s.12; ss. (3) (4) of s. 65, repealed 1950, c. 53, s. 9; s. 67, repealed 1947, c. 75, s. 14; ss. (3) of s. 69, repealed 1947, c. 75, s. 15; s. 78, repealed 1932, c. 45, s. 10; ss. (3) of s. 81, repealed 1945, c. 33, s. 2; s. 86, repealed 1950, c. 53, s. 12.
30	Government Employees Compensation	Repealed 1947, c. 18, s. 14.
31	Contingencies	Repealed 1951 (2nd Sess.), c. 12, s. 101.
32	Copyright	Consolidated, except par. (m) of s. 2, repealed 1931, c. 8, s. 2(2); par. (q) of s. 2, repealed 1931, c. 8, s. 2(3); s. 8, repealed 1931, c. 8, s. 4; ss. (3) of s. 20, repealed 1931, c. 8, s. 7; s. 30, repealed 1931, c. 8, s. 8; s. 40, repealed 1931, c. 8, s. 9; ss.(3) of s. 44, repealed 1950, c. 50, s. 10; s. 47, spent.
33	Admiralty	Repealed 1934, c. 31, s. 36.
34	Exchequer Court	Consolidated, except s. 4, repealed 1928, c. 23, s. 1; s. 8, repealed 1944–45, c. 3, s. 2; ss. (1) of s. 12, repealed 1947, c. 33, s. 1; s. 14, repealed 1928, c. 23, s. 2; s. 18, repealed 1949 (2nd Sess.), c. 5, s. 1; par. (c) of ss. (1) of s. 19, repealed 1938, c. 28, s. 1; s. 22, repealed 1928, c. 23, s. 3; s. 36, repealed 1928, c. 23, s. 4; ss. (1) (2) of s. 82, repealed 1949 (2nd Sess.), c. 5, s. 2; s. 85, repealed 1949 (2nd Sess.), c. 5, s. 3; s. 87, repealed 1928, c. 23, s. 5.
35	Supreme Court	Consolidated, except ss. 4, 6, 9, repealed 1949 (2nd Sess.), c. 37, s. 1; s. 14, repealed 1951 (2nd Sess.), c. 25, s. 1; ss. (2) of s. 32, repealed 1928, c. 9, s. 1; ss. (2) of s. 33, repealed 1928, c. 9, s. 2; s. 36, repealed 1949 (2nd Sess.), c. 37, s. 2; s. 37, repealed 1930, c. 44, s. 1; ss. 38–44, repealed 1949 (2nd Sess.), c. 37, s. 2; s. 54, repealed 1949 (2nd Sess.) c. 37, s. 3; s. 65, repealed 1949 (2nd Sess.), c. 37, s. 4; s. 85, repealed 1949 (2nd Sess.), c. 37, s. 5.
36	Criminal Code	Not repealed and not consolidated.
37	Extradition	Consolidated.
38	Identification of Criminals	Consolidated, except ss. (1) of s. 2, repealed 1947, c. 35, s. 1.
39	Cullers	Repealed 1949, c. 11, s. 1.
40	Currency	Consolidated, except s. 5, repealed 1931, c. 48, s. 1 "17 (2)"; ss. (2) of s. 20, repealed 1950, c. 50, s. 10; ss. (3) of s. 21, repealed 1950, c. 50, s. 10.
41	Dominion Notes	Pursuant to 1934, c. 34, s. 2, repealed by Proclamation, March 11, 1935: 68 *Canada Gazette*, Pt. 2, p. 1968.
42	Customs	Consolidated, except par. (g) of ss. (1) of s. 2, repealed 1936, c. 19, s. 1; pars. (l) (r) of ss. (1) of s. 2, repealed 1936, c. 30, s. 1; s. 3, repealed 1931, c. 55, s. 14; ss. (1) of s. 24, repealed 1936, c. 19, s. 2; s. 35, repealed 1948, c. 41, s. 2; s. 36, repealed 1930 (2nd Sess.), c. 2, s. 1; s. 37, repealed 1930 (2nd Sess.), c. 2, s. 2; ss. (1) of s. 38, repealed 1948, c. 41, s. 3; ss. (4) of s. 38, repealed 1948, c. 41, s. 3;

R.S., 1952.   5992

even after the 1952 revision. We now know that the *Criminal Code* was revised in 1927, but it is a good idea to see if there were any changes to the polygamy section between 1927 and 1952. One way to find this out is to look at the Table of Public Statutes and Responsible Ministers (Illustration 7.2) for the sessional volume that preceded the 1952 revision.

ILLUSTRATION 7.2

TABLE OF PUBLIC STATUTES AND RESPONSIBLE MINISTERS, RSC 1952

vi		*Table of Public Statutes*
Subject-Matter	R.S. 1927 Chap.	Amendments in years 1907–1952
C		
Consolidation Revenue and Audit *See* Financial Administration............................	178	1931, c. 27, C.S.; 1950, c. 50, s. 10, Rep. 1951 (2 Sess.), c. 12, s. 101.
Consumer Credit (Temporary Provisions)....	....	1950-51, c. 3; 1951 (1 Sess.), c. 14.
Contingencies (*See* Financial Administration)..	31	Rep. 1951 (2 Sess.), c. 12, s. 101.
Continuation of Transitional Measures (*See* Transitional Measures, Continuation of).		
Convention with U.S. (Sockeye Salmon Fisheries)............................	....	1930, c. 10.
Copper, Bounty on............................	....	1923, c. 40; 1928, c. 25.
Copyright............................	32	1931, c. 8; 1935, c. 18; 1936, c. 28; 1938, c. 27; 1950, c. 50, s. 10.
Corrupt Practices Inquiries..................	51	
Criminal Code............................	36	1930, c. 11; 1931, c. 28; 1932, cc. 7, 8, 9, 28; 1932-33, cc. 25, 53; 1934, cc. 11,47; 1935, cc. 36, 56; 1936, c. 29; 1938, c. 44; 1939, c. 30; 1943-44, c. 23; 1944-45, c. 35; 1946, cc. 5, 20; 1947, cc. 31, 55; 1947-48, cc. 39, 40; 1949 (2 Sess.), cc. 2, 13; 1950, cc. 11, 12; 1951 (1 Sess.), cc. 25, 47; 1952, cc. 22, 39.

There are quite a few amendments to look at, as the table does not specify which sections of the Act have been amended. As a shortcut we can look at the wording of the polygamy section as it was in 1927 and see if it is substantially similar to the wording in 1953–54. If it is, then we would not have to look at each of these amendments. The index to the statutes in volume V, which is organized by subject, will lead us to the appropriate section in the 1927 revision (Illustration 7.3).

It is immediately apparent that something is different, as polygamy is listed in the index as being in two sections of the statute, whereas in 1953–54 it was only in one section. So we will start by looking at RSC 1927, c 36, ss 310 and 948 as identified by the index.

ILLUSTRATION 7.3

SUBJECT INDEX, RSC 1927

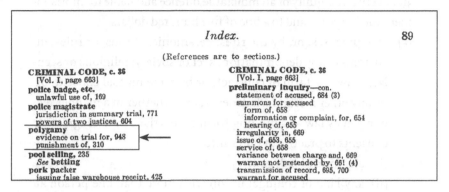

Index.   89

(References are to sections.)

CRIMINAL CODE, c. 36
[Vol. I, page 663]
police badge, etc.
  unlawful use of, 169
police magistrate
  jurisdiction in summary trial, 771
  powers of two justices, 604
polygamy
  evidence on trial for, 948
  punishment of, 310
pool selling, 235
  See betting
pork packer
  issuing false warehouse receipt, 425

CRIMINAL CODE, c. 36
[Vol. I, page 663]
preliminary inquiry—con.
  statement of accused, 684 (3)
  summons for accused
    form of, 658
    information or complaint, for, 654
    hearing of, 655
    irregularity in, 669
    issue of, 653, 655
    service of, 658
    variance between charge and, 669
    warrant not pretended by, 661 (4)
    transmission of record, 695, 700
    warrant for accused

Tracing Section 310 — Punishment of Polygamy

Because polygamy now spans two sections (section 310 (Punishment of Polygamy) and section 948 (Evidence on Trial for Polygamy)), our research will have to follow each of these sections further back, starting with section 310. As you can see, the wording here is substantially different and so it will be necessary to look at all the amending statutes between 1927 and 1953–54. It should be noted that while the wording is quite different here than in the later versions of the section, these differences may or may not be significant. As Bastarache J noted in his dissent in *Marche v Halifax Insurance Co*:

> Thus, it is possible to conclude that "even dramatic changes in wording are meant to simplify or otherwise modernize the style rather than to change the substance of the provision": Sullivan, at p. 477; see also R. v. McIntosh, [1995] 1 S.C.R. 686 (S.C.C.), at paras. 62-75. I maintain this is the case in the present appeal.[6]

Without reproducing those statutes here, none of the amending statutes amended section 310 or 948. So, it is clear that changes to the wording occurred during the revision of the *Criminal Code*. This will be a key point in time to research when building the legislative history for this section of the statute (see Chapter 8).

---

6   *Marche,* above note 2 at para 103.

Here is the text of section 310 from RSC 1927:

310. Every one is guilty of an indictable offence and liable to imprisonment for five years, and to a fine of five hundred dollars

(a) who practises, or, by the rites, ceremonies, forms, or rules, or customs of any denomination, sect or society, religious or secular, or by any form of contract, or by mere mutual consent, or by any other method whatsoever, and whether in a manner recognized by law as a binding form of marriage or not, agrees or consents to practise or enter into

(i) any form of polygamy,

(ii) any kind of conjugal union with more than one person at the same time, or

(iii) what among the persons commonly called Mormons is known as spiritual or plural marriage; or

(b) who lives, cohabits, or agrees or consents to live or cohabit in any kind of conjugal union with a person who is married to another or with a person who lives or cohabits with another or others in any kind of conjugal union; or

(c) celebrates, is a party to, or assists in any rite or ceremony which purports to make binding or to sanction any of the sexual relationships mentioned in paragraph (a) of this section; or

(d) procures, enforces, enables, is a party to, or assists in the compliance with, or carrying out of, any form, rule or custom which so purports; or

(e) procures, enforces, enables, is a party to, or assists contract in the execution of, any form of contract which so purports, or the giving of any consent which so purports. RS, c 146, s 310.

The source reference for this section leads us back to RS c 146, s 310. The Statutes of Canada were previously revised in 1906 and that is where we will turn to next.

Revised Statutes of Canada c 146, s 310

310. Every one is guilty of an indictable offence and liable to imprisonment for five years, and to a fine of five hundred dollars,

(a) who practises, or, by the rites, ceremonies, forms, rules, or customs of any denomination, sect or society, religious or secular, or by any form of contract, or by mere mutual consent, or by any other method whatsoever, and whether in a manner recognized by law as a binding form of marriage or not, agrees or consents to practise or enter into

 (i) any form of polygamy

 (ii) any kind of conjugal union with more than one person at the same time, or union;

 (iii) what among the persons commonly called Mormons is known as spiritual or plural marriage; or,

(b) who lives, cohabits, or agrees or consents to live or cohabit in any kind of conjugal union with a person who is married to another or with a person who lives or cohabits with another or others in any kind of conjugal union; or,

(c) celebrates, is a party to, or assists in any rite or Celebrating ceremony which purports to make binding or to sanction any of the sexual relationships mentioned in paragraph (a) of this section; or,

(d) procures, enforces, enables, is a party to, or assists in the compliance with, or carrying out of, any form, rule or custom which so purports; or,

(e) procures, enforces, enables, is a party to, or assists in the execution of, any form of contract which so purports, or the giving of any consent which so purports. 63–64 V, c 46, s 3.

The wording in the 1906 revision is the same as the wording in the 1927 revision so there were no changes between 1906 and 1927. The source reference has an interesting twist. Rather than referring to a chronological year, the note refers to 63–64 V, c 46, s 3. The numbers 63–64 V refer to the sixty-third and sixty-fourth years of the reign of Queen Victoria (1900). If you are looking at the statute volumes in print, you will see the regnal years indicated on the spine of the statute volumes. If you are unsure of the date, a quick internet search for regnal years will give you the information you need.

The Criminal Code Amendment Act, 1900, 63–64 Vict, c 46, s3

We now turn to *The Criminal Code Amendment Act, 1900,* 63–64 V, c 46, s 3. Section 3 of this statute is a huge section that includes many amendments to the *Criminal Code.* You will need to read through until you find the polygamy section. Once you find it, you will see that the section number of the previous version was 278.

> 278. Every one is guilty of an indictable offence and liable to imprisonment for five years, and to a fine of five hundred dollars,
>
> (a) who practises, or, by the rites, ceremonies, forms, rules or customs of any denomination, sect or society, religious or secular, or by any form of contract, or by mere mutual consent, or by any other method whatsoever, and whether in a manner recognized by law as a binding form of marriage or not, agrees or consents to practise or enter into
>
>   (i)   any form of polygamy;
>
>   (ii) any kind of conjugal union with more than one person at the same time; or
>
>   (iii) what among the persons commonly called Mormons is known as spiritual or plural marriage; or
>
> (b) who lives, cohabits, or agrees or consents to live or cohabit in any kind of conjugal union with a person who is married to another, or with a person who lives or cohabits with another or others in any kind of conjugal union; or
>
> (c) celebrates, is a party to, or assists in any such rite or ceremony which purports to make binding or to sanction any of the sexual relationships mentioned in paragraph (a) of this section; or
>
> (d) procures, enforces, enables, is a party to, or assists in the compliance with, or carrying out of, any such form, rule or custom which so purports; or
>
> (e) procures, enforces, enables, is a party to, or assists in the execution of, any such form of contract which so purports, or the giving of any such consent which so purports.

You will also see that this section does not have a source reference; however the first line of section 3 tells us that this statute is amending *The Criminal Code 1892,* which can be found at 55–56 Vict c 29 s 278.

ILLUSTRATION 7.4

THE CRIMINAL CODE AMENDMENT ACT, 1900, 63–64 VICT, C 46, S 3

63-64 VICTORIA.

CHAP. 46.

An Act further to amend the Criminal Code, 1892.

[Assented to 18th July, 1900.]

HER Majesty, by and with the advice and consent of the Senate and House of Commons of Canada, enacts as follows :—

1. This Act may be cited as *The Criminal Code Amendment Act*, 1900. Short title.

2. This Act shall come into force on the first day of January, 1901. Coming into force.

→ **3.** *The Criminal Code*, 1892, is amended in the manner set forth in the following schedule :— 1892, c. 29, amended.

SCHEDULE.

Section **3.**—By repealing sub-paragraph (i) of paragraph (*e*) as that sub-paragraph is enacted by chapter 40 of the statutes of 1895, and substituting the following therefor :—
" (i.) In the province of Ontario, the Court of Appeal for Ontario."
And by repealing sub-paragraph (i) of paragraph (*y*) and substituting the following therefor :—
" (i.) In the province of Ontario, the High Court of Justice for Ontario."

So now, we will go back to *The Criminal Code 1892*, 55–56 Vict c 29 s 278. Here, once again, the wording is similar to the 1900 version:

278. Every one is guilty of an indictable offence and liable to imprisonment for five years, and to a fine of five hundred dollars,

(a) who practises, or, by the rites, ceremonies, forms, rules or customs of any denomination, sect or society, religious or secular, or by any form of contract, or by mere mutual consent, or by any other method whatsoever, and whether in a manner recognized by law as a binding form of marriage or not, agrees or consents to practise or enter into

(i) any form of polygamy;

(ii) any kind of conjugal union with more than one person at the same time; or

(iii) what among the persons commonly called Mormons is known as spiritual or plural marriage; or

(b) who lives, cohabits, or agrees or consents to live or cohabit in any kind of conjugal union with a person who is married to another, or with a person who lives or cohabits with another or others in any kind of conjugal union; or

(c) celebrates, is a party to, or assists in any such rite or ceremony which purports to make binding or to sanction any of the sexual relationships mentioned in paragraph (a) of this section; or

(d) procures, enforces, enables, is a party to, or assists in the compliance with, or carrying out of, any such form, rule or custom which so purports; or

(e) procures, enforces, enables, is a party to, or assists in the execution of, any such form of contract which so purports, or the giving of any such consent which so purports. 53 V, c 37, s 11.

53 V c 37 s 11, *An Act Further to Amend the Criminal Law*

The source reference then refers to 53 V c 37 s 11, *An Act Further to Amend the Criminal Law*. This is where the polygamy section was first added to the statute in 1890. This date will be crucial when you are building your legislative history.

RSC, c 161 amended

11. The following sections are hereby added to the last cited Act:

5. Every one who practises, or, by the rites, ceremonies, forms, rules or customs of any denomination, sect or society, religious or secular, or by any form of contract, or by mere mutual consent, or by any other method whatsoever, and whether in a manner recognized by law as a binding form of marriage or not, agrees or consents to practise or enter into

(a) Any form of polygamy; or

(b) Any kind of conjugal union with more than one person at the same time; or

(c) What among the persons commonly called Mormons is known as spiritual or plural marriage; or

(d) Who lives, cohabits, or agrees or consents to live or cohabit, in any kind of conjugal union with a person who is married to another, or with a person who lives or cohabits with another or others in any kind of conjugal union; and

2. Every one who,

(a) Celebrates, is a party to, or assists in any such rite or ceremony which purports to make binding or to sanction any of the sexual relationships mentioned in sub-section one of this section; or

(b) Procures, enforces, enables, is a party to, or assists in the compliance with, or carrying out of, any such form, rule or custom which so purports; or

(c) Procures, enforces, enables, is a party to, or assists in consent, the execution of any such form of contract which so purports, or the giving of any such consent which so purports, is guilty of a misdemeanor, and liable to imprisonment for five years and to a fine of five hundred dollars; and

3. In any charge or indictment for any offence mentioned in sub-section two of this section it shall be sufficient to describe the offence in the language of that sub-section applicable, thereto; and no averment or proof of the method in which the sexual relationship charged was entered into, agreed to, or consented to, shall be necessary in any such indictment, or upon the trial of the person thereby charged; nor shall it be necessary upon such trial to prove carnal connection had or intended to be had between the parties implicated.

The note introducing section 3 indicates that the section is amending chapter 161 of the previous revision (*An Act respecting Offenses Relating to the Law of Marriage*), which is RSC 1887 but does not indicate which section is being amended; this is a clue that the polygamy section did not exist earlier. A look at the statute shows that polygamy was not included in this Act. From this we can conclude that the eventual polygamy section of the *Criminal Code* was first added in 1887.

And here your research into the evolution of section 310 ends.

Tracing the Evolution of Section 948 (Evidence on Trial for Polygamy)
As we noted from the index to the *Revised Statutes of Canada* 1927, two separate sections of the *Criminal Code* concern polygamy. Having traced the evolution of section 310 back to its inception, it is now time to trace section 948:

> 948. In the case of any indictment under section three hundred and ten (b), (c) and (d), no averment or proof of the method in which the sexual relationship charged was entered into, agreed to or consented to, shall be necessary in any such indictment, or upon the trial of the person thereby charged; nor shall it be necessary upon such trial to prove carnal connection had or intended to be had between the persons implicated. RS, c 146, s 948.

The source reference in the *Revised Statutes of Canada* 1927 leads us to the previous revision, RSC 1906, c 146, s 948:

> 948. In the case of any indictment under section three hundred and ten (b), (c) and (d), no averment or proof of the method in which the sexual relationship charged was entered into, agreed to or consented to, shall be necessary in any such indictment, or upon the trial of the person thereby charged; nor shall it be necessary upon such trial to prove carnal connection had or intended to be had between the persons implicated. 55–56 V, c 29, s 706.

There were no changes to the wording of the statute between 1896 and 1927. We are now being referred to 55–56 Vic, c 39, s 706. Notice that the section number has changed from section 948 to section 706, but the wording is the same in both the older and newer sections:

> 706. In the case of any indictment under section two hundred and seventy-eight (b), (c) and (d), no averment or proof of the method in which the sexual relationship charged was entered into, agreed to or consented to, shall be necessary in any such indictment, or upon the trial of the person thereby charged; nor shall it be necessary upon such trial to prove carnal connection had or intended to be had between the persons implicated. 53 V, c 37, s 11.

The source reference 53 V, c 37, s 11 now cites the same statute and section number as the previous section 310—Punishment of Polygamy. This statute, *An Act to Amend the Criminal Law*, 1890 53 Vic, c 37, s 11, introduces polygamy into the *Criminal Code*. From here, as with section 278, we trace the statute back to c 161 of the previous *Revision* (see above). Finally, we have traced both sections of the Act back to the original statute.

As noted above, courts will use the evolution of the wording of a statute as evidence of legislative intent, but often not without looking at the history of a statute as well. And so, the next step in our journey will be to trace the legislative history of the statute.

5) Researching Legislative Evolution Checklist

For additional assistance, there is a comprehensive overview of the resources available for updating statutes and regulations in *Updating Statutes and Regulations for All Canadian Jurisdictions* (5th ed).[7]

Current Statutes Online

- Go to the online legislation databases for the jurisdiction you are researching. These databases include current consolidated statutes from the most recent revision onward (1985 federally and 1990 in Ontario, for example). You will also find annual statutes included in these databases.
- Locate the statute you are researching. The federal (*Justice Laws Canada*) and Ontario (e-Laws) government sites also provide links to previous versions of the statutes for comparison.
- The source reference, if available, will also provide an indication of changes to each section since the last revision. e-Laws provides a source reference at the end of each section. A limited number of statutes also include a drop-down menu of "section amendments with date in force" at the end of each section.

---

7 Nancy McCormack & Nathalie Leonard, *Updating Statutes and Regulations for All Canadian Jurisdictions*, 5th ed (Toronto: Carswell, 2012) at 179.

ℰ To ensure you have located each and every change, check the Tables of Public Statutes, which lists all legislation (even repealed legislation).

When You Have a Current Statute and Need to Look at Prior Legislative Changes in Print

ℰ Look at the section of the current statute that you are researching.

ℰ Look at the source reference, which appears at the bottom of the section or the Table of Public Statutes. Either source will indicate changes to the section since the statute's inception or since the most recent revision.

ℰ Look at the amending statutes identified in the source reference or table for changes to the text of your statute.

ℰ Do this repeatedly until you reach the earliest incarnation of the statutes.

ℰ During this process you will need to make note of any changes in the language of the section that might be significant when looking at legislative intent.

ℰ If you hit a roadblock and can't see a source reference, look at the Table of Public Statutes for the year prior to the year with no source reference. This should put you back on track or indicate that you have reached the end of your task.

Researching Legislative History

ℰ Where you find changes to the wording of your section, consult the debates (and other materials such as committee debates and commission reports) from that time period in order to ascertain whether Parliament or the legislatures has given any indication as to the intent of those changes.

chapter eight

How to Trace the Legislative History of a Statute

A. TIMELINE OF THE POLYGAMY SECTION OF THE *CRIMINAL CODE OF CANADA*

What do we know about polygamy in the statutes from looking at the legislative evolution?

❧ *An Act Relating to the Law of Marriage*, RSC 1886, c 161
No mention of polygamy in this statute.

❧ *An Act to Further Amend the Criminal Law*, SC 1890, c 37, s 11
Polygamy added to the Act. This is where you would start looking for House and Senate debates to understand why this provision was added and what the intention of Parliament was when it added this section. You might also look for royal commission reports as well as committee evidence and debates.

❧ *Criminal Code 1892*, SC 1982, c 29, ss 278 and 706
In 1892, all the criminal statutes in Canada were consolidated and amalgamated, resulting in the *Criminal Code 1892*. In the new Code, the wording and meaning of the polygamy section was essentially the same as in the earlier version. The major difference being that the provision is now split into two, section 278 is almost identical to the earlier sections 5(1) and (2), section 706 is similar to section 5(3). Since no substantial changes have been made to the wording or meaning of the text, then it is not

necessary to look at the debates or other sources of legislative intent at this time.

❦ Criminal Code Amendment Act, 1900, 63–64 Vict, C 46, s 5

Section 278 was amended by making minor changes to the wording and numbering of the provision but there were no substantive changes. Section 706 was not amended.

❦ Criminal Code, RSC 1906, c 146, ss 310 and 948

The text of the provision is the same, only the section numbers have changed.

❦ Criminal Code, RSC 1927, c 36, ss 310 and 948

This wording and the section numbers are the same as in the 1906 revision. The *Criminal Code* was not included in the revised *Statutes of Canada 1952* but was still in force as it had not been repealed and had not been consolidated since the 1927 revision. Why? Because a royal commission was appointed in 1951 to make recommendations for a complete overhaul of the *Criminal Code*. The text of this royal commission can be located through the Privy Council Office's very useful "Commissions of Inquiry" page at www.pco-bcp.gc.ca/index.asp?lang=eng&Page=information&Sub=commissions.

❦ Criminal Code, SC 1953–1954, c 51, s 243

By 1954 this overhaul was completed and there were some changes made to the polygamy section. The two provisions referring to polygamy were merged into one and the wording was changed, excluding all references to Mormons. In order to understand why this section was changed, it is a good idea to look at the bills, House and Senate debates, royal commission reports or committee evidence, and debates to determine if there was a change in the intention of Parliament that needs to be considered.

❦ Revised Statutes of Canada 1970 and Revised Statutes of Canada 1985 to present.

The text of the provision is unchanged.

B. HOW TO TRACE THE HISTORY OF THE STATUTE

From our research into the evolution of the statute, we can see that there are two key points in the history of the polygamy section of the *Criminal Code* that could provide indicators as to the intent of this piece of legislation. The first is 1890 when polygamy was added to the criminal law, and the second was in the early 1950s, when the wording of the section was changed and updated.

The most important resource when determining legislative intent is the parliamentary debates. For federal legislation, you will need to consult both the House of Commons and Senate debates.

The Introduction of the Statute in 1890

House of Commons Debates

When using the debates, the best place to start is the index.

The 1890 House of Commons Debates has two indexes: a speaker index and a subject index. Since we do not know any of the speakers at this point, we will start by looking at the subject index. There is no entry in the subject index for polygamy, but there is one for criminal law that looks like it might be relevant.

ILLUSTRATION 8.1

HOUSE OF COMMONS DEBATES 1890, SUBJECT INDEX

lxiv INDEX.

COMMITTEES—*Continued.*
BRESAYLOR HALF-BREEDS: Rep. presented (Mr. *Mc Neill*) 4732 (ii).
DEBATES, OFFICIAL: M. for Sp. Com. (Mr. *Bowell*) 4.
—— List of Members, vii.
—— 1ST REP. OF COM.: M. to conc. (Mr. *Desjardins*) 1261 (i), 3153 (ii).
—— 2ND REP.: presented (Mr. *Desjardins* 3368 (ii)
—— 3RD REP.: presented (Mr. *Davin*) 4396.
—— M. (Mr. *Davin*) to conc., 4578 (ii).
—— Amt. (Mr. *Curran*) to ref, back, 4578 (ii).
EXPIRING LAWS: List of Members, 34 (i).
LIBRARY OF PARLIAMENT, JOINT: M. (Sir *John A. Macdonald*) 31 (i).
PRINTING, JOINT COM.: M. (Sir *John A. Macdonald*) 31.
—— List of Members, 31 (i).
—— M. (Sir *Hector Langevin*) to add names, 1651 (i).
—— 3RD REP.: M. (Mr. *Bergin*) to conc., 1856 (i).
—— objection (Mr. *Blake*) 440 (ii).
—— 6TH REP.: M. (Mr. *Taylor*) to conc., 4658 (ii).
—— 9TH REP.: M. (Mr. *Bergin*) to conc., 4928 (ii).
PRIVATE BILLS (MISCELLANEOUS): List of Members, 35 (i).
PRIVILEGES AND ELECTIONS: List of Members, 33 (i).
—— M. (Mr. *Girouard*) to employ shorthand writer 2098 (i).
—— REP. presented (Mr. *Girouard*) 4397 (ii).
PUBLIC ACCOUNTS; List of Members, 35 (i).
—— NON-MEETING: Remarks (Sir *Richard Cartwright*) 2596 (ii).
RAILWAYS AND CANALS, &C.: List of Members, 34 (i).

CORNWALL CANAL: in Com. of Sup., 2275 (i).
—— LETTER OF MR. PAGE: prop. Res. (Mr. *Bergin*) 1122 (i).
CORSETS, CLASPS, &C.: in Com. of Ways and Means, 3485 (ii).
COTTON CORDAGE, &C.: in Com. of Ways and Means, 3392 (ii)
—— DENIMS, &C.: in Com. of Ways and Means, 3400 (ii).
—— TWINE: in Com. of Ways and Means, 3541 (ii).
COTÉ, F., PET. *re* DAMAGES TO PROPERTY BY I.C.R.: M. for copies * (Mr. *Fiset*) 1713 (i).
COURT HOUSE, MONTREAL, COST OF CONSTRUCTION: M. for Ret. (Mr. *Curran*) 2188 (i).
COVE HEAD HARBOR SURVEYS, REPS. OF ENGINEERS, &C.: M. for copies (Mr. *Davies, P.E.I.*) 1065 (i).
CRANE ISLAND MAIL SERVICE: Ques. (Mr. *Choquette*) 121 (i).
Criminal Law (seduction, &c.) Amt. B. No. 65 (Sir *John Thompson*). 1°, 342 (i); 2°, 3161; in Com., 3164, 3368; 3° m. and Amt. (Mr. *Bergin*) 3411; neg. (Y. 36, N. 124) 3446; Amt. (Mr. *Mitchell*) 3447; Amt. (Mr. *Tisdale*) to Amt. 3454; neg. (Y. 71, N. 98) 3457; Amt. neg. (Y. 74, N. 88) 3458; Amts. (Messrs. *Blake* and *Mc Neill*) neg. and 3°, 3460 (ii). (53 *Vic.*, c. 37.) ←
CRIMINAL STATISTICS: in Com. of Sup., 498 (i).

The subject index refers us to the *Criminal Law Amendment* Bill No 65. Since this is the only entry on the criminal law in this index, we are likely in the right place. The index entry gives a surprising amount of information: who introduced the bill, where to find each reading and the debates, as well as the citation to the statute. This is a concrete clue that we are looking at the correct entry, because 53 Vict, c 37 is, as we know from our evolution research, the statute that introduces polygamy to Canadian law.

First Reading

Start by looking at *Hansard* for the date of first reading when the bill was introduced. When ministers introduce a bill at first reading, they might provide some context or information that could be useful in discerning legislative intent. In this instance, Minister of Justice Sir John Thompson introduced the bill and explicitly noted that one of the purposes of this bill was to "make more effectual provision for the suppression of polygamy."[1]

Debates on Second Reading

On second reading, the Minister of Justice went on to explain further the intent of bill as a whole and the polygamy section in detail:

> Section 9 deals with the practice of polygamy, which I am not aware
> yet exists in Canada, but which we are threatened with; and I think
> it will be much more prudent that legislation should be adopted at
> once in anticipation of the offence, if there is any probability of its
> introduction, rather than we should wait until it has become estab-
> lished in Canada.[2]

Committee Stage

When a bill goes to a committee for discussion it can be referred to a separate committee or to the Committee of the Whole House, usually shortened to the Committee of the Whole. The Committee of the Whole includes all members of Parliament. In this case, Bill 65 was referred to the Committee of the Whole and the discussion took place immediately after second reading.

---

1   *House of Commons Debates*, 6-4 (7 February 1890) at 342 (Sir John Thompson).
2   *Ibid* at 3163 (Sir John Thompson).

At the committee stage, members examine and discuss the meaning and purpose of each clause of the bill and propose amendments to the bill on a clause-by-clause basis. During the course of the lengthy discussion, members of Parliament questioned the minister and the prime minister as to the purpose and meaning of this section of the bill and members proposed minor changes to the wording of the bill and to the punishment for polygamy that were accepted. The committee debates, not included here because of their length, can be found in House of Commons Debates, 4th session, 6th Parliament.[3]

The two changes to the wording of this section of bill were:

From: (b) Any kind of conjugal union with more than one person of the opposite sex at the same time . . . .

To: (b) Any kind of conjugal union with more than one person at the same time . . . .

At that time, the members of Parliament could not conceive of a conjugal union with anyone other than a person of the opposite sex, so that the words "opposite sex" were considered to be "surplusage."[4]

The penalty section was changed

From: Is guilty of a misdemeanor, and liable to imprisonment for two years, or to a fine of five hundred dollars, or to both such.

To: Is guilty of a misdemeanor, and liable to imprisonment for five years and to a fine of five hundred dollars.

The penalty was increased to create a greater deterrent to the practice of polygamy.

While the changes to the wording were not significant, some of the other discussion and explanation of the intent of the bill is illustrative. The purpose of this section of the bill was to enable immigration from the Mormon community with the same rights as all Canadians on becoming citizens, including serving on juries and voting, while at the same time ensuring that the practice of polygamy was suppressed in keeping with the values of the time.

---

3   *Ibid* at 3172–183.

4   *House of Commons Debates*, 6-4 (10 April 1890) at 3177 (Hon Mr Mulock).

Third Reading

The bill with its changes was passed on third reading and referred to the Senate.[5] Senate debates are used in the same way as House of Commons debates when it comes to discerning legislative intent.[6]

Debates of the Senate

As with the House of Commons debates, the Senate debates have a Speaker (Index to Senators) and a Subject index. The Subject index is the best place to start locating discussion of this bill. This index provides information on where to find discussion of the bill for all readings as well as the date of royal assent.

ILLUSTRATION 8.2

SENATE DEBATES 1980, SUBJECT INDEX

1st R.*, 333.
2nd R.*, 348.
3rd R.*, 373.
Assent, 564.
Chinamen at Niagara, The Explanation.
Mr. Abbott, 515.
See *Tax.*

Clapp Divorce B. (I).—*Mr. Clemow.*
1st R.*, 44.
2nd R.*, 130.
11th Rep. of Com. considered, m. (*Mr. Clemow*), Mr. McInnes, Mr. Kaulbach, Mr. Power, Mr. Abbott, Mr. Howlan, Mr. Flint, Mr. Read, Mr. Dever, Mr. Dickey, Mr. Lougheed, Mr. Macdonald, B.C., Mr. Poirier, Mr. Robitaille, Mr. McKindsey, Mr. McCallum, Mr. McInnes, B.C., Mr. Prowse, Mr. Reesor, Mr. Alnon, Mr. Haythorne, Mr. Bellerose, 498-514.
M. rejected on div'n.: C. 8 ; N.C. 35, 513.
Suggestion to expunge corresp. from Records, (Mr. Read), 513.

Coinage, Gold, in Canada, Resolutions concerning.
m. (*Mr. McInnes*, B.C.), that it is expedient to establish, 170-1.
Discussion : Mr. Kaulbach, Mr. Howlan, Mr. Wark, Mr. MacInnes (Burlington), 172 ; Mr. Scott, Mr. Power, Mr. Dever, Mr. McKay, 173 ; Mr. Boulton, 174 ; Mr. Reid (B.C.), Mr. Abbott, 175.
M. withdr., 177.

2nd R.*, 153.
In Com. of W., discussed : Mr. Abbott, Mr. Miller, 199.
Amt. moved and agreed to, Rep. from Com. as amended, concurred in, 199.
3rd R., and passed as amended, 199.
Assent, 564.

Criminal Law Further Amt. B. (65)—*Mr. Abbott.*
1st R.*, 515.
2nd. R. m. (*Mr. Abbott*), 583.
Discussed : Mr. Macdonald, Mr. Kaulbach, Mr. Abbott, Mr. Power, 583-6.
M. agreed to, 586.
2nd R., 586.
In Com. of W., discussed : Mr. Abbott, Mr. Power, Mr. Scott, Mr. Dickey, Mr. Sanford, Mr. Reesor, Mr. Drummond, Mr. Macdonald, Mr. Lougheed, Mr. DeBoucherville, Mr. O'Donohoe, Mr. Girard, Mr. Kaulbach, Mr. Masson, Mr. Perley, Mr. Prowse, Mr. Pelletier, Mr. Sullivan, Mr. Murphy, Mr. Ross, 648-58.
Progress reported, 658.
Resumed : Mr. Abbott, Mr. Power, Mr. De Boucherville, 681-3.
Rep. from Com. with Amts., 683.
3rd R.*, and passed, 683.
Concurr. in Commons Amts., discussed : Mr. Abbott, Mr. DeBoucherville, 780.
Assent, 904.

---

5   *Ibid* at 3460.
6   "§129 The House of Commons Debates and the Debates of the Senate of Canada or Hansard are admissible in a court of law to aid in the interpretation, construction and application of statutes so long as a court remains mindful of the limited reliability and weight of Hansard evidence." CED 4th (online) *Parliament and Legislature*, Parliament of Canada: House of Commons: Parliamentary Publications: Official Report of Debates (I.3.(j).(ii)).

First Reading in the Senate

The bill was introduced into the Senate on 22 April 1980, with no debate or discussion, by John Abbott in his role as Leader of the Government in the Senate.

Second Reading in the Senate

In the second reading of the bill (30 April 1890), as discussion commences, John Abbott indicates that the goal of the bill is to prevent Mormon polygamy from coming into Canada. One suggested amendment articulated by Senator MacDonald was that "no one holding views which Mormons do should be allowed to vote or serve on juries."[7] According to John Abbott, the "bill is not directed against any particular religion or sect or Mormon more than anyone else: it is directed at polygamists"[8] and the changes suggested by MacDonald were outside the purview of criminal law. After this discussion, the motion was passed to send the bill onto the Committee of the Whole.

Senate Committee

As with the House, this bill was directed to the Committee of the Whole for discussion.

The clause-by-clause discussion on this section of the bill focused mainly on jury duty and voting rights. Abbott makes it clear that these issues are out of the scope of the bill and the clause was adopted.

Third Reading in the Senate

After some brief discussion, the bill was passed.

Royal Assent

On 16 May 1890, the bill received royal assent and became Chapter 37 of the 1890 *Statutes of Canada*.

The Revision of the Statute in 1953–54

Use of Secondary Sources

We know from tracing the evolution of the statute that the only major changes to the polygamy section after 1890 occurred during the revision of the *Criminal Code* in 1953–54.

---

7   *Senate Debates*, 6:4 (25 April 1890) at 584 (Hon Mr MacDonald).
8   *Senate Debates*, 6:4 (25 April 1890) at 584 (Hon Mr Abbott).

Because the revision of the *Criminal Code* was a huge undertaking, it is a good idea not to go directly to the debates, but instead to see if you can find any kind of history or background documents that would help you zero in on relevant debates or discussion.

There is, in fact, a chronology of the revision on the BC Courthouse Libraries website that is very helpful. There are often resources like this available that you can use to start your research. This is a good tactic to consider when looking at the history or evolution of omnibus bills or any statute with a complex history.

Key Points in the Chronology

- Although the process of revision began in 1949, it wasn't until 1952 that things started to really get moving.
- May 1951: The Royal Commission on the Revision of the *Criminal Code* was established.
- February 1952: The committee's report, including a draft bill, were submitted to the minister of justice and then tabled in the House in April 1952.
- May 1952: Bill H-8 is introduced to the Senate (ahead of being introduced into the House) and referred to the Senate Banking and Commerce Subcommittee for review.
- June 1952: The Senate Committee did not recommend the bill continue without revision.
- November 1952: (a new session) Bill H-8 was reintroduced in the Senate as Bill O and once again referred to the Senate Banking and Commerce Subcommittee, and it passed on third reading with amendments in December of that year.
- January 1953: Bill 93 was introduced into the House of Commons (with same text as Bill O) and referred to a special committee.
- Between February and May, the committee's report was tabled, and the bill underwent review and debate.
- May 1953: An election was called, and the bill died on the Order Paper.
- November 1953: The bill is reintroduced to the House as Bill 7 with the same text as the earlier bill, but with amendments recommended by the special committee.

❦ Between December 1953 and June 1954: The bill passed through all readings in the House and Senate.

❦ June 1954: The bill receives royal assent.

❦ 1 April 1955: *Criminal Code*, SC 1953–54, c 51 proclaimed into force.[9]

What Is Important Here?

Look at the royal commission and committee reports as well as the debates.

The Royal Commission Report

The mandate for the royal commission was to revise the text and remove ambiguities and inconsistencies in the law. The report makes many recommendations, but none have any real effect on the intent of polygamy provisions:

> The 1954 *Criminal Code* followed the work of the Royal Commission on the Revision of the Criminal Code, appointed in 1951 with terms of reference relating primarily to updating and simplifying the provisions of the *Criminal Code*. The Commission presented its final report and a draft bill to the government on February 22, 1952, and these were tabled in the House of Commons on April 7, 1952. The Commission's working materials indicate a suggestion to add the words "or enters into" after "practises" in paragraph (a), line 1, ins. 310 of the 1927 *Criminal Code*, and a note on a draft of Appendix C to the final report stated, "Clause 243 effects some condensation of section 310 relating to polygamy, and incorporates the rule as to evidence relevant thereto which now appears in section 948." However, the final report itself made no comment on the polygamy provision.[10]

---

9   British Columbia Courthouse Libraries, "What Is the History of the 1995 *Criminal Code* Revision" (16 April 2018), online: www.courthouselibrary.ca/how-we-can-help/our-legal-knowledge-base/what-history-1955-criminal-code-revision.

10 Craig E Jones & Deborah Strachan, "Section 293 Legislative History Brief—Submitted by the Attorneys General of British Columbia and Canada" at para 14, online: https://docs.google.com/file/d/0B-URIT52yhx4MzkxZDY2YTAtODkzNyooYjU3LTlkZDktOTdiMjQzMmExMzY2/edit?hl=en#.

The Debates

Although the revision of the *Criminal Code* was discussed in some detail, there is no indication in the debates that there were any changes to the original intention of Parliament with respect to polygamy. The removal of the clauses referring to Mormons received no discussion in Parliament.

C. A PRACTICAL APPLICATION

This legislative history was applied in *Reference Re: Section 293 of the Criminal Code of Canada*[11] in which the Province of British Columbia asked the court to declare whether the prohibition on polygamy is consistent with the *Charter of Rights and Freedoms*.

One of the briefs presented to the court in this case was an extensive legal history compiled by the British Columbia and federal Attorneys General. The researchers who compiled this history did an extremely careful job of the research, including looking at the National Archives for Committee working materials.[12] This is a perfect example of how a legislative evolution and history can be compiled and presented.

What the Judge Said

Chief Justice Bauman of the British Columbia Supreme Court referred to this brief a number of times in his judgment and dedicated an entire section of his judgment to "The Purpose and Interpretation of Section 293."[13] Eventually he upheld the constitutional validity of section 293 of the *Criminal Code*, noting that:

> [903] Polygamy was not prohibited because it was a religious belief of the early Mormon settlers. It was the practice of polygamy and the harms with which it was associated that concerned Canadian lawmakers.

---

11   *Reference Re: Section 293 of the Criminal Code of Canada*, 2011 BCSC 1588 [*Polygamy Reference*].

12   Above note 10.

13   *Polygamy Reference*, above note 11 at paras 903–4.

[904] I find that the prohibition was prompted by largely secular concerns with the perceived harms associated with the practice of polygamy to women, children, society and the institution of monogamous marriage.

chapter nine

Interpretation of Treaties with Indigenous Peoples

Treaties with Indigenous peoples are "are agreements made between the Government of Canada, Indigenous groups and often provinces and territories that define ongoing rights and obligations on all sides."[1] There are two (or more) equal partners to every treaty, as treaties were, and are, "the primary means by which diplomatic relations were conducted between Britain [and then Canada] and Aboriginal peoples."[2] In addition, treaty rights are constitutionally "recognized and affirmed"[3] by section 35 of the Canadian Constitution. As with statutes, if there is disagreement about the meaning of a treaty, the courts will be expected to interpret that meaning.

Ideally, when the courts are considering the meaning of a treaty, both parties' understanding of the terms of the treaty should be considered equally. However, this has not always been the case. As Borrows and Rotman note:

---

1   Government of Canada, "Treaties, Agreements and Negotiations," online: *Crown-Indigenous Relations and Northern Affairs Canada* www.rcaanc-cirnac.gc.ca/eng/1100100028574/1529354437231.

2   John J Borrows & Leonard I Rotman, *Aboriginal Legal Issues: Cases, Materials & Commentary*, 5th ed (Markham, ON: LexisNexis Canada, 2018) at 281 [Borrows & Rotman, *Aboriginal Legal Issues*].

3   *Constitution Act, 1982*, s 35, being Schedule B to the *Canada Act 1982* (UK), 1982, c 11.

Treaties ... are best understood in their historical and cultural context.... These agreements were made between parties with different world views, languages and cultures. *While courts have historically privileged the written terms of treaties* [emphasis added], it must be remembered the Indigenous peoples' own laws and understandings of the agreements made form an equally important part of a treaty's context and understanding such that treaties cannot be interpreted without such input.[4]

A. INTENTION

As with statutes, one approach to discerning the meaning of a treaty is to look at its intention by examining "the specific facts relating to the intentions and understanding of the treaty signatories ...."[5] As Cory J noted in *R v Badger*, relying solely on accepted rules of construction when interpreting the meaning of a treaty without looking at its context would give priority to the written text and devalue the Indigenous signatories' understanding of the agreement:

> [W]hen considering a treaty, a court must take into account the context in which the treaties were negotiated, concluded and committed to writing. The treaties, as written documents, recorded an agreement that had already been reached orally and they did not always record the full extent of the oral agreement .... The treaties were drafted in English by representatives of the Canadian government who, it should be assumed, were familiar with common law doctrines. Yet, the treaties were not translated in written form into the languages ... of the various Indian nations who were signatories. Even if they had been, it is unlikely that the Indians, who had a history of communicating only orally, would have understood them any differently. As a result, it is well settled that the words in the treaty must not be interpreted in their strict technical sense nor subjected to rigid modern rules of construction. Rather, they must be interpreted in the sense

---

4   Borrows & Rotman, *Aboriginal Legal Issues*, above note 2 at 281–82.
5   Mary Locke Macaulay, *Aboriginal Treaty Rights and Practice* (Toronto: Thompson Reuters, 2000) (loose-leaf updated 2018, release 1) ch 9 at 9-6 [Macaulay, *Treaty Rights*].

that they would naturally have been understood by the Indians at the time of the signing.[6]

One of the ways to establish the intention of the signatories is through the examination of extrinsic evidence alongside the text of the treaty itself. Extrinsic evidence in treaty interpretation goes beyond historical documents to include oral histories and expert testimony. Because of the broad range of resources allowed, researching the extrinsic evidence to be used in treaty interpretation can provide some challenges. As the process of conducting this type of research can be quite complex and time consuming, it should most likely be left to historical researchers.

B. STATUTORY INTERPRETATION AND TREATY INTERPRETATION

The courts have "developed a set of interpretive rules, specific to treaty interpretation, that are largely modelled on statutory canons of construction,"[7] like Driedger's modern principle. The cannons for treaty interpretation "include the large, liberal and generous interpretation of treaties, with ambiguities resolved in favour of the aboriginal people, as understood by the aboriginal signatories, and interpreted flexibly, with the use of extrinsic evidence."[8] In the case of treaty interpretation, the Crown's intent can be equated with legislative intent in statutory interpretation.[9]

In her dissent in *R v Marshall*, McLachlan J summarised and listed the current principles of treaty interpretation that have been set out in previous Court decisions:

> This Court has set out the principles governing treaty interpretation on many occasions. They include the following.

---

6   *R v Badger*, [1996] 1 SCR 771 at para 52.

7   Aimée Craft, "Treaty Interpretation: A Tale of Two Stories," Canadian Bar Association Working Paper (6 April 2011) at 5, online: www.cba.org/cba/cle/PDF/ABOR11_Craft_Paper.pdf [Craft, *Treaty Interpretation*].

8   *Ibid* at 12.

9   *Ibid* at 23.

1. Aboriginal treaties constitute a unique type of agreement and attract special principles of interpretation: ...

2. Treaties should be liberally construed and ambiguities or doubtful expressions should be resolved in favour of the aboriginal signatories: ...

3. The goal of treaty interpretation is to choose from among the various possible interpretations of common intention the one which best reconciles the interests of both parties at the time the treaty was signed: ...

4. In searching for the common intention of the parties, the integrity and honour of the Crown is presumed: ...

5. In determining the signatories' respective understanding and intentions, the court must be sensitive to the unique cultural and linguistic differences between the parties: ...

6. The words of the treaty must be given the sense which they would naturally have held for the parties at the time: ...

7. A technical or contractual interpretation of treaty wording should be avoided: ...

8. While construing the language generously, courts cannot alter the terms of the treaty by exceeding what "is possible on the language" or realistic: ...

9. Treaty rights of aboriginal peoples must not be interpreted in a static or rigid way. They are not frozen at the date of signature. The interpreting court must update treaty rights to provide for their modern exercise. This involves determining what modern practices are reasonably incidental to the core treaty right in its modern context ....[10]

C. THE USE OF EXTRINSIC EVIDENCE TO INTERPRET HISTORIC TREATIES IN THE COURTS

Treaties formed between 1701 to 1923 are considered historic treaties. Although there are written versions of some treaties available, they are not always considered to be "a conclusive record of the actual terms of

---

10   *R v Marshall*, [1999] 3 SCR 456 at para 78 [*Marshall*].

the treaty."[11] These treaties were often negotiated and agreed upon verbally with the terms written up after the fact. The written versions of the treaty were not always consistent with what the Indigenous signatories believed they had agreed to and the treaties were very often recorded only in English, which "many of the Aboriginal Signatories did not understand"[12] or read. Further, some treaties were "confirmed orally but not ... reduced to writing."[13] As a result, the courts have begun to allow the use of extrinsic evidence, rather than just the written text, to assist in treaty interpretation. The types of extrinsic aids allowed have included oral histories, primary documents (minutes of negotiating sessions for example), and testimony from expert witnesses.

D. THE EVOLUTION OF THE USE OF EXTRINSIC EVIDENCE FOR TREATY INTERPRETATION

Originally, the courts were reluctant to look at extrinsic evidence in treaty interpretation cases, just as they were when they applied the exclusionary rule to the interpretation of statutes. However, as the use of extrinsic evidence in statutory interpretation evolved, the use of extrinsic evidence in treaty interpretation evolved as well. In 1988 in *R v Horse*,[14] Estey J rejected the use of extrinsic evidence, except in the case of ambiguity:

> I have some reservations about the use of this material as an aid to interpreting the terms of Treaty No. 6. In my view the terms are not ambiguous. The normal rule with respect to interpretation of contractual documents is that extrinsic evidence is not to be used in the absence of ambiguity; nor can it be invoked where the result would be to alter the terms of a document by adding to or subtracting from the written agreement.[15]

---

11   Kerry Wilkins, *Essentials of Canadian Aboriginal Law* (Toronto: Thomson Reuters, 2018) at § 363 [Wilkins, *Essentials*].

12   *Quebec (Attorney General) v Moses*, 2010 SCC 17, cited in Wilkins, *Essentials*, above note 11 at § 366.

13   Craft, *Treaty Interpretation*, above note 7 at 16.

14   *R v Horse*, [1988] 1 SCR 187.

15   *Ibid* at para 34.

In 1990, in *R v Sioui*, Lamer J saw ambiguity and as a result referred to a variety of historical documents as extrinsic evidence as an aid to interpreting a treaty, advocating a flexible approach when necessary:

> As this Court recently noted in *R. v. Horse*, [1988] 1 S.C.R. 187, at p. 201, extrinsic evidence is not to be used as an aid to interpreting a treaty in the absence of ambiguity or where the result would be to alter its terms by adding words to or subtracting words from the written agreement. This rule also applies in determining the legal nature of a document relating to the Indians. However, a more flexible approach is necessary as the question of the existence of a treaty within the meaning of s. 88 of the *Indian Act* is generally closely bound up with the circumstances existing when the document was prepared . . . . In any case, the wording alone will not suffice to determine the legal nature of the document before the Court. On the one hand, we have before us a document the form of which and some of whose subject-matter suggest that it is not a treaty, and on the other, we find it to contain protection of fundamental rights which supports the opposite conclusion. The ambiguity arising from this document thus means that the Court must look at extrinsic evidence to determine its legal nature. . . .[16]

The appellant agreed that certain of these documents, namely Murray's Journal, letters and instructions, should be included in the record provided this Court considered that their admissibility was justified by the concept of judicial notice. I am of the view that all the documents to which I will refer, whether my attention was drawn to them by the intervener or as a result of my personal research, are documents of a historical nature which I am entitled to rely on pursuant to the concept of judicial knowledge.[17]

In fact, Lamer J consulted an extensive list of historical documents in order to "identify more accurately the historical context essential to the resolution of this case."[18]

---

16   *R v Sioui*, [1990] 1 SCR 1025 at para 58.
17   *Ibid* at para 60.
18   *Ibid*.

In this case, the Court looked at a number of historical documents, including:

- Adam Shortt & Arthur G Doughty, eds, *Documents relating to the Constitutional History of Canada 1759–1791*, 2nd and rev ed (Ottawa: King's Printer, 1918) Part I.
- Cadwallader Colden, *The History of the Five Indian Nations of Canada* (London: T Osborne, 1747).
- François Xavier Garneau, *Histoire du Canada français*, t 3 (Montréal: Les Amis de l'Histoire, 1969).
- Jésuites, *Relations des jésuites contenant ce qui s'est passé de plus remarquable dans les missions des Pères de la Compagnie de Jésus dans la Nouvelle France*, vol 2 (Québec: Augustin Côté, 1858).
- Sir William Johnson, *The Papers of Sir William Johnson*, vols I, III, X, XIII, prepared for publication by the Division of Archives and History of the University of the State of New York (Albany: University of the State of New York, 1921 to 1962).
- John Knox, *An Historical Journal of the Campaigns in North-America for the Years 1757, 1758, 1759 and 1760*, Vol 2 (London: W Johnston & J Dodsley, 1769).
- John Knox, *Appendix to an Historical Journal of the Campaigns in North America for the Years 1757, 1758, 1759 and 1760*, vol 3 (Toronto: Champlain Society, 1916).
- NAM MacKenzie, "Indians and Treaties in Law" (1929) 7 *Canadian Bar Review* 561.
- Louis-Joseph Montcalm, *Journal du Marquis de Montcalm durant ses campagnes en Canada de 1756 à 1759*, Publié sous la direction de H-R Casgrain (Québec: L-J Demers & Frère, 1895).
- James Murray, *Governor Murray's Journal of the Siege of Quebec* (Toronto: Rous & Mann Ltd, 1939).
- EB O'Callaghan, ed, *Documents Relative to the Colonial History of New York*, vol 7 (Albany, NY: Weed, Parsons and Co, 1861).
- Eugène Ortolan, *Des moyens d'acquérir le domaine international ou propriété d'État entre les nations* (Paris: Amyot, 1851).
- Québec. Archives de Québec, *Rapport de l'archiviste de la Province de Québec pour 1923–1924* (Québec: Imprimeur du Roi, 1924).

☞ Maurice Ratelle, *Contexte historique de la localisation des Atti-kameks et des Montagnais de 1760 à nos jours* (Québec: Ministère de l'énergie et des ressources, 1987).

☞ Jack Stagg, *Anglo-Indian Relations in North America to 1763* (Ottawa: Research Branch, Indian and Northern Affairs Canada, 1981).

☞ Emmerich de Vattel, *The Law of Nations or Principles of the Law of Nature*, vol I2, book 3 (London: Newbury, 1760).[19]

In the 1999 *R v Marshall* decision, the use of extrinsic evidence was allowed even in the absence of ambiguity:

In *R. v. Marshall (Marshall No. 1)*, the majority (Binnie J.) itemized the reasons for the embrace of extrinsic evidence. The first draws on the rules of interpretation in ordinary contract law and deduces that the acceptance of such evidence in that law must apply all the more in the context of treaties between Indian peoples and the Crown. The second relies on case law that makes clear "that extrinsic evidence of the historical and cultural context of a treaty may be received even absent any ambiguity on the face of the treaty." The third points out that "it would be unconscionable for the Crown to ignore the oral terms while relying on written terms." In order for the Court's assumptions about the Crown's approach to treaty making (honourable), and for its own approach to treaty interpretation (flexible) to achieve their objectives, i.e., determination of the common intention of the parties at the time of the treaty, extrinsic evidence must be admitted and considered.[20]

The use of extrinsic evidence in treaty interpretation continued to evolve and by 1997, in *Delgamuukw v British Columbia*, oral histories were allowed as tools for interpretation in addition to historical documents.

---

19 *Ibid.*

20 J Timothy S McCabe, "Proof of Treaty Rights: Extrinsic Evidence" in J Timothy S McCabe, *The Law of Treaties Between the Crown and Aboriginal Peoples* (Markham, ON: LexisNexis Canada, 2010) citing *Marshall*, above note 10.

This appeal requires us to apply not only the first principle in *Vander-peet* but the second principle as well, and adapt the laws of evidence so that the aboriginal perspective on their practices, customs and traditions and on their relationship with the land, are given due weight by the courts. In practical terms, this requires the courts to come to terms with the oral histories of aboriginal societies, which, for many aboriginal nations, are the only record of their past. Given that the aboriginal rights recognized and affirmed by s. 35(1) are defined by reference to pre-contact practices or, as I will develop below, in the case of title, pre-sovereignty occupation, those histories play a crucial role in the litigation of aboriginal rights.[21]

E. WHERE TO FIND EXTRINSIC AIDS TO TREATY INTERPRETATION

1) Types of Historical Resources

Mary Locke Macaulay in *Aboriginal Treaty Rights and Practice*[22] provides an excellent and detailed overview of the type of evidence that has been admissible in treaty interpretation and the grounds on which this is so. Before researching, consult this text.

a) Existing Scholarship

As with all research, it makes sense to consult secondary sources to save time, to identify key resources, and to build your own understanding of the subject matter before approaching the primary sources. These secondary sources could include treatises and journal articles on Indigenous history generally or on the treaties themselves. One good place to orient yourself would be the Indigenous and Northern Affairs Canada (INAC) website. (This website is in transition as INAC will soon be divided into Indigenous Services Canada and Crown-Indigenous Relations and Northern Affairs Canada but will contain the same or a similar range of resources.)

---

21   *Delgamuukw v British Columbia*, [1997] 3 SCR 1010 at para 84 [*Delgamuukw*].
22   Macaulay, *Treaty Rights*, above note 5.

 Treaty Research Reports, online: *Indigenous and Northern Affairs Canada* www.aadnc-aandc.gc.ca/eng/1100100028653/ 1100100028654.

b) Unpublished Primary Documents

These documents can be defined as the "earliest written records involving contact with aboriginal people were produced by explorers, missionaries, police, Government Indian agents … surveyors, settlers and early anthropologists."[23] These records are likely to be housed in a variety of archives or libraries.[24] This research is likely to be very complex and some considerations for researchers will be finding out who was there, who they were reporting to, and where they would likely be filing their reports.[25]

c) Oral History

The courts have given oral history evidence the same weight as other forms of evidence, although their admissibility is judged on a case-by-case basis:

> Notwithstanding the challenges created by the use of oral histories as proof of historical facts, the laws of evidence must be adapted in order that this type of evidence can be accommodated and placed on an equal footing with the types of historical evidence that courts are familiar with, which largely consists of historical documents. This is a long-standing practice in the interpretation of treaties between the Crown and aboriginal peoples.[26]

Oral histories "for many Aboriginal Nations are the only record of their past."[27] They are the "unwritten cultural, historical and

---

23   *Ibid*, ch 7 at 7-4.
24   *Ibid*.
25   *Ibid*, ch 7 at 7-5.
26   *Delgamuukw*, above note 21 at para 87.
27   *Delgamuukw*, *ibid*, cited in Aimée Craft, "Reading Beyond the Lines: Oral Understandings and Aboriginal Litigation" (Paper delivered at Canadian Institute for the Administration of Justice Conference, Winnipeg, MB, 11 October 2013, revised December 2013), online: *Canadian Institute for the Administration of Justice*

spiritual knowledge passed down by family and community members to others over time."[28]

Researching and documenting an oral history will not be the role of the librarian; that is best left to the Indigenous community, historians, and other experts. The role of the librarian will be to assist and support researchers in locating existing oral histories and material, as well as being aware of the types of oral history evidence that is admissible in the course.

Types of Oral History Evidence
• Elder Testimony

Elder testimony can include not only oral history but also demonstrations, "(songs, dances, culturally significant objects or activities on the land)."[29] An Elder's authority comes from the community that recognizes and acknowledges their ability to speak on behalf of that community.[30] The Federal Court of Canada has developed *Practice Guidelines on Elder Testimony and Oral History*,[31] as it is incumbent on the courts to find a balance between "cultural sensitivity, while meeting the requirements of fairness and truth finding."[32]

• Interview transcripts

These can be either recent or historical. If a document is over thirty years old, it may be admissible as an "ancient document." Admissibility

---

Public Interest Law Centre https://ciaj-icaj.ca/wp-content/uploads/documents/import/2013/843.pdf?id=703&1534795163 [Craft, "Reading"].

28   Leigh Ogston, ed, *Researching the Indian Land Question in B.C.: An Introduction to Research Strategies & Archival Research for Band Researchers* (Vancouver: Union of British Columbia Indian Chiefs, 1998) at s 6.01, cited in Darwin Hanna, "Oral Traditions: Practical Considerations for Communities in Light of the *Delgamuukw* Decision" (2000) at 5, online: http://fngovernance.org/ncfng_research/considerations.pdf.

29   Craft, "Reading," above note 27 at 14.

30   *Ibid.*

31   Federal Court of Canada, *Practice Guidelines for Aboriginal Law Proceedings* (April 2016) Section D, "Elder Testimony and Oral History," online: www.fct-cf.gc.ca/Content/assets/pdf/base/Aboriginal%20Law%20Practice%20Guidelines%20April-2016%20(En).pdf.

32   Craft, "Reading," above note 27 at 23.

is contingent of whether these have been appropriately safeguarded and documented.[33] Some bands may maintain their own archives.

- Affidavits

Affidavits sworn by Elders that contain oral history are admissible as evidence.[34]

F.   GUIDES TO RESEARCH

- ☙ "Aboriginal Law Research Guide," online: *University of Victoria Library* http://libguides.uvic.ca/c.php?g=690502&p=4996588.
- ☙ Bennet Ellen McCardle, *Indian History and Claims: A Research Handbook* (Ottawa: Department of Indian and Northern Affairs Canada, 1983).
- ☙ "Indigenous Law/Indigenous Legal Traditions Guide," online: *University of Victoria Library* https://libguides.uvic.ca/iluvic.
- ☙ "Indigenous Studies: Text and Primary Source Databases Guide," online: *University of Toronto Library* https://guides. library.utoronto.ca/c.php?g=250519&p=1670892#s-lg-box-5089168.

G.   GUIDES TO UNDERSTANDING INDIGENOUS METHODOLOGIES

- ☙ "Indigenous Research Methodologies Libguide," online: *University of British Columbia Library* http://guides.library.ubc.ca/ IndigResearch.
- ☙ Margaret Kovach, *Indigenous Methodologies: Characteristics, Conversations, and Contexts* (Toronto: University of Toronto Press, 2009).
- ☙ Heidi Kiiwetinepinesiik Stark, "Stories as Law: A Method to Live By" in Chris Andersen & Jean M O'Brien, eds, *Sources and Methods in Indigenous Studies* (London: Routledge, 2017).

---

33   *Ibid* at 30–31.
34   *Ibid* at 32.

H. ETHICAL RESEARCH PRACTICES

᷎ "The First Nations Principles of OCAP," online: *First Nations Information Governance Centre* https://fnigc.ca/ocapr.html.

᷎ "Royal Commission on Aboriginal Peoples—Ethical Guidelines for Research" (1993), online: www.wrrb.ca/sites/default/files/public_registry/15.%20RCAP_Guidelines_1993.pdf.

I. MODERN TREATIES OR COMPREHENSIVE LAND CLAIMS

Modern treaties are different from historical treaties in that they are seen to be the "product of lengthy negotiations between well-resourced and sophisticated parties"[35] and are often accompanied by implementing legislation.[36] As these treaties are much better documented and understood by all parties, interpretation will give greater weight to the treaty text than it does with historical treaties,[37] although the canons of treaty interpretation previously set out by the courts still apply.[38]

---

35 *Beckman v Little Salmon/Carmacks First Nation*, 2010 SCC 53, cited in Wilkins, *Essentials*, above note 11 at § 366.

36 Borrows & Rotman, *Aboriginal Legal Issues*, above note 2 at 380.

37 Wilkins, *Essentials*, above note 11 at § 367.

38 Borrows & Rotman, *Aboriginal Legal Issues*, above note 2 at 380.

chapter ten

Statutory Instruments, Royal Prerogative, and Delegated Legislation

A. WHAT ARE STATUTORY INSTRUMENTS?

The federal *Statutory Instruments Act* defines statutory instruments generally as:

"statutory instrument"

(a) means any rule, order, regulation, ordinance, direction, form, tariff of costs or fees, letters patent, commission, warrant, proclamation, by-law, resolution or other instrument issued, made or established

    (i) in the execution of a power conferred by or under an Act of Parliament, by or under which that instrument is expressly authorized to be issued, made or established otherwise than by the conferring on any person or body of powers or functions in relation to a matter to which that instrument relates, or

    (ii) by or under the authority of the Governor in Council, otherwise than in the execution of a power conferred by or under an Act of Parliament.[1]

---

1 *Statutory Instruments Act*, RSC 1985, c S-22, s 2(i).

Regulations, which will be the main focus of this chapter, are included in the above definition but also have a further, more specific definition:

> "regulation" means a statutory instrument
> (a) made in the exercise of a legislative power conferred by or under an Act of Parliament, or
> (b) for the contravention of which a penalty, fine or imprisonment is prescribed by or under an Act of Parliament,
>
> and includes a rule, order or regulation governing the practice or procedure in any proceedings before a judicial or quasi-judicial body established by or under an Act of Parliament, and any instrument described as a regulation in any other Act of Parliament.[2]

Each province has legislation that covers statutory instruments, most often called regulations Acts. Unlike the federal *Statutory Instruments Act*, most of these provincial statutes do not define statutory instruments and regulations separately as the federal statute does.

The definition of statutory instruments can be complex, but it can be summed up as follows:

> Statutory instruments are documents issued under the authority of a statutory provision that mentions the instrument by name, as a noun, as well as instruments issued under royal prerogative.[3]

B. ROYAL OR CROWN PREROGATIVE

This text will not be focusing on interpreting the intention of Crown or royal prerogative, but it is still important to understand what royal prerogative is and how it works. Some statutory instruments, in the form of orders or orders in council, are produced as a result of executive action and may be subject to judicial interpretation.[4]

---

2   *Ibid.*

3   Paul Salembier, *Regulatory Law and Practice in Canada* (Markham, ON: Lexis-Nexis, 2004) at 35–36 [Salembier].

4   See, for example, *Canada (Prime Minister) v Khadr*, 2010 SCC 3 [*Khadr*].

In Canada, royal or Crown prerogative is an executive rather than a legislative power. It is exercised by custom and does not depend on legislation for its authority. The commonly accepted definition of royal prerogative is that it is "the residue of discretionary or arbitrary authority, which at any given time is left in the hands of the Crown"[5] or as Peter Hogg says, "the powers and privileges accorded by the common law to the Crown."[6] The Queen delegates these powers to the Governor General and the provincial Lieutenant Governors as well as to the prime minister, provincial premiers, and Cabinet ministers in both the federal and provincial governments:[7]

> In representing the Sovereign in Canada, the Governor General and Lieutenant Governors have duties that cover a broad range of responsibility; among them are: the summoning and dissolution of Parliament/Legislature, the swearing in of the Ministry, the reading of the Speech from the Throne, the granting of Royal Assent and the use of reserve powers.[8]

Part III of the Constitution outlines the executive power of the Crown in Canada. Some examples of federal royal prerogative are

> the conduct of foreign affairs, including the making of treaties and the declaration of war ... the appointment of the Prime Minister (by the Governor General) and other ministers (by the Governor General on the advice of the Prime Minister), the issue of passports, the creation of Indian Reserves and the conferring of honours.[9]

---

5   AV Dicey, *Introduction to the Study of the Law of the Constitution*, 10th ed (London: Macmillan, 1959) at 424.

6   PW Hogg, *Constitutional Law of Canada* (Scarborough, ON: Carswell, 2007) (loose-leaf updated 2011, release 1) ch 1 at 1-18 [Hogg, *Constitutional*].

7   Ronald I Chefins, "The Royal Prerogative and the Office of Lieutenant Governor" (2000) 23:1 *Canadian Parliamentary Review*, online: www.revparl.ca/english/issue.asp?param=74&art=163.

8   "The Governor General and the Lieutenant Governors," online: *The Royal Family: Canada* www.royal.uk/canada.

9   Hogg, *Constitutional*, above note 6 (loose-leaf updated 2013, release 1) ch 1 at 1-20–1-21.

These powers are not unlimited and may be displaced or abrogated by a statute if that statute contains a "clear and express statutory provision"[10] that limits those powers. If prerogative is limited by a statute, then "the Crown must comply with the terms of the statute."[11]

Each province has a Lieutenant Governor who is the Crown's delegate and who has the same base of authority as the Governor General. "[A] Lieutenant Governor, when appointed, is as much the representative of Her Majesty for all purposes of provincial government as the Governor General himself is for all purposes of Dominion government."[12] The premiers and Cabinet ministers also have powers granted to them by royal prerogative. For example, provincial Cabinet ministers have the power to make appointments by prerogative.[13]

1) Review of Royal Prerogative by the Courts

Royal prerogative in itself cannot be the subject of review by the courts, but the way in which it is used can be, as a means to ensure that "prerogative powers be exercised in conformity with the *Charter of Rights*."[14] For example, in *Canada (Prime Minister) v Khadr*, the Supreme Court has stated:

> [36] In exercising its common law powers under the royal prerogative, the executive is not exempt from constitutional scrutiny .... It is for the executive and not the courts to decide whether and how to exercise its powers, but the courts clearly have the jurisdiction and the duty to determine whether a prerogative power asserted by the Crown does in fact exist and, if so, whether its exercise infringes the *Charter* ... or other constitutional norms ....[15]

---

10   *Operation Dismantle Inc v Canada*, [1983] 1 FC 745 (CA).
11   Peter W Hogg, Patrick J Monahan, & Wade K Knight, *Liability of the Crown*, 4th ed (Toronto: Carswell, 2011) at 121.
12   *Maritime Bank of Canada (Liquidators of) v New Brunswick (Receiver-General)*, [1892] AC 437 at 443 (JCPC), cited in *Canada (Attorney General) v Ontario (Attorney General)* (1894), 23 SCR 458 and *Canada v Bank of Nova Scotia* (1885), 11 SCR 1.
13   Ontario, "Public Appointments," online: www.pas.gov.on.ca/scripts/en/generalInfo.asp.
14   Hogg, *Constitutional*, above note 6 (loose-leaf updated 2013, release 1) ch 1 at 1-21.
15   *Khadr*, above note 4 at para 36.

C. ORDERS IN COUNCIL

Orders in council (OIC) are documents that are created by the Governor in Council, in other words the Governor General acting on the advice of Cabinet,[16] which memorialize and give force to Cabinet decisions. These orders are "legal documents which can be used in a court of law."[17] Some are produced by the exercise of royal prerogative and others (regulations) are made under the authority of an enabling Act.

The Privy Council Office provides guidelines for the making and publication of OICs (other than regulations). One requirement is that these orders be accompanied by explanatory notes that are written "in plain language ... [and that] should include, detailed information about the issue at play, the objectives pursued, relevant background information, as well as related implications or impacts."[18]

1) Where to Find Orders in Council

Orders in council are numbered and identified with a Privy Council (PC) number,[19] and some may additionally be provided with a statutory instrument (SI) number if they are published in the *Canada Gazette*, Part II. As an example, the *Order Amending the Canadian Passport Order* published in the *Gazette* has both a PC number (PC 2015-563) and an SI number (SI/2015-33).[20] Other OICs with a more local or specific purpose will not be published in the *Gazette* and will only be given a PC number.[21] Regulations can be differentiated from statutory instruments as their numbering begins with SOR rather than SI. For reasons

---

16   Salembier, above note 3 at 12.
17   Government of Canada, "Process Guide for Governor in Council Submission (Other than Regulations)," online: *Privy Council Office* www.canada.ca/en/privy-council/services/orders-in-council/process-guide-governor-council-submissions.html.
18   *Ibid.*
19   Wendy Hubley & Micheline Beaulieu, "Locating Canadian Orders in Council" (2001) 26:1 *Canadian Law Library Review* 8.
20   *Order Amending the Canadian Passport Order*, SI/2015-33 (2015), online: www.gazette.gc.ca/rp-pr/p2/2015/2015-05-20/html/si-tr33-eng.php.
21   See, for example, *Appointment of IAN E. WILSON of Ottawa, Ontario, to be Librarian and Archivist of Canada*, PC 2004-0988.

of confidentiality or national security, many orders in council are not published; for example, an order relating to an individual's passport would not be published.[22]

Official versions of OICs are published in the *Canada Gazette*, Part II. The print version of the *Canada Gazette* dating from 1841 to the present can be found in various law and government documents libraries.[23] Online versions of the *Canada Gazette* are also available from 1841–1997 on the Library and Archives Canada website;[24] from 1998 to the present on the *Canada Gazette* website.[25]

Unofficial versions of OICs are also available from the Privy Council's searchable *Orders in Council Database*, from 1990 to present[26] (certified copies can be purchased from the Privy Council Office), as well as from the Library and Archives Canada's *Orders in Council Database 1867–1910*.[27]

A good example of an order in council: SI/2004-113 Order Amending the *Canadian Passport Order* is available at https://laws-lois.justice.gc.ca/PDF/SI-81-86.pdf. As you will see, this order is created by "Other Than Statutory Authority." Section 3(4) indicates that the order does not limit royal prerogative.

D. REGULATIONS

Regulations are a form of delegated legislation. Delegated legislation derives its authority from statutes rather than from royal or Crown prerogative. Sometimes called subordinate legislation, delegated legislation is a form of law that is not enacted directly in Parliament or in the provincial legislatures, as statutes are, but instead is enacted by designated bodies, administrative agencies, or individuals (ministers

---

22   OIC Database Search Page, online: *Privy Council Office* www.pco-bcp.gc.ca/oic-ddc.asp.
23   Library and Archives Canada, "A Nation's Chronicle: *The Canada Gazette*," online: www.collectionscanada.gc.ca/canada-gazette/index-e.html.
24   *Canada Gazette*: Archives, online: www.gazette.gc.ca/rp-pr/archives-eng.html.
25   *Canada Gazette*, online: www.gazette.gc.ca/rp-pr/publications-eng.html.
26   Above note 22.
27   *Orders in Council Database 1867–1910*, online: *Library and Archives Canada* www.bac-lac.gc.ca/eng/discover/politics-government/orders-council/Pages/search.aspx.

or their representatives, for example) who have been given the authority to do so by those legislative bodies through enabling legislation.[28] These bodies do not have the power to make legislation themselves above and beyond the power granted to them by the enabling legislation.[29] As with statutes, delegated legislation has the force of law. It must be constitutional and, in addition, must be consistent "with the objects, purposes and scope of the enabling statute."[30]

Regulations are the most predominant form of delegated legislation. Some other forms of delegated legislation can be rules (e.g., rules of court), municipal bylaws, or territorial ordinances.[31] Guidelines or policies are also "akin" to regulations and can be considered binding if the enabling statute so states.[32]

1) Do Regulations Have the Force of Law? What Is Their Authority?

Regulations have the force of law. Executive legislation (including regulations) has a legal force "equivalent to statute law."[33] Because the body or person delegated to make regulations is authorized to do so by the Parliament or legislature, the act of delegation confers the force of law on any instruments created under that authority.[34]

As noted above, regulations are made under the authority of an enabling statute by the person or body prescribed by the statute to have that authority. But this authority is not unlimited. Regulations

---

28 Guy Régimbald, *Canadian Administrative Law*, 2d ed (Markham, ON: LexisNexis, 2015).

29 *Ibid.*

30 *Ibid* at 158.

31 John Mark Keyes, *Executive Legislation*, 2d ed (Markham, ON: LexisNexis, 2010) at 24 [Keyes].

32 Régimbald, above note 28 at 151–52.

33 Keyes, above note 31 at 31.

34 "The true view of the effect of this type of legislation is that the subordinate body in which the law-making authority is vested by it is intended to act as the agent or organ of the legislature and that the acts of the agent take effect by virtue of the antecedent legislative declaration (express or implied) that they shall have the force of law." See *Re George Edwin Gray* (1918), 57 SCR 150 at 170.

must not go beyond the "objective and scope"[35] of the enabling statute or contravene the Constitution or the *Charter*. Further, if the enabling Act is found to be unconstitutional, then the regulations pursuant to that Act are considered to be unconstitutional as well.[36]

2) What Is the Purpose and Value of Regulations?

The main purpose of regulations is to "spell out the fine points of the subject matter covered in their 'enabling statute.'"[37] While statutes establish the government's policy in broad strokes, regulations, in contrast, are narrower in focus and set out the details that support the application of that policy.[38] And because they are more specific and detailed, regulations "are far more likely to have a direct impact on our daily lives"[39] than their parent statutes. As a very simple, hypothetical example, a statute might indicate that there is a fine for speeding and the regulation associated with that statute would provide the amount of that fine.

Regulations are a valuable tool for ensuring timeliness and administrative efficiency in the law-making process. Every bill is read three times in each House (or in the legislature) as well as being vetted by a committee on its way to becoming a statute. By contrast, regulations can be made into law much more quickly, therefore making it easier for governments to "adjust rules to changing conditions"[40] when they occur. Referring to the example above, it would be time consuming and expensive to go through the entire process of creating

---

35 Régimbald, above note 28 at 154.

36 *Ibid* at 155; Denys C Holland & John P McGowan, *Delegated Legislation in Canada* (Toronto: Carswell, 1989).

37 Maureen Fitzgerald & Susan Barker, *Legal Problem Solving*, 7th ed (Toronto: LexisNexis Canada, 2016) at 181.

38 Michael Taggart, "From 'Parliamentary Powers' to Privatization: The Chequered History of Delegated Legislation in the Twentieth Century" (2005) 55 *University of Toronto Law Journal* 575 at 587.

39 *Ibid*, and Bryan P Schwartz et al, "Democratizing the Regulation Making Process in Manitoba: Drawing on National and International Best Practices" (2012) 35:2 *Manitoba Law Journal* 1.

40 Keyes, above note 31 at 10.

or amending a statute in order to set or change the amount of a fine. It is far more efficient to flesh out the law with regulations, as regulations are very often so specific that they "would be unlikely to warrant the full consideration of the house."[41] As Keyes notes, "It is unrealistic to expect parliamentary bodies to make all the law. Delegation allows this task to be shared."[42]

In addition to the advantages of efficiency and timeliness, there is also the question of expertise. It is impossible for legislators and legal drafters to be experts in every field of endeavour and therefore it makes sense to have public servants rather than legislators make specific regulations in the "complex and technical"[43] areas in which they are experts.[44]

3) Some Controversies About Regulations

One of the main principles of the rule of law is that law must be both known and knowable. Regulations, however, are a little-known form of legislation and, as indicated from the example below, are not readily understood. The nature of regulations makes it "difficult for most to comprehend the meaning or application of a regulation, that is, even if they know where to look to find [it]."[45] One step in the direction of making the law known is to make regulations more accessible than they have been in the past. To that end, all the government websites, as well as the Canadian Legal Information Institute (CanLII), provide free access to regulations through links from their enabling statutes. Access, however, does not guarantee that the regulations will be knowable in the sense that the public understands their meaning and authority. Regulations may have far reaching powers and yet they receive less "attention and publicity"[46] than statutes and may be

---

41 Linda Reid, "Oversight of Regulations by Parliamentarians" (Winter 2010) *Canadian Parliamentary Review* 7 at 7, online: www.revparl.ca/33/4/33n4_10e_Reid.pdf.

42 Keyes, above note 31 at 68.

43 UK HC, *Report of Committee on Ministers' Powers* (Cmd 4060, 1932) at 51–52, cited in Schwartz et al, above note 39 at 10.

44 Keyes, above note 31.

45 Reid, above note 41 at 8.

46 *Ibid.*

passed without "notice by the public or press."[47] And when they are noticed in the press, it is often because the regulation is controversial or misunderstood. In 2010, during the G20 summit in Toronto, the provincial government passed a regulation[48] that defined the perimeter of the G20 security zone as a public work and therefore under the jurisdiction of the *Public Works Protection Act*[49] (since repealed). This Act gave police and security officers the authority to ask for identification, to search anyone attempting to enter into a public work (without warrant), and to refuse admission to public works when deemed necessary.[50] The regulation, which was made on June 2 with a revocation date of June 28 and was published in the *Ontario Gazette* on July 3, simply defined the G20 perimeter as a public work. On June 2, the *Toronto Star* published an article entitled "G20 Law Gives Police Sweeping Powers to Arrest People," in which it stated:

> Ontario has secretly passed an unprecedented regulation that empowers police to arrest anyone near the G20 security zone who refuses to identify themselves or agree to a police search.[51]

The article further went on to quote one lawyer as saying that "It's just unbelievable you would have this kind of abuse of power where the cabinet can create this offence without having it debated in the Legislature, ... it was just done surreptitiously, like a mushroom growing under a rock at night."[52] In reality, the controversial powers given to police and security officers had existed in the *Public Works Protection Act* since 1939,[53] but because the regulation itself was not

---

47 *Ibid.*
48 *Designation of Public Works*, O Reg 233/10. (This regulation was very short lived. It was made on 2 June 2010, filed on 14 June 2010, published on e-Laws 16 June 2010 and printed in the *Ontario Gazette* on 3 July 2010, but had a revocation date of 28 June 2010.)
49 *Public Works Protection Act*, RSO 1990, c P.55 repealed by *Security for Electricity Generating Facilities and Nuclear Facilities Act*, 2014, SO 2014, c 15, Schedule 1, s 1.
50 Jennifer Yang, "G20 Law Gives Police Sweeping Powers to Arrest People" *Toronto Star* (25 June 2010), online: www.thestar.com/news/gta/g20/2010/06/25/g20_law_gives_police_sweeping_powers_to_arrest_people.html.
51 *Ibid.*
52 *Ibid.*
53 *Public Works Protection Act*, SO 1939, (2nd Sess), c 10.

subject to legislative scrutiny, the public's understanding of its purpose and value was limited to the way in which it was characterized in the press.

The strongest and most prevalent criticism of regulations, however, is that contrary to our fundamental democratic principles, regulations have the same force of law as statutes, even though they are not subject to the same parliamentary scrutiny.[54] To counter that argument, it should be noted that regulations are only created under the authority of their enabling acts and that the individuals or bodies that are responsible for making regulations are "usually democratically elected individuals; cabinet ministers and municipal councils."[55] Further, while regulations do not go through the same parliamentary scrutiny as legislation, and only Quebec and the federal government provide some weak provisions for public consultation,[56] some jurisdictions do have committees "of elected representatives … [to] … scrutinize delegated legislation on the basis of criteria designed to detect the abuse of power."[57] In addition, the federal government "in response to concerns raised by parliamentarians and the public about the widespread use of regulations, … has passed several acts that provide for the parliamentary review of proposed regulations" either in committee or the house as a whole.[58] At present these are:

- *The Official Languages Act*
- *The Emergencies Act*
- *The Firearms Act*
- *The Referendum Act*
- *The Tobacco Act*
- *The Canadian Small Business Financing Act*

---

54 Reid, above note 41.
55 Keyes, above note 31 at 68.
56 Edward Clark, *Delegated Legislation and the Duty to Be Fair in Canada* (LLM thesis, University of Toronto Faculty of Law, 2008) [Unpublished].
57 Keyes, above note 31 at 68.
58 Peter Bernhardt & Michael Dewing, *Parliamentary Committee Review of Regulations*, Library of Parliament. Publication No 2005-63-E (2008), online: https://lop.parl.ca/sites/PublicWebsite/default/en_CA/ResearchPublications/200563E [Bernhardt & Dewing].

  ❦ *The Immigration and Refugee Protection Act*
  ❦ *The Assisted Human Reproduction Act*
  ❦ *The Citizenship Act*
  ❦ *The Quarantine Act*
  ❦ *The Human Pathogens and Toxins Act*
  ❦ *The Canadian Consumer Product Safety Act*[59]

Finally, and most importantly, regulations are subject to judicial interpretation both for adherence to the intent of their enabling Act as well as their constitutionality.[60]

4) Judicial Interpretation of Regulations

Regulations are interpreted in the court in the same way that statutes are. Judges use Driedger's modern principle as a guide:[61]

> Today there is only one principle or approach, namely, the words of an Act are to be read in their entire context and in their grammatical and ordinary sense harmoniously with the scheme of the Act, the object of the Act, and the intention of Parliament.[62]

Or, as paraphrased by Deschamps J in *Glykis v Hydro-Québec*:

> A statutory provision must be read in its entire context, taking into consideration not only the ordinary and grammatical sense of the words, but also the scheme and object of the statute, and the intention of the legislature. *This approach to statutory interpretation must also be followed, with necessary adaptations, in interpreting regulations.*[63]

These necessary adaptations include ensuring that the regulation is read "in the context of its authorizing statute,"[64] because, as Binnie J

---

59 *Ibid.*

60 Keyes, above note 31 at 68.

61 Ruth Sullivan, *Sullivan on the Construction of Statutes*, 6th ed (Markham, ON: LexisNexis Canada, 2014) § 13.18 [Sullivan, *Construction*, 6th].

62 Elmer Dreidger, *Construction of Statutes* (Toronto: Butterworths, 1974) at 67.

63 *Glykis v Hydro-Québec*, 2004 SCC 60 at para 5 [emphasis added].

64 Elmer Dreidger, *Construction of Statutes*, 2d ed (Toronto: Butterworths, 1983) at 247.

notes in *Bristol-Myers Squibb Co v Canada (Attorney General)*, "the scope of the regulation is constrained by its enabling legislation."[65]

E. USING EXTRINSIC AIDS TO DETERMINE REGULATORY INTENT

Given that Driedger's modern principle has been accepted as a guide for interpreting regulations as well as for interpreting statutes, it is important to identify the extrinsic sources that can be used as tools for this type of interpretation in cases where the wording or language of a regulation is not clear.

F. LEGISLATIVE EVOLUTION

Even though the concept of legislative evolution refers to textual changes within a statute or regulation, legislative evolution is considered to be an *extrinsic* aid to the interpretation of regulations.[66] One example of the use of the evolution of a regulation is the Nova Scotia case *Municipal Enterprises Ltd v Nova Scotia (Attorney General)*,[67] an appeal case in which the "sole issue . . . is one of statutory interpretation":[68] specifically the intention of regulations under the *Gasoline and Diesel Oil Tax Act*. During the course of the original trial, the judge "traced the evolution of the *GDOTA* and its Regulations from 1926 to 1981 to identify their original purpose and any trends reflecting new policies or whether they have remained constant."[69] As part of their appeal, the appellants argued that the trial judge had given "undue weight"[70] to legislative history (including legislative evolution). The appeal was dismissed. In her findings, Glube CJNS explicitly noted that in order to avoid an absurdity "it was appropriate for the trial

---

65 *Bristol-Myers Squibb Co v Canada (Attorney General)*, [2005] 1 SCR 533 at para 38 [*Bristol-Myers*].

66 Sullivan, *Construction*, 6th, above note 61 at 661.

67 *Municipal Enterprises Ltd v Nova Scotia (Attorney General)*, 2003 NSCA 10.

68 *Ibid* at para 2.

69 *Ibid* at para 18.

70 *Ibid* at para 70.

judge to consider factors such as the debates from the Nova Scotia House of Assembly; [and] *the evolution of the act and its regulations*" [emphasis added].[71]

G. LEGISLATIVE HISTORY

1) Regulatory Impact Analysis Statements (Federal)

The most important and accessible extrinsic aid for interpreting *federal* regulations is the Regulatory Impact Analysis Statement (RIAS). RIASs are published in the *Canada Gazette*, Part I, and they have "the status of an official public document of the Government of Canada"[72] and have been a mandatory component of a regulation since 1986.[73]

The purpose of the RIAS is to explain:

- the elements of the regulatory proposal, including what problems or situations it addresses and what it is meant to achieve;
- what alternatives to regulation have been considered;
- what are the anticipated costs and benefits of the regulations;
- what consultations have been carried out and what opportunities Canadians have had to be heard;
- what is the response of the department or agency to the concerns voiced or suggestions made;
- what mechanisms are built in to ensure compliance with the regulations once they are in force;
- how the effectiveness of the regulations will be measured.[74]

The courts have articulated their admissibility:

[156] It has long been established that the usage of admissible extrinsic sources regarding a provision's legislative history and its

---

71   *Ibid* at para 77.

72   France Houle, "Regulatory History Material as an Extrinsic Aid to Interpretation: An Empirical Study of the Use of RIAS by the Federal Court of Canada" (2006) 19 *Canadian Journal of Administrative Law and Practice* 151 at 152.

73   *Ibid*.

74   Government of Canada, *Guide to Making Federal Acts and Regulations: Part 3— Making Regulation*, online: *Privy Council Office* www.canada.ca/en/privy-council/ services/publications/guide-making-federal-acts-regulations.html.

context of enactment could be examined .... [I]n order to confirm the purpose of the impugned regulation, the intended application of an amendment to the regulation or the meaning of the legislative language, it is useful to examine the RIAS, prepared as part of the regulatory process (see Sullivan, at pp. 499-500). McGillis J. in Merck 1999, at para. 51, indicated:

> ... a Regulatory Impact Analysis Statement, which accompanies but does not form part of the regulations, reveals the intention of the government and contains " ... information as to the purpose and effect of the proposed regulation."

[157] The use of the RIAS to determine both the purpose and the intended application of a regulation has been frequent in this Court and others, and this across a wide range of interpretive settings.[75]

2) Regulatory Impact Statements in the Provinces

Each of the provinces requires that some element of regulatory analysis be provided during the making of a regulation in the form of a report, memorandum, or checklist (see Table 10.1, below). They are most often considered to be confidential Cabinet documents and so their use in the courts as evidence of intent is rare but it is still permissible. As one example, the Nova Scotia Court of Appeal in *Enterprise Cape Breton Corp v Hogan* referred to the appellant's claim that:

> the Minister of Labour's Report and Recommendation to the Executive Council had stipulated that the purpose of the amendments to the Regulations was to eliminate redundancy, in that the types of income previously listed in s. 20(c) would normally be included in regular wages, or salary, anyway. Thus, ECBC argued that the Report and Recommendation reflected a legislative intention not to limit the types of income that could be considered as earnings under the Act.[76]

---

75   *Bristol-Myers*, above note 65 at paras 156–57.
76   *Enterprise Cape Breton Corp v Hogan*, 2013 NSCA 33 at para 59.

H. OTHER EXTRINSIC AIDS TO THE INTERPRETATION OF REGULATIONS

As with statutes, the courts have allowed other types of regulatory history material to be used as evidence of intent. In 1984 (prior to the RIAS requirements being put into place) the Federal Court in *New Brunswick Broadcasting Co, Ltd v Canadian Radio-Television & Telecommunications Commission*[77] allowed the Royal Commission on Newspapers' (The Kent Commission) report to be admitted as "evidence of the situation and context in which the order in council [i.e., SOR/82-746] was passed."[78] The court also allowed a speech federal Minister of State (Multiculturalism) Jim Fleming made to journalism students at the University of Western Ontario, in which he set out the government's intended responses to that report, which included the creation of the regulation in question. In another case, *Friesen v Canada*,[79] the Supreme Court referred to not only the RIAS but a Department of Finance Release[80] in making its decision.

In some cases, you may need to check for *Hansard* evidence as well. A few federal statutes include a provision that requires its attendant regulations be tabled before the parliament.[81] As noted earlier these are:

- *The Official Languages Act*
- *The Emergencies Act*
- *The Firearms Act*
- *The Referendum Act*
- *The Tobacco Act*
- *The Canadian Small Business Financing Act*
- *The Immigration and Refugee Protection Act*
- *The Assisted Human Reproduction Act*

---

77 *New Brunswick Broadcasting Co, Ltd v Canadian Radio-Television & Telecommunications Commission*, [1984] 2 FC 410 (CA).

78 *Ibid.*

79 *Friesen v Canada*, [1995] 3 SCR 103.

80 Canada, Department of Finance, Release No 87-09, "New Measures to Prevent Tax Avoidance from Offsets of Losses and Other Deductions" (15 January 1987).

81 Bernhardt & Dewing, above note 58.

- *The Citizenship Act*
- *The Quarantine Act*
- *The Human Pathogens and Toxins Act*
- *The Canadian Consumer Product Safety Act*[82]

Since more statutes might be added to this list in the future, check the "Regulations" provision of the statute to see if the tabling requirement exists. As an example, section 66(1) of the *Assisted Human Reproduction Act* states:

> 66 (1) Before a regulation is made under section 65, the Minister shall lay the proposed regulation before each House of Parliament.[83]

Even if there is not a requirement that proposed regulations be tabled, it is a good idea to check *Hansard* for any commentary on the intent of proposed regulations, whether you are researching federal or provincial regulations. Sometimes the debates will make explicit references to regulations and their intent in their discussion of proposed legislation. In 1980, for example, this occurred during debates on Bill 188, a bill that amended Ontario's *Highway Traffic Act* to include standards for transportation of handicapped persons, in response to a question on what the regulations would look like. The Minister of Transportation and Communications responded:

> The new regulations will help in terms of making sure that there are safety devices available in those buses, that there are proper tie-down or hold-down facilities and many other things.[84]

Sometimes judges will make inferences from the debates as to the intent of a regulation. In *R v Brown*, a case on the constitutionality of section 3.7 of the *Races, Contests and Stunts* regulation, O Reg 455/07, Cuthbertson JP looked at the Ontario debates for evidence of legislative intent and reached the following conclusion:

---

82   *Ibid.*

83   *Assisted Human Reproduction Act*, SC 2004, c 2, s 66(1).

84   Ontario, Legislative Assembly, *Official Report of Debates (Hansard)*, 31-4th, No 138 (11 December 1980) at 5218 (James Wilfred Snow), cited in Elizabeth Bruton, "Time Travelling: Intent Behind Regulations" (2016) 41 *Canadian Law Library Review* 20.

In summary, the references throughout the lengthy debates on Bill 203 to speeding, excessive speeding and speeding over 50 kph greater than the speed limit are numerous. I am satisfied that the Legislature was aware of and debated these issues, as it contemplated Bill 203. The resulting subsection 3.7 of O. Reg. 455/07 flows from the debates.[85]

I.　WHERE TO FIND REGULATIONS

1)　CanLII (Canadian Legal Information Institute)

You can find unofficial versions of current consolidated regulations for all Canadian jurisdictions for no cost on CanLII (www.canlii.org). While they are not official, these regulations are usually accurate because the justice departments of each of the jurisdictions provides CanLII with the content. Because CanLII provides statutes and regulations for all jurisdictions, it is a useful resource for doing comparative work across jurisdictions. Additionally, the database provides point-in-time, side-by-side comparisons of historical versions of regulations that are extremely useful if you are compiling a record of the legislative evolution of a particular regulation.

2)　Government Websites

Not all government websites provide official consolidated versions of regulations. If your research requires the official version, consult the regulations as enacted, which usually appear as part of the *Gazettes* for each respective jurisdiction.

85　*R v Brown*, 2009 ONCJ 6.

TABLE 10.1: WHERE TO FIND FEDERAL REGULATIONS

[*Note*: Links to URLs are current to May 2019]

Governing Legislation	☞ *Statutory Instruments Act*, RSC 1985, c S-22 ☞ *Statutory Instruments Regulations*, CRC, c 1509
Committee	Standing Joint Committee for the Scrutiny of Regulations www.parl.gc.ca/CommitteeBusiness/AboutCommittees. aspx?Cmte=REGS&Mode=1&Parl=38&Ses=1&Language=E
Process	Federal regulations are created by a thirteen-step process. This process starts by developing the policy that the regulation is meant to implement as well as the instructions for the drafters. It is at this step where the first draft of the Regulatory Impact Analysis Statement (RIAS) should be written. This policy is then sent on for departmental approval. Once the policy is approved, the regulation is drafted and then sent back to the department for sign off. After that it goes to the Privy Council Office (PCO), which ensures that the regulation does not stray from the intent of the RIAS. Then it is forwarded onto the Treasury Board, which will either exempt it from pre-publication (in rare instances), in which case it is made a regulation by the Governor in Council. In most cases the proposed regulation is then sent for pre-publication, i.e., publication in the *Canada Gazette*, Part I. At this point the public has an opportunity to comment on the proposed regulation. After the pre-publication period ends the regulation is once more examined by the originating department. If changes are suggested, the regulations go back to the drafters for those changes to be made. Once the sponsoring department is happy with the regulation it is send to the minister for sign off. Once the minister signs off then the regulation, along with its ministerial recommendation and supporting documentation, is sent to the Privy Council Office for final approval. After final approval from the PCO, the regulation is made by the Governor in Council in two stages. The Treasury Board first approves the regulation for enactment and then it is sent to the Governor General to sign. Once the Governor General signs the regulation it is considered to be enacted. At this point the regulation is sent to be registered by the Orders in Council Division of the PCO. At this point it is given a registration number (e.g., SOR/82-746) as well as a PC number. Regulations come into force on the day they are registered unless a different coming into force date is specified. They are then published in the *Canada Gazette*, Part II.[86]

---

86   Salembier, above note 3, gives a highly detailed breakdown of each of the thirteen steps.

TABLE 10.1: WHERE TO FIND FEDERAL REGULATIONS

Documentation	*Regulatory Impact Analysis Statement*

Where They Can Be Found	**Pre-publication**
	 Canada Gazette Part I: Notices and Proposed Regulations (published weekly)
	   ☛ 2012–present
	     Online: *Canada Gazette*
	     www.gazette.gc.ca/rp-pr/publications-eng.html#a1
	   ☛ 1998–2011
	     Online: *Canada Gazette* Archives
	   ☛ A link to the Consolidated Index is provided along with each annual volume of the *Gazette*.
	   ☛ 1947–1997
	     Online: Library and Archives Canada
	     www.collectionscanada.gc.ca/databases/canada-gazette
	
	 Regulations as Enacted with Regulatory Impact Analysis Statements
	 Canada Gazette Part II: Official Regulations (published every two weeks)
	   ☛ 1998–present
	     Online: *Canada Gazette* Archive
	     www.gazette.gc.ca/rp-pr/publications-eng.html
	   ☛ 1947–1997
	     Online: Library and Archives Canada
	     www.collectionscanada.gc.ca/databases/canada-gazette
	     001060-100.04-e.php
	
	 Canada Gazette
	   ☛ 1867–1946 (Dominion of Canada)
	     Online: Library and Archives Canada
	     www.collectionscanada.gc.ca/databases/canada-gazette/
	     001060-100.04-e.php
	   ☛ Became the official *Gazette* of the Dominion of Canada in 1869.
	
	 Current Consolidated Regulations
	   ☛ *Consolidated Regulations*
	     Online: Justice Laws Canada
	     http://laws-lois.justice.gc.ca/eng/regulations
	   ☛ This is an ongoing consolidation that is usually updated every two weeks.

TABLE 10.1: WHERE TO FIND FEDERAL REGULATIONS

Where They Can Be Found	**Historical Consolidated Regulations**

    🍂 *Statutory Orders and Regulations: Consolidation 1949*:
        Online: Library and Archives Canada
        www.collectionscanada.gc.ca/databases/canada-gazette
        001060-100.02-e.php
    🍂 *Statutory Orders and Regulations: Consolidation 1955*:
        Online: Library and Archives Canada
        www.collectionscanada.gc.ca/databases/canada-gazette
        001060-100.02-e.php
    🍂 *Consolidated Regulations of Canada 1976* (in print only)
    🍂 These do not have an index, but they are organized alphabetically by the name of the enabling Act.

Use the Consolidated Index to Statutory Instruments: Table 1 (see below) to locate the relevant enabling Act.

Finding Tools/ Indexes	*Canada Gazette Part I: Index*

    🍂 Annual Index 1947–1971
    🍂 Quarterly Index (not cumulative) 1972 onwards

To access the index to *Canada Gazette: Part I*, go to the *Canada Gazette* main page at www.gazette.gc.ca/rp-pr/publications-eng.html, and select the Gazette for the year you are researching. You will see links to each of the quarterly indexes at the bottom of the page.

    🍂 Cumulative from 1955 to present
    🍂 *I-Table of Regulations, Statutory Instruments (other than Regulations) and other documents*
        This table lists the regulations by name and refers to the enabling Act.
    🍂 *II-Table of Regulations, Statutory Instruments (other than Regulations) and other documents arranged by Statute*
        This table is organized by the enabling Act. It provides the SOR numbers and history of each section of the regulations, which is useful if you are researching the evolution of a particular regulation.
    🍂 *Canada Gazette (Dominion of Canada) 1867–1946*
    🍂 Each volume has an index.

Notes	The online versions of the *Canada Gazette* have been official since 1 April 2003.

The online versions of the consolidated regulations have been official since 1 June 2009.

TABLE 10.2: WHERE TO FIND PROVINCIAL AND TERRITORIAL REGULATIONS

[*Note*: Links to URLs are current to May 2019]

Alberta Regulations	
Governing Legislation	☙ *Regulations Act*, RSA 2000, c R-14 ☙ *Regulations Act Regulation*, Alta Reg 288/1999 ☙ Regulations are defined in the *Interpretation Act* (see appendix)
Committee/ Oversight	Internal Cabinet review
Documentation	Internal Cabinet documents — not available to the public.

Where They Can Be Found	**Regulations as Enacted**
	☙ *Alberta Gazette* Part II
	    Online: www.qp.alberta.ca/Alberta_Gazette.cfm
	☙ Published every two weeks
	☙ Previous issues back to 1995
	    www.qp.alberta.ca/alberta_gazette.cfm?page=gazette_2014_pt2.cfm
	
	Current Consolidated Regulations
	☙ Online: *Alberta Queen's Printer*
	    www.qp.alberta.ca/Laws_Online.cfm
	    Updated frequently
	☙ Online: CanLII
	    www.canlii.org/en/ab/laws/regu
	    CanLII provides current consolidated versions as well as some previous versions of regulations.
	
	Historical Issues
	☙ Online: Our Future Our Past: Alberta Law Collection: 1905–1990
	    https://cdm22007.contentdm.oclc.org/digital/collection/p22007coll9
	☙ 1905–1990 (Regulations appear in part 2 from 1957 onwards)
	☙ 1990–1995, in print only

Finding Tools/ Indexes	Index of Regulations Filed Under the *Regulations Act* ☙ Online: *Alberta Queens Printer* www.qp.alberta.ca/alberta_gazette.cfm?page=gazette_current_issue_pt2.cfm ☙ Cumulative index of in force regulations from 1960
British Columbia Regulations	
Governing Legislation	*Regulations Act*, RSBC 1996, c 402 *Regulations Regulation*, BC Reg 394/83
Oversight/ Administration	Registrar of Regulations

TABLE 10.2: WHERE TO FIND PROVINCIAL AND TERRITORIAL REGULATIONS

Documentation	Regulatory impact checklist and regulatory count[87]
Where They Can Be Found	**Regulations as Enacted** ☙ *British Columbia Gazette Part II* Online: *British Columbia Queen's Printer* www.bclaws.ca/civix/content/bcgaz2/bcgaz2/?xsl=/templates/browse.xsl ☙ From October 2001 ☙ Published every two weeks ☙ In print from 1958 **Current Consolidated Regulations** ☙ Online: BC Laws: Statutes and Regulations www.bclaws.ca/civix/content/complete/statreg/?xsl=/templates/browse.xsl ☙ Online: CanLII www.canlii.org/en/bc/laws/index.html Includes previous versions **Archived Consolidated Regulations** ☙ Online: BC Laws: Archived Regulation Consolidations www.bclaws.ca/archive-reg.html (from Consolidation 60, April 2003 onwards)
Notes	There are no regulations prior to 1958.[88] Any regulatory orders that were published before that were converted into regulations and published in the 1958 *Gazette*.
Finding Tools/ Indexes	Index of Current BC Regulations, online: www.bclaws.ca/civix/content/regulationbulletin/regulationbulletin/618009051/?xsl=/templates/browse.xsl ☙ Cumulative from 1958 ☙ Published quarterly
Finding Tools/ Indexes	BC Regulations Bulletins, online: www.bclaws.ca/civix/content/regulationbulletin/regulationbulletin/618009051/?xsl=/templates/browse.xsl ☙ From 1999 onwards ☙ Provides dates of deposit and links to regulations

---

87 British Columbia, Ministry of Small Business and Red Tape Reduction, Regulatory Reform Policy (June 2016), online: www2.gov.bc.ca/assets/gov/government/about-the-bc-government/regulatory-reform/pdfs/final_regulatory_reform_policy_-_aug_2016.pdf.

88 BC Courthouse Library, online: www.courthouselibrary.ca/how-we-can-help/our-legal-knowledge-base/where-can-i-find-pre-1958-bc-regulations.

TABLE 10.2: WHERE TO FIND PROVINCIAL AND TERRITORIAL REGULATIONS

Manitoba Regulations

Governing Legislation	*Statutes and Regulations Act*, CCSM c S207
	Official Copy Regulation, Man Reg 131/2014
	The Regulatory Accountability Act, SM 2017, c 21 (assented to 2 June, some sections coming into force on proclamation — pending as of 13 January 2019)
Committee/ Oversight	Standing Committee on Statutory Regulations and Orders of the Legislative Assembly
	❦ Regulatory Accountability Committee
	❦ Regulatory Accountability Secretariat
Documentation	Regulatory Impact Statement
	❦ provided as advice to Cabinet and not available to the public
Where They Can Be Found	**Regulations as Enacted**
	❦ Regulations of Manitoba (2000–)
	http://web2.gov.mb.ca/laws/regs/index_annual.php
	❦ *Manitoba Gazette Part II–*
	In print from 1960
	Current Consolidated Regulations
	❦ http://web2.gov.mb.ca/laws/regs/index.php
Finding Tools/ Indexes	Table of Consolidated Regulations.
	❦ http://web2.gov.mb.ca/laws/regs/index.php
	Includes links to archived versions of regulations that were in force after 1 May 2014
Notes	With some exceptions, regulations are to be tabled in the Assembly within the first fifteen days of the commencement of a new session.[89]

New Brunswick Regulations

Governing Legislation	*Regulations Act*, RSNB 2011, c 218
	General Regulation (Regulations Act), NB Reg 91-160
Oversight/ Administration	Attorney General
	Registrar of Regulations
Documentation	Memorandum to the Executive Council

---

89   *Statutes and Regulations Act*, CCSM c S207, s 22(1).

TABLE 10.2: WHERE TO FIND PROVINCIAL AND TERRITORIAL REGULATIONS

Where They Can Be Found	**Regulations as Enacted** ❦ Annual Volumes ❦ Online from 2000 www2.gnb.ca/content/gnb/en/departments/jag/attorney-general/content/acts_regulations/content/annual_volumes_ofregulations.html ❦ In print from 1963 **Royal Gazette** ❦ Online from 2000 www2.gnb.ca/content/gnb/en/departments/jag/attorney-general/content/royal_gazette.html **Current Consolidated Regulations** ❦ http://laws.gnb.ca/en/BrowseTitle ❦ Link from enabling Act
Finding Tools/ Indexes	Cumulative Index of New Brunswick Regulations from 1964 www.gnb.ca/0062/acts/BBR-2017/CI-2017-e.pdf

Newfoundland and Labrador Regulations

Governing Legislation	*Statutes and Subordinate Legislation Act*, RSNL 1990, c S-27 *Subordinate Legislation Regulations*, CNLR 995/96
Oversight/ Administration	Registrar (defined as the Legislative Counsel)
Where They Can Be Found	**Regulations as Passed** ❦ *Newfoundland and Labrador Gazette* (called the *Newfoundland Gazette* until 21 December 2001) ❦ Annual Volumes from 2001 www.assembly.nl.ca/legislation/sr/annualregs/ ❦ *Newfoundland Gazette Part II Regulations* In print from 1978 to 2001[90] **Current Consolidated Regulations** ❦ Consolidated Statutes and Regulations www.assembly.nl.ca/legislation/sr/consolidation **Point in Time Regulations** ❦ From 1 August 2010 www.assembly.nl.ca/legislation/sr/pointintime/pittitleindex2.htm

---

90   Nancy McCormack & Nathalie Leonard, *Updating Statutes and Regulations for All Canadian Jurisdictions*, 5th ed (Toronto: Carswell, 2012) at 179.

TABLE 10.2: WHERE TO FIND PROVINCIAL AND TERRITORIAL REGULATIONS

Notes	Regulations were re-gazetted in 1978–79 — as a result, issues of the *Newfoundland Gazette* published from 7 July 1978 to 20 July 1979 contained all existing subordinate legislation.
Finding Tools/ Indexes	Table of Regulations 1978–1995 www.assembly.nl.ca/legislation/sr/historicallegislation/ HisSLRegisters/1978-1995/default.htm
	Annual Register of Subordinate Legislation (1996–2017) www.assembly.nl.ca/legislation/sr/lists/CurSLRegister/default.htm

Northwest Territories Regulations

Governing Legislation	*Statutory Instruments Act*, RSNWT 1988, c S-13 *Statutory Instruments Regulations*, RRNWT 1990, c S-19
Oversight/ Administration	Registrar of Regulations
Documentation	No requirement for documentation
Where They Can Be Found	**As published** 🐦 *Northwest Territories Gazette Part II*, online: www.justice.gov.nt.ca/en/northwest-territories-gazette 🐦 Online from 1994 🐦 In print from 1979 **Historical Consolidated Regulations** 🐦 *Revised Regulations of the Northwest Territories, 1980* In print 🐦 *Revised Regulations of the Northwest Territories, 1990* In print **Current Consolidated Regulations** 🐦 www.justice.gov.nt.ca/en/legislation (to locate the regulation, browse to the enabling legislation) 🐦 Can also be searched directly at www.justice.gov.nt.ca/en/legislation-search
Finding Tools	"History of Regulations" Index in the *Revised Regulations of the Northwest Territories, 1980* *Table C: Table of Regulations of the Northwest Territories Forming Part of the Revised Regulations of the Northwest Territories, 1990, and New Regulations and Including . . . .* Published annually as part of the index to the *Gazette* www.justice.gov.nt.ca/en/northwest-territories-gazette/ #gn-filebrowse-0 🐦 Online since 1994

TABLE 10.2: WHERE TO FIND PROVINCIAL AND TERRITORIAL REGULATIONS

Nova Scotia Regulations

Governing Legislation	*Regulations Act*, RSNS 1989, c 393 *Regulations under the Regulation Act*, NS Reg 42/99
Oversight/ Administration	Registrar of Regulations
Documentation	Report and Recommendation (Non-confidential parts might be published in the *Gazette* along with the regulation.[91])
Where They Can Be Found	**Regulations as Passed** ❧ *Royal Gazette Part II* https://novascotia.ca/just/regulations/rg2/issues.htm ❧ Online from 2001 ❧ In print from 1977 **Historical Regulations** ❧ 1942 — Rules and Regulations ❧ 1943–1973 — Published in the Annual Statute Volumes ❧ 1973–1977 — Tabled Regulations of Nova Scotia **Current Consolidated Regulations** ❧ https://novascotia.ca/just/regulations/regsxact.htm
Finding Tools	Index of Regulations for the *Royal Gazette Part II* Online from 1996 https://novascotia.ca/just/regulations/rg2/indexes.htm

Nunavut Regulations

Governing Legislation	*Statutory Instruments Act*, RSNWT (Nu) 1988, c S-13 *Statutory Instruments Regulations*, RRNWT (Nu) 1990, c S-19
Oversight/ Administration	Registrar of Regulations
Documentation	Supporting documents must "address legal considerations, financial implications, consultations conducted and alternatives to regulating."[92] These are Cabinet documents and not available to the public.

---

91   Salembier, above note 3 at 152.
92   *Ibid* at 155.

TABLE 10.2: WHERE TO FIND PROVINCIAL AND TERRITORIAL REGULATIONS

Notes	"The Nunavut Act, S.C. 1993, c.28 as amended brought Nunavut into being on April 1,1999 (s.3) and provided, at s.29, that the ordinances of the Northwest Territories and the laws made under them effective March 31, 1999 will be duplicated for Nunavut."[93]
	Given Nunavut's distinct legislative history, locating current regulations will take more than one step. Although the website provides "Current Consolidated Regulations," these are not always completely up to date. You will also have to check the *Gazettes* subsequent to the most recent Table of Regulations, which is dated 2014. The Nunavut Legislation "Instruction on How to Search Webpage" provides a useful step-by-step checklist for searching for statutes and regulations.
Where They Can Be Found	**Regulations as Passed** ✾ *Nunavut Gazette Part II* ✾ Online from 1999 www.nunavutlegislation.ca/en/nunavut-gazette/2017/part-2
	Historical Consolidated Regulations ✾ Existing Law on the Creation of Nunavut, 1 April 1999 www.nunavutlegislation.ca/en/consolidated-law/original?title=A
	Current Consolidated Regulations ✾ www.nunavutlegislation.ca/en/consolidated-law/current?
Finding Tools	Tables of Regulations ✾ From 1999–2014 www.nunavutlegislation.ca/en/tables-of-regulations
Ontario Regulations	
Governing Legislation	*Legislation Act, 2006*, SO 2006, c 21, Schedule F
Oversight/ Administration	Standing Committee on Regulations and Private Bills Registrar of Regulations
Documentation	Confidential Cabinet documents — not available to the public
Where They Can Be Found	**Regulations as Passed** ✾ Source Law on e-Laws from 2000: www.ontario.ca/laws ✾ In print 1944–current ✾ Internet Archive from 1944–2007 http://archive.org/search.php?query=axt-4498%20AND%20collection%3Atoronto&page=2

---

93   "Legislation," online: *Nunavut Court of Justice Law Library* www.nunavutcourts.ca/ 2014-09-05-13-12-02.

TABLE 10.2: WHERE TO FIND PROVINCIAL AND TERRITORIAL REGULATIONS

Where They Can Be Found	**Gazettes** 🦫 *Ontario Gazette Part II* From 2000: www.ontario.ca/search/ontario-gazette **Historical Consolidated Regulations** 🦫 Consolidated Regulations of Ontario 1950 🦫 Revised Regulations of Ontario, 1960, 1970, 1980, 1990 In print and on the Internet Archive http://archive.org/search.php?query=%22Revised%20 Regulations%22%20AND%20collection%3A%22toronto%22 &sort=date **Current Consolidated Regulations** 🦫 Ontario e-Laws From 2000: www.ontario.ca/laws **Period in Time Regulations on e-Laws** 🦫 Historical versions of regulations for comparison going back to 2 January 2004 www.ontario.ca/laws
Notes	Since 1944, the law requires that regulations be published in the *Ontario Gazette*. Earlier regulations may be obtained by checking through orders in council, although coverage may not be complete.
Finding Tools	Legislative Tables: Regulations www.ontario.ca/laws/regulations A list of Ontario's consolidated and unconsolidated regulations. Indicates the statute under which the regulation was made, whether the regulation is on e-Laws, whether any laws amended the regulation, or any change notices were given affecting it, and whether it has been revoked or identified as spent. Table of Regulations 🦫 1990–2001 In annual statute volumes in print Table or Index to Regulations in the *Gazette* 🦫 From 1944 in print or on the Internet Archive.

Prince Edward Island

Governing Legislation	None. However, the *Interpretation Act*, RSPEI 1988, c I-8 provides a definition of a regulation (See Appendix 1).

TABLE 10.2: WHERE TO FIND PROVINCIAL AND TERRITORIAL REGULATIONS

Oversight/ Administration	Standing Committee on Rules, Regulations, Private Bills and Privileges Legislative Counsel Office
Documentation	Executive Council Memorandum. Confidential Document. Not available to the public.

Where They Can Be Found	**Regulations as Passed**
	✓ *Royal Gazette* Part II
	✓ Online from 1999
	   www.princeedwardisland.ca/en/royalgazette
	✓ In print
	
	Historical Consolidated Regulations
	✓ Revised in 1985 and published as a looseleaf service from 1985 to 1998
	
	Current Consolidated Regulations
	✓ www.princeedwardisland.ca/en/legislation/all/all/l
	   Located via the enabling legislation.

Finding Tools	Table of Regulations ✓ www.princeedwardisland.ca/sites/default/files/publications/ leg_table_regs.pdf Consolidated — amendments since 1979
Québec Regulations	
Governing Legislation	*Regulations Act,* CQLR c R-18.1
Oversight/ Administration	Comité de legislation Quebec National Assembly "The National Assembly may, in accordance with its standing orders, vote the disallowance of any regulations or any pre-scriptions of a regulation."[94]
Documentation	Impact Study or Impact Assessment relating to the costs on businesses
Notes	Proposed regulations are published in the *Gazette* for public comment for 45 days (minimum) unless otherwise indicated in the case of urgency or if there are fiscal implications.[95]

---

94   *Regulations Act*, CQLR c R-18.1, s 21.
95   *Ibid*, ss 8–14.

TABLE 10.2: WHERE TO FIND PROVINCIAL AND TERRITORIAL REGULATIONS

Where They Can Be Found	**Regulations as Passed** ❦ *Gazette* officielle du Québec — Part 2 — Laws and Regulations www3.publicationsduquebec.gouv.qc.ca/gazetteofficielle/loisreglements.fr.html ❦ From 1996 ❦ In print from 1973 **Historical Revisions** ❦ Revised Regulations of Quebec 1981 **Current Consolidated Regulations** ❦ From LégisQuébec http://legisquebec.gouv.qc.ca/en/BrowseChapter?corpus=regs ❦ Organized by name of regulation
Finding Tools	Tableau des modifications et Index sommaire; Recueil de lois et des règlements du Québec. In print and online via subscription *Gazette* officielle du Québec Partie 2 — Lois et règlements Annual Index

Saskatchewan Regulations

Governing Legislation	*Regulations Act, 1995*, SS 1995, c R-16.2 *Regulations Act Regulations, 1997, The*, RRS c R-16.2 Reg 1
Oversight/ Administration	Intergovernmental Affairs and Justice Committee Registrar of Regulations
Documentation	Memorandum with cost benefit and impact analyses, information about communication and consultation with stakeholders.[96] Confidential Cabinet document
Where They Can Be Found	**Regulations as Passed** *Saskatchewan Gazette* ❦ From 1991 ❦ Part II — Revised Regulations ❦ Part III — Unrevised Regulations ❦ http://publications.saskatchewan.ca/#/categories/1511 ❦ In print from 1964 **Current Consolidated Regulations** http://publications.saskatchewan.ca/#/categories/1507 ❦ Regulations of Saskatchewan In print, looseleaf — cumulative from 1983

---

96   Salembier, above note 3 at 170.

TABLE 10.2: WHERE TO FIND PROVINCIAL AND TERRITORIAL REGULATIONS

Finding Tools	Legislative Tables of Regulations http://publications.saskatchewan.ca/#/categories/1858
	Legislative Tables of Repealed Regulations http://publications.saskatchewan.ca/#/categories/1859
	Law Society of Saskatchewan — Saskatchewan Regulations Database https://library.lawsociety.sk.ca/databasespub/regulations2002.htm

	The Saskatchewan Regulations database indexes all revised and unrevised regulations published in the *Saskatchewan Gazette* since 1 January 2000 with links to the full text. Includes:
	  🖝 regulations made pursuant to a particular statute since 2000
	  🖝 the "coming into force" dates for new regulations
	  🖝 amendments to existing regulations since 2000

	Annual Indexes *Saskatchewan Gazette* In print from 1964
Yukon Regulations	
Governing Legislation	*Regulations Act*, RSY 2002, c 195
Oversight/ Administration	Registrar of Regulations
Documentation	Submission to Cabinet. Confidential Cabinet Documents.

Where they can be found	**Regulations as Passed**
	  🖝 New regulations since most recent consolidation
	    www.gov.yk.ca/legislation/regs_new.html
	  🖝 *Yukon Gazette Part II*
	    Online from 2000
	    http://gazette.gov.yk.ca/part2_search.html
	
	Current Consolidated Regulations
	  🖝 www.gov.yk.ca/legislation/legislation/page_a.html

Finding Tools	Index of Regulations www.gov.yk.ca/legislation/regs/regs_a.html *Yukon Gazette* Annual Index Online from 2000 A link to each Annual Index is provided along with each annual volume of the *Gazette*.

chapter eleven

Tracing the Evolution and History of a Regulation

As noted in Chapter 10, the rules of interpretation that apply to statutes also apply to regulations:

> A statutory provision must be read in its entire context, taking into consideration not only the ordinary and grammatical sense of the words, but also the scheme and object of the statute, and the intention of the legislature. *This approach to statutory interpretation must also be followed, with necessary adaptations, in interpreting regulations.*[1]

Even though the concept of legislative evolution refers to textual changes within a statute or regulation, legislative evolution is considered to be an *extrinsic* aid to the interpretation of regulations.[2] One example of the use of the evolution of a regulation is the Nova Scotia case *Municipal Enterprises Ltd v Nova Scotia (Attorney General)*,[3] an appeal case in which the "sole issue … is one of statutory interpretation"[4]—specifically the intention of regulations under the *Gasoline and Diesel Oil Tax Act*. During the course of the original trial, the trial judge "traced the evolution of the *GDOTA* and its Regulations from

---

1   *Glykis v Hydro Quebec* 2004 SCC 60 at para 5 [emphasis added].
2   Ruth Sullivan, *Sullivan on the Construction of Statutes*, 6th ed (Markham, ON: LexisNexis, 2014) at 661 [Sullivan, *Construction*, 6th].
3   *Municipal Enterprises Ltd v Nova Scotia (Attorney General)*, 2003 NSCA 10.
4   *Ibid* at para 2.

1926 to 1981 to identify their original purpose and any trends reflecting new policies or whether they have remained constant."[5] As part of their appeal, the appellants argued that the trial judge had given "undue weight"[6] to legislative history (including legislative evolution). The appeal was dismissed. In her findings, Glube CJNS explicitly noted that in order to avoid an absurdity, "it was appropriate for the trial judge to consider factors such as the debates from the Nova Scotia House of Assembly; [and] *the evolution of the act and its regulations.*"[7]

A. LEGISLATIVE EVOLUTION

As with tracing the evolution of a statute, we will use Sullivan's definition of legislative evolution as the basis for researching the evolution of a regulation:

> **Legislative evolution** is "the evolution of a legislative provision [consisting] of successive enacted versions from inception to the version in place when the relevant facts occur."[8]

1) Tracing the Evolution of a Regulation

Tracing the evolution of a regulation starts with the current regulation and working backward, making note of any changes of meaning or wording in a regulation and flagging when those changes occurred, as they can be used as the basis for locating the legislative history of the regulation.

2) The Source Reference

One important tool to be aware of when tracing legislative evolution is the source reference. Start by locating the current regulation, either on the government websites or on CanLII (www.canlii.org). If the jurisdiction you are researching uses source references, you will see

---

5　*Ibid* at para 18.
6　*Ibid* at para 70.
7　*Ibid* at para 77 [emphasis added].
8　Sullivan, *Construction*, 6th, above note 2 at 660.

the source reference at the end of the section that you are researching. The source reference will give you the citation to the previous versions of that section, either going back to its inception if it came into being prior to the previous revision, or to the previous revision if it is an older regulation.

The source reference appears at the end of each section of a regulation for most jurisdictions. This note will indicate the source of the original regulation as well as any changes up until the current consolidation. The citation for the source reference usually follows the same pattern for each jurisdiction. For the provincial unrevised regulations, you will see an indication of the jurisdiction, a short form for the word regulation, an ordinal number, and an indication of the year. The structure of the citation may differ from province to province, so in British Columbia you might see BC Reg 200/2001, while in Newfoundland and Labrador you might see NLR 17/05. The *McGill Guide*[9] provides a complete list of citation styles for each jurisdiction in Rule 2.5 (Regulations). The citations for revised regulations are less predictable, so it is best to consult the *McGill Guide* if you are not sure how to interpret a source reference. Federal regulations have their own citation convention, unrevised regulations are cited SOR/year-regulation number (SOR/2001-16), and revised regulations are cited CRC and chapter number (CRC, c 167).

3) Tracing the Evolution of a Recent Regulation

Here is an example of tracing a recent regulation back using the definitions section of O Reg 223/08: *Professional Misconduct* under *Early Childhood Educators Act, 2007*, SO 2007, c 7, Schedule 8. While this example is specific to Ontario, these instructions can be generalized to cover other jurisdictions as well. As this is a current regulation, the best place to begin your research is e-Laws, the Ontario Government's official source of statutes and regulations (www.ontario.ca/laws).

---

9   McGill Law Journal, *Canadian Guide to Uniform Legal Citation*, 8th ed (Toronto: Carswell, 2014) or any subsequent editions [*McGill Guide*].

4) Source References Method: Current Regulation

Use e-Laws to locate the current regulation.

> *Early Childhood Educators Act, 2007*
> ONTARIO REGULATION 223/08
> PROFESSIONAL MISCONDUCT
>
> *Definitions*
> 1. In this Regulation,
> "guardian" includes a person, children's aid society or corporation that
> has legal custody of the child; "member" means a member of the Col-
> lege; "profession" means the profession of early childhood education.
> O Reg 223/08, s 1; O Reg 357/15, s 1.

From this you can see that this regulation was introduced in 2008
(O Reg 223/08 is the current regulation number) and amended in 2015
(O Reg 357/15).

To check the history of this regulation, you would look at both
O Reg 359/15 and O Reg 223/08. To locate the original regulations as
passed, check the "Source Law" volumes (limiting your search to
Regulations as Filed) that are available on e-Laws or select each of the
versions from the box at the top of the current regulation. Searching
Source Law will provide information relating to the enactment of
the regulation that might be useful for future research. Looking at
the versions will simply give you the text of the regulation. Another
alternative would be to look at the point-in-time versions of the regulation on CanLII. Searching CanLII will give you the same information as you will see by looking at the historical versions on e-Laws.

5) Amending Regulation

The section of O Reg 359/15 that amends section 1, located through
Source Law, looks like this:

> Ontario Regulation 359/15 made under the *Early Childhood Educators*
> *Act, 2007*
> Made: October 30, 2015

Approved: November 25, 2015

Filed: November 27, 2015

Published on e-Laws: November 27, 2015

Printed in *The Ontario Gazette*: December 12, 2015

AMENDING O REG 223/08 (PROFESSIONAL MISCONDUCT)

1. The definition of "child" in section 1 of Ontario Regulation 223/08 is revoked.

The date that the regulation was filed can be important for two reasons: It may tell you when the regulation came into force (in most jurisdictions regulations come into force on filing unless an alternative date is specified) and the filing date gives you a time frame to look at if you were looking for any possible discussion of why this section of the regulation was revoked.

6) Original Regulation

Ontario Regulation 223/08 made under the *Early Childhood Educators Act, 2007* (located through Source Law) looks like this:

Made: May 13, 2008

Approved: June 17, 2008

Filed: June 19, 2008

Published on e-Laws: June 23, 2008

Printed in *The Ontario Gazette*: July 5, 2008

PROFESSIONAL MISCONDUCT

Definitions

1.   In this Regulation,

"child" means a person under the age of 18 years;

"guardian" includes a person, children's aid society or corporation that has legal custody of the child;

"member" means a member of the College;

"profession" means the profession of early childhood education.

7) Using a Finding Tool

Another approach to tracing a regulation back is to use a finding tool such as a Table of Regulations. Tables of regulations are often online on the government websites as well as available in print. The Ontario government, for example, provides a table of regulations ordered by enabling legislation that provides a list of regulations and their amending regulations. A search for the *Early Childhood Educators Act* lists all its regulations and amendments including the "Professional Misconduct Regulation." This approach is slightly less efficient than looking directly at the regulations online as it adds an additional step, but it does provide a useful list of all the amendments in one place. It also does not specify which of the sections of the regulation were amended. A table or an index is your best option for tracing back the evolution of the regulation if the jurisdiction you are researching does not provide source references for its regulations.

8) Source References Method: Older Regulation

While tracing the evolution of a recent regulation can be straight-forward, tracing the evolution of an older regulation has its own set of complexities. You may need to consult the print or an online print equivalent as well as a table of regulations in order to build a comprehensive record of the evolution of a particular regulation.

The following example was chosen because it illustrates how deeply you can dive into the evolution of a regulation. The "Duties of Teachers" section of *Ontario Schools for the Blind and the Deaf*, RRO 1990, Reg 296 under the *Education Act*, RSO 1990, c E.2 goes back many years. Although the wording of the regulation does not change significantly over the years, the process is illustrative of some of the hiccups that you might experience along the way when you are tracing a regulation back to its inception.

As this is a current in-force regulation, the best starting point is e-Laws.

The text of the current consolidated version of section 15 reads:

Duties of Teachers

15. A person employed to teach at a School shall, in addition to the duties of a teacher under the Act,

(a) be responsible for effective instruction in the subjects assigned to him or her by the Superintendent, the management of his or her classes and the discipline in his or her classroom;

(b) co-operate with officials of the Ministry and the Superintendent for the purposes of planning and evaluating the program of instruction;

(c) make adequate provision in his or her daily program for the individual differences of the pupils in his or her classes so that each pupil may experience a reasonable amount of success;

(d) prepare for use in his or her class or classes such teaching plans and outlines as are required by the Superintendent and submit the plans and outlines to the Superintendent on request;

(e) assist in maintaining discipline in the School and in fostering school spirit and morale; and

(f) carry out such supervisory duties as may be assigned by the Superintendent. RRO 1990, Reg 296, s 15

As you can see from the source reference this regulation previously appeared in the Revised Regulations of Ontario 1990, Regulation number 296. As there are no other references included in the source reference, it is safe to assume that this regulation has not been amended between 1990 and the currency date of the version of e-Laws. (You can locate the currency date by clicking on the link provided with every statute and regulation.)

By contrast, if you were to use the Table of Regulations, you would see a list of all the amendments to the regulation but not in which section specifically.

As you know from the source reference that this section of the regulation has not been amended since the regulations were revised in 1990, then your next step would be to locate RRO 1990, Reg 296, either in the print RRO or an online equivalent.

ILLUSTRATION 11.1

ONTARIO TABLE OF REGULATIONS

www.ontario.ca/laws/regulations

- existed on December 31, 1990 and were consolidated in the Revised Regulations of Ontario, 1990 (R.R.O. 1990)
- existed on December 31, 1990, but because they were considered to be of limited application or effect, were not included in the R.R.O. 1990 and continued in unconsolidated form (see the Schedule in volume 9 of the R.R.O. 1990)
- were filed with the Registrar of Regulations on or after January 1, 1991

Table

Search: schools for the Blind and the Deaf

Enabling Statute	Regulation	Citation	Notes	On e-Laws	Legislative History	Spent or revoked on (d/m/y)	Revoked by (O. Reg.)
Education Act, R.S.O. 1990, c. E.2	ONTARIO SCHOOLS FOR THE BLIND AND THE DEAF	R.R.O. 1990, Reg. 296		Yes	323/04, 447/05, 133/08, 177/10, 202/11		

1 - 1 of 1 results (5,558 records)   ‹ Back   1   Next ›

RRO 1990, Reg 296, s 15

Duties of Teachers

15. A person employed to teach at a School shall, in addition to the duties of a teacher under the Act,

(a) be responsible for effective instruction in the subjects assigned to him or her by the Superintendent, the management of his or her classes and the discipline in his or her classroom;

(b) co-operate with officials of the Ministry and the Superintendent for the purposes of planning and evaluating the program of instruction;

(c) make adequate provision in his or her daily program for the individual differences of the pupils in his or her classes so that each pupil may experience a reasonable amount of success;

(d) prepare for use in his or her class or classes such teaching plans and outlines as are required by the Superintendent and submit the plans and outlines to the Superintendent on request;

(e) assist in maintaining discipline in the School and in fostering school spirit and morale; and

(f)　carry out such supervisory duties as may be assigned by the Superintendent.
RRO 1980, Reg 268, s 15

Looking at section 15 you will see that the wording has not changed between 1990 revision and the current consolidated version. You will, however, see a source reference that leads you to RRO 1980, Reg 268, section 15. The single source reference indicates that there were no changes to the provision between RRO 1980 and RRO 1990. Since the wording has not changed, there would be no reason to go and look for any indications of a change in legislative intent for this point in time.

RRO 1980, Reg 268, s 15

DUTIES OF TEACHERS

15.　A person employed to teach at a School shall, in addition to the duties of a teacher under the Act,

(a)　be responsible for effective instruction in the subjects assigned to *him* by the Superintendent, the management of his classes and the discipline in *his* classroom;

(b)　co-operate with officials of the Ministry and the Superintendent for the purposes of planning and evaluating the program of instruction;

(c)　make adequate provision in *his* daily program for the individual differences of the pupils in his classes so that each pupil may experience a reasonable amount of success;

(d)　prepare for use in *his* class or classes such teaching plans and outlines as are required by the Superintendent and submit the plans and outlines to the Superintendent on request;

(e)　assist in maintaining discipline in the School and in fostering school spirit and morale; and

(f)　carry out such supervisory duties as may be assigned by the Superintendent.

O Reg 555/79, s 15

The only change to the text of this section between 1980 and 1990 was to gender neutralize the language; changing *his* to *his or her*, and *him* to *him or her*. The source reference leads us to O Reg 555/79, s 19. As this reference is not leading us to a previous revision, this could mean that this section of the regulation was either introduced for the first time or an existing regulation was amended in 1979. The only way to find out is to look at that amendment.

O Reg 555/79, s 15

> DUTIES OF TEACHERS
>
> 15. A person employed to teach at a School shall, in addition to the duties of a teacher under the Act,
>
> (a) be responsible for effective instruction in the subjects assigned to him by the Superintendent, the management of his classes and the discipline in his classroom;
>
> (b) co-operate with officials of the Ministry and the Superintendent for the purposes of planning and evaluating the program of instruction;
>
> (c) make adequate provision in his daily program for the individual differences of the pupils in his classes so that each pupil may experience a reasonable amount of success;
>
> (d) prepare for use in his class or classes such teaching plans and outlines as are required by the Superintendent and submit the plans and outlines to the Superintendent on request;
>
> (e) assist in maintaining discipline in the School and in fostering school spirit and morale; and
>
> (f) carry out such supervisory duties as may be assigned by the Superintendent.
>
> O Reg 555/79, s 15

The wording of the regulation is the same as the subsequent iteration, but the source reference is now at a dead end, as it is referencing the regulation that we are already looking at. It is always a good idea to confirm whether this really is the end of the road by looking at the Table of Regulations for the year prior to 1979.

The Table of Regulations filed under *The Regulations Act* to 31 December 1978 shows that there were indeed regulations under a similar Act. These regulations appeared in 1976, 1975, and RRO 1970. A quick look at O Reg 119/76 and O Reg 81/75 shows that neither includes any clauses relating to the duties of teachers. Since these regulations only amend parts of RRO 1970 Reg 198, it would be a good idea to look at the 1970 revision as a whole.

ILLUSTRATION 11.2

TABLE OF REGULATIONS FILED UNDER THE *REGULATIONS ACT*

TO 31 DECEMBER 1978

1216 TABLE OF REGULATIONS

	Regulation No.		Date of Gazette
	R.R.O. 1970	O. Reg.	
Department of Colleges and Universities Act—*Continued* (*See now* **Ministry of Colleges and Universities Act, 1971**) (*title of Act changed April 1st, 1972, See S.O. 1972, c. 1, s. 12 (1)*) Colleges of Applied Arts and Technology—*Continued*			
Centennial	172	......	....
Conestoga	173	......	....
Confederation	174	......	....
Durham	175	......	....
Fanshawe	176	......	....
George Brown	177	......	....
Georgian	178	......	....
Humber	179	......	....
Lambton	180	......	....
Loyalist	181	......	....
Mohawk	182	......	....
Niagara	183	......	....
Northern	184	......	....
St. Clair	185	......	....
St. Lawrence	186	......	....
Seneca	187	......	....
Sheridan	188	......	....
Sir Sandford Fleming	189	......	....
Department of Education Act (*See* **Ministry of Education Act**) (*See* **Education Act, 1974**, *See S.O. 1974, c. 109*)			
General Legislative Grants	193	......	....
General Legislative Grants	194	......	....
General Legislative Grants	...	59/71	Feb. 13/71
amended	...	74/71	Feb. 27/71
amended	...	532/71	Jan. 8/72
amended	...	791/74	Nov. 2/74
General Legislative Grants	...	124/71	Apr. 10/71
General Legislative Grants	...	98/72	Mar. 18/72
General Legislative Grants	...	242/72	June 3/72
General Legislative Grants	...	308/73	June 9/73
Municipal Recreation Directors' Certificates and Arena Managers' Certificates	...	392/71	Sept. 25/71
(*Now under Ministry of Culture and Recreation Act, 1974*) Ontario Schools for the Blind and Ontario Schools for the Deaf	198	......	....
amended	...	81/75	Feb. 22/75
amended	...	119/76	Feb. 21/76
Programs of Recreation	200	......	....
Purchase of Milk	201	......	....
Teachers' Contracts	208	......	....
Department of Labour Act (*See now* **Ministry of Labour Act**) (*title of Act changed April 1st, 1972, See S.O. 1972, c. 1, s. 82 (1)*)			
Department of Municipal Affairs Act (*See now* **Municipal Affairs Act**) (*title of Act changed April 1st, 1972, See S.O. 1972, c. 1, s. 104 (1)*)			

RRO 1970 Reg 198, s 14

> DUTIES OF TEACHERS
>
> 14. A teacher at a School shall,
>
> (a) be responsible for effective instruction in the subjects assigned to him, the management of his classes and the discipline in his classroom;
>
> (b) co-operate with the Superintendent, Assistant Superintendent, the Instructors in Professional Training and the Dean of Residences, in securing a suitable selection, arrangement and correlation of the subject matter and materials of instruction;
>
> (c) prepare for use of his classes a daily teaching outline based on the courses of study;
>
> (d) assist in maintaining discipline in the school and in fostering school spirit and morale;
>
> (e) carry out the supervisory duties assigned by the Superintendent; and
>
> (f) make adequate provision in his daily program for the individual differences of the pupils in his classes so that each pupil may experience a reasonable amount of success.
>
> O Reg 28/63, s 14

Yes, section 14 of RRO 1970, Reg 198 has a section on the duties of teachers and refers us to O Reg 28/63 in the source reference section.

O Reg 28/63, s 14

> DUTIES OF TEACHERS
>
> 14. A teacher at a School shall,
>
> (a) be responsible for effective instruction in the subjects assigned to him, the management of his classes and the discipline in his classroom;
>
> (b) co-operate with the Superintendent, Assistant Superintendent, the Instructors in Professional Training and the Dean of Residences, in securing a suitable selection, arrangement and correlation of the subject matter and materials of instruction;

(c) prepare for use of his classes a daily teaching outline based on the courses of study;

(d) assist in maintaining discipline in the school and in fostering school spirit and morale;

(e) carry out the supervisory duties assigned by the Superintendent; and

(f) make adequate provision in his daily programme for the individual differences of the pupils in his classes so that each pupil may experience a reasonable amount of success.

O Reg 28/63 does have a section on the duties of teachers but no source reference. A look at the Revised Regulations for 1960 shows that the "Duties of Teachers" does appear in 1960.

RRO 1960, Reg 90, s 15

DUTIES OF TEACHERS

15. A teacher at a School shall,

(a) be responsible for effective instruction in the subjects assigned to him, the management of is classes and the discipline in his classroom;

(b) co-operate with the Superintendent, Assistant Superintendent, and the Instructors in Professional Training in securing a suitable selection, arrangement and correlation of the subject matter and materials of instruction;

(c) prepare for use of his classes a daily teaching outline based on the courses of study;

(d) assist in maintaining discipline in the school and in fostering school spirit and morale;

(e) carry out the supervisory duties assigned by the Superintendent; and

(f) make adequate provision in his daily programme for the individual differences of the pupils in his classes so that each pupil may experience a reasonable amount of success.

O Reg 111/59, s 15

From here, the source reference directs us back to O Reg 111/59.

O Reg 111/59, s 15

DUTIES OF TEACHERS

15. A teacher at a School shall

(a) be responsible for effective instruction in the subjects assigned to him, the management of his classes, and the discipline in his classroom;

(b) co-operate with the Superintendent, Assistant Superintendent, and the Instructors in Professional Training in securing a suitable selection, arrangement, and correlation of the subject matter and materials of instruction;

(c) prepare for use of his classes a daily teaching outline based on the courses of study;

(d) assist in maintaining discipline in the school and in fostering school spirit and morale;

(e) carry out the supervisory duties assigned by the Superintendent; and

(f) make adequate provision in his daily programme for the individual differences of the pupils in his classes so that each pupil may experience a reasonable amount of success.

This version has similar wording to the subsequent regulation but does not provide a source reference to an earlier version. Have we finally reached the end of the trail? A look at the *Index of Regulations* from 1958 does not have an entry for Schools for the Blind and Deaf under the *Department of Education Act, 1954*. A further look at the *Index to the Consolidated Regulations of Ontario 1950* also does not show any regulations relating to Schools for the Blind and Deaf so it looks like we have legitimately reached the end of the line.

The process as shown above has not revealed any dramatic changes to the legislation, but this is not something you would know unless you have done the research. And further, sometimes the absence of change has just as much significance as change in the eyes of the law.

9) Building Legislative History of a Regulation

Although the terms legislative evolution and legislative history are often used interchangeably (and somewhat confusingly) by the courts, we are following Ruth Sullivan's definition of legislative history for the purposes of this text:

> A legislative history includes "everything that relates to [a statute's] conception, preparation and passage ... from the earliest proposals to royal assent. This includes reports of law reform commissions, ... ; departmental and committee studies and recommendations; proposals and memoranda submitted to Cabinet; the remarks of the minister responsible for the bill; materials tabled or otherwise brought to the attention of the legislature during the legislative process including explanatory notes; materials published by the government during the legislative process, such as explanatory papers or press releases; legislative committee hearings and reports; debates ... ; the records of motions to amend the bill; regulatory impact analysis statements; and more."[10]

a) Provincial

In most provinces, the documents that support the creation of a regulation are confidential and not available to researchers. The content or proposed content of a regulation might have been discussed, tangentially, in the legislature,[11] and so researching *Hansard* for that jurisdiction might yield some results, but this is rare and infrequent. You may want to check the *Hansard* for any committees that have oversight of the regulations to see if there has been some discussion there.

b) Federal

A Regulatory Impact Analysis Statement (RIAS) is used to form the legislative history for federal regulations and has been deemed

---

10   Ruth Sullivan, *Sullivan on the Construction of Statutes*, 5th ed (Markham, ON: LexisNexis, 2008) at 593.

11   Elizabeth Bruton, "Time Travelling: Intent Behind Regulations" (2016) 41 *Canadian Law Library Review* 20.

admissible in court as evidence of regulatory intent. As described in the regulations chapter, a RIAS explains:

- the elements of the regulatory proposal, including what problems or situations it addresses and what it is meant to achieve;
- what alternatives to regulation have been considered;
- what are the anticipated costs and benefits of the regulations;
- what consultations have been carried out and what opportunities Canadians have had to be heard;
- what is the response of the department or agency to the concerns voiced or suggestions made;
- what mechanisms are built in to ensure compliance with the regulations once they are in force;
- how the effectiveness of the regulations will be measured.[12]

10) Locating a Regulatory Impact Analysis Statement (RIAS)

The Regulatory Impact Analysis Statement is published in the *Canada Gazette*, Part II along with the proposed regulation. Once the regulation is registered, in force, and consolidated on the Justice Laws website, the RIAS is no longer included with the regulation. RIASs are considered to be extrinsic to the text of the regulation, so remember to check the *Canada Gazette*, Part II when you are looking for extrinsic evidence of legislative intent.

---

12   Government of Canada, Privy Council Office, "Guide to Making Federal Acts and Regulations: Part 3—Making Regulation," online: www.pco-bcp.gc.ca/index.asp?lang=eng&page=information&sub=publications&doc=legislation/part3-eng.htm.

B. RESEARCH SUMMARY AND CHECKLIST

Checklist

Tracing the Evolution of a Regulation
- ❦ Look at the section of the current regulation that you are researching.
- ❦ Look at the source reference that appears at the bottom of the section or at the Table of Regulations for the jurisdiction you are researching. These tools will indicate changes to the section since the regulation's inception or since the most recent revision.
- ❦ Look at the amending regulations identified by the source reference or table for changes to the text of your regulation.
- ❦ Do this repeatedly until you reach the earliest incarnation of the regulation.
- ❦ During this process you will need to make note of any changes in the language of the section that might be significant when looking at legislative intent.
- ❦ If you hit a roadblock and can't see an historical note, look at the Table of Regulations for the year prior to the year with no historical note. This should put you back on track or indicate that you have reached the end of your task.

Toolbox

Federal

Consolidated Index of Statutory Instruments
- ❦ Table II: Table of Regulations, Statutory Instruments (Other than Regulations) and Other Documents Arranged by Statute.
- ❦ http://laws.justice.gc.ca/eng/IndexStatutoryInstruments only includes in-force regulations.
- ❦ For regulations you will have to look at the index for the time it was in force.
- ❦ Some are exempt from publication—see *Statutory Instruments Regulations*, online: http://laws-lois.justice.gc.ca/eng/regulations/ C.R.C.,_c._1509/page-2.html?txthl=publication#s-15.

appendix one

Definitions of Regulations

FEDERAL

Statutory Instruments Act, RSC 1985, c S-22

. . .

Definitions

2(1) In this Act,

prescribed means prescribed by regulations made pursuant to this Act;

regulation means a statutory instrument
(a) made in the exercise of a legislative power conferred by or under an Act of Parliament, or
(b) for the contravention of which a penalty, fine or imprisonment is prescribed by or under an Act of Parliament,
and includes a rule, order or regulation governing the practice or procedure in any proceedings before a judicial or quasi-judicial body established by or under an Act of Parliament, and any instrument described as a regulation in any other Act of Parliament;

regulation-making authority means any authority authorized to make regulations and, with reference to any particular regulation or proposed regulation, means the authority that made or proposes to make the regulation;

statutory instrument

(a) means any rule, order, regulation, ordinance, direction, form, tariff of costs or fees, letters patent, commission, warrant, proclamation, by-law, resolution or other instrument issued, made or established

    (i) in the execution of a power conferred by or under an Act of Parliament, by or under which that instrument is expressly authorized to be issued, made or established otherwise than by the conferring on any person or body of powers or functions in relation to a matter to which that instrument relates, or

    (ii) by or under the authority of the Governor in Council, otherwise than in the execution of a power conferred by or under an Act of Parliament,

but

(b) does not include

    (i) any instrument referred to in paragraph (a) and issued, made or established by a corporation incorporated by or under an Act of Parliament unless

      (A) the instrument is a regulation and the corporation by which it is made is one that is ultimately accountable, through a Minister, to Parliament for the conduct of its affairs, or

      (B) the instrument is one for the contravention of which a penalty, fine or imprisonment is prescribed by or under an Act of Parliament,

    (ii) any instrument referred to in paragraph (a) and issued, made or established by a judicial or quasi-judicial body, unless the instrument is a rule, order or regulation governing the practice or procedure in proceedings before a judicial or quasi-judicial body established by or under an Act of Parliament,

    (iii) any instrument referred to in paragraph (a) and in respect of which, or in respect of the production or other disclosure of which, any privilege exists by law or whose contents are limited to advice or information intended only for use or assistance in the making of a decision or the determination of policy, or in the ascertainment of any matter necessarily incidental thereto, or

(iv) a law made by the Legislature of Yukon, of the Northwest Territories or for Nunavut, a rule made by the Legislative Assembly of Yukon under section 16 of the *Yukon Act*, of the Northwest Territories under section 16 of the *Northwest Territories Act* or of Nunavut under section 21 of the *Nunavut Act* or any instrument issued, made or established under any such law or rule.

Determination of whether certain instruments are regulations

(2) In applying the definition regulation in subsection (1) for the purpose of determining whether an instrument described in subparagraph (b)(i) of the definition statutory instrument in that subsection is a regulation, that instrument shall be deemed to be a statutory instrument, and any instrument accordingly determined to be a regulation shall be deemed to be a regulation for all purposes of this Act.

. . .

PROVINCES

Alberta

Regulations Act, RSA 2000, c R-14

. . .

1(1) In this Act,

. . .

(f) "regulation" means a regulation as defined in the *Interpretation Act* that is of a legislative nature.

(2) The following are not regulations within the meaning of subsection (1)(f):

(a) a regulation, rule, order, bylaw or resolution of

(i) a local authority,

(ii) a corporation incorporated under a public Act, or

      (iii) a corporation incorporated by or under a private Act;

  (b) a General Council Policy of the Metis Settlements General Council incorporated under the Metis Settlements Act;

  (c) a proclamation;

  (d) a document adopted or incorporated by reference in a regulation.

Interpretation Act, RSA 2000, c I-8

1(1) In this Act,

. . .

  (c) "regulation" means a regulation, order, rule, form, tariff of costs or fees, proclamation, bylaw or resolution enacted

      (i) in the execution of a power conferred by or under the authority of an Act, or

      (ii) by or under the authority of the Lieutenant Governor in Council,

      but does not include an order of a court made in the course of an action or an order made by a public officer or administrative tribunal in a dispute between 2 or more persons;

British Columbia

Regulations Act, RSBC 1996, c 402

1 In this Act:

. . .

"regulation" means a regulation, as defined in the *Interpretation Act*,

  (a) made under a power in an Act where the word "regulation", "regulations", "prescribe", "prescribes" or "prescribed" is used in conferring the power, or

  (b) identified in the Schedule,

but does not include

  (c) material adopted by reference,

  (d) a regulation adopted by reference, and

  (e) a regulation, as defined in the *Interpretation Act*, of a corporation unless the regulation is identified in the Schedule;

Interpretation Act, RSBC 1996, c 238

1 In this Act, or in an enactment:

   ...

"regulation" means a regulation, order, rule, form, tariff of costs or fees, proclamation, letters patent, commission, warrant, bylaw or other instrument enacted

(a) in execution of a power conferred under an Act, or

(b) by or under the authority of the Lieutenant Governor in Council, but does not include an order of a court made in the course of an action or an order made by a public officer or administrative tribunal in a dispute between 2 or more persons;

Manitoba

Statutes and Regulations Act, CCSM c S207

1 The following definitions apply in this Act.

   ...

"regulation" means a regulation, rule, order or by-law to which Part 3 applies or to which the former *Regulations Act* applied.

   • Part 3
      (a) every regulation, rule, order or by-law that
         (i) is made or approved in the execution of a power conferred by or under an Act,

PART 3
ORIGINAL REGULATIONS

Application of Part

8 (1) Subject to subsection (2), this Part applies to the following:

(a) every regulation, rule, order or by-law that
   (i) is made or approved in the execution of a power conferred by or under an Act,
   (ii) is made or approved by the Lieutenant Governor in Council, a minister or group of ministers, an individual or a government agency, and

(iii) either

    (A) is of a legislative nature, or

    (B) governs practice or procedure in quasi-judicial proceedings and is made or approved in the execution of a power conferred by a provision that uses the word "regulation" in conferring the power;

(b) every regulation or rule that

    (i) is made in the execution of a power conferred by or under an Act, and

    (ii) governs practice or procedure in judicial proceedings.

New Brunswick

Regulations Act, RSNB 2011, c 218

1 The following definitions apply in this Act.

. . .

"regulation" means a regulation, rule, order, by-law or other instrument made under the authority of an Act of New Brunswick but does not include (règlement)

(a) a by-law or resolution of a local authority or of a corporation, body corporate or company incorporated or continued under the laws of New Brunswick,

(b) a regulation, rule, order, by-law or other instrument made under the authority of a private Act,

(c) a proclamation of the commencement of an Act or any provision of an Act, or an alteration to or revocation of a proclamation, or an order of the Lieutenant-Governor in Council under which a proclamation is issued, or an order of the Lieutenant-Governor in Council altering or revoking such order,

(d) a regulation, rule, order, by-law or other instrument made under the authority of an Act which excludes the application of this Act,

(e) a regulation, rule, order, by-law or other instrument of an administrative nature as distinguished from a legislative nature, or

(f) a regulation, rule, order, by-law or other instrument identified in accordance with the regulations.

Newfoundland and Labrador

Interpretation Act, RSNL 1990, c I-19

2. (1) In this Act

...

(b) "regulation" includes a rule, rule of court, order prescribing
regulations, tariff of costs or fees, form, by-law, resolution, or
order made in the execution of a power given by statute;

Northwest Territories

Statutory Instruments Act, RSNWT 1988, c S-13

1. (1) In this Act,

...

"regulation" means a statutory instrument (a) made in the exercise
of a legislative power conferred by or under an Act, or (b) for the
contravention of which a penalty, fine or imprisonment is imposed
by or under an Act, and includes a rule, order or regulation governing the practice or procedure in any proceedings before a judicial
or quasi-judicial body established by or under an Act, but does not
include a bylaw, resolution, order or directive of a local authority;

"statutory instrument" means any rule, order, regulation, direction,
form, tariff of costs or fees, commission, warrant, proclamation,
bylaw, resolution or other instrument issued, made or established

(a) in the execution of a power conferred by or under an Act, by
or under which such instrument is expressly authorized to be
issued, made or established otherwise than by the conferring
on any person or body of powers or functions in relation to a
matter to which such instrument relates, or

(b) by or under the authority of the Commissioner, but does not
include

(c) any such instrument issued, made or established by a corporation incorporated by or under an Act unless the instrument is a
regulation and the corporation by which it is made is one that

is ultimately accountable through the Commissioner to the Legislative Assembly for the conduct of its affairs,

(d) any such instrument issued, made or established by a judicial or quasi-judicial body, unless the instrument is a rule, order or regulation governing the practice or procedure in proceedings before a judicial or quasi-judicial body established by or under an Act, or

(e) any such instrument in respect of which, or in respect of the production or other disclosure of which, any privilege exists by law or whose contents are limited to advice or information intended only for use or assistance in the making of a decision or the determination of policy, or in the ascertainment of any matter necessarily incidental to that.

Nova Scotia

Regulations Act, RSNS 1989, c 393

2. In this Act,

...

(g) "regulation" means a rule, order, proclamation, regulation, by-law, form, resolution or tariff of costs or fees made in the exercise of a legislative power conferred by or under an Act of the Legislature

(i) by the Governor in Council,

(ii) by the minister presiding over any department of the public service of the Province or by any official of such department, whether or not such regulation is subject to the approval of the Governor in Council,

(iii) by any board, commission, agency or body listed in the Schedule to this Act or added thereto by the Governor in Council in accordance with this Act, whether or not such regulation is subject to the approval of the Governor in Council, or

(iv) the exercise of which power is declared by the Act conferring it to be a regulation within the meaning of this Act,

but does not include a rule, order, proclamation, regulation, by-law, form, resolution or tariff of costs or fees made by

(v) a local authority, or

(vi) a corporation incorporated by private or public Act of the Legislature or by the board of directors or the board of management of such corporation unless it is a board, commission, agency or body listed in the Schedule or added thereto by the Governor in Council in accordance with this Act.

Nunavut

Same as Northwest Territories

Ontario

Legislation Act, 2006, SO 2006, c 21, Schedule F

17. In this Part,

...

"regulation" means a regulation, rule, order or by-law of a legislative nature made or approved under an Act of the Legislature by the Lieutenant Governor in Council, a minister of the Crown, an official of the government or a board or commission all the members of which are appointed by the Lieutenant Governor in Council, but does not include,

(a) a by-law of a municipality or local board as defined in the *Municipal Affairs Act*, or

(b) an order of the Ontario Municipal Board.

Prince Edward Island

Interpretation Act, RSPEI 1988, c I-8

1. In this Act

...

(e) *"regulation"* means a regulation, order, rule, form, tariff of costs regulation or fees, proclamation or bylaw enacted

(i) in the execution of a power conferred by or under the authority of an Act, or

(ii) by or under the authority of the Lieutenant Governor in Council, but does not include an order of a court or an order made by a public officer or administrative tribunal in a dispute between two or more persons;

Quebec

Regulations Act, CQLR c R-18.1

1. In this Act,

"regulation" means a normative instrument of a general and impersonal nature, made under an Act and having force of law when it is in effect.

Saskatchewan

The Interpretation Act, 1995, SS 1995, c I-11.2

2. In this Act:

...

"regulation" means a regulation, order, rule, rule of court, form, tariff of costs or fees, proclamation, letter patent, bylaw or resolution enacted in the execution of a power conferred by or pursuant to the authority of an Act, but does not include:

(a) an order of a court made in the course of an action; or

(b) an order made by a public officer or administrative tribunal in a dispute between two or more persons;

Yukon

Interpretation Act, RSY 2002, c 125

1(1) In this Act,

...

"regulation" includes any rule, rule of court, order prescribing regulations, tariff of costs or fees, form, bylaw, resolution, or order made in the execution of a power given by an enactment.

appendix two

Federal, Provincial, and Territorial Parliamentary Libraries and Archives in Canada

Jurisdiction	Parliamentary Library	Archives
Federal	Library of Parliament Parliament of Canada Ottawa, ON K1A 0A9 Toll-free (Canada): 1 (866) 599-4999 Phone: 613-992-4793 TTY: 613-995-2266 Email: info@parl.gc.ca Website: www.lop.parl.gc.ca/ About/Library/VirtualLibrary/ index-e.asp	Library and Archives Canada 395 Wellington Street Ottawa, ON K1A 0N4 Phone: 613-996-5115 or 1-866-578-7777 TTY: 613-992-6969 or 1-866-299-1699 Fax: 613-995-6274 Website: www.bac-lac.gc.ca/ eng/Pages/home.aspx
Alberta	Legislature Library Legislative Assembly of Alberta 216 Legislature Building 10800-97 Avenue Edmonton, AB T5K 2B6 Phone: 780-427-2473 Email: library@assembly.ab.ca Website: www.assembly.ab.ca/lao/ library/index.htm	Provincial Archives of Alberta 8555 Roper Road Edmonton, AB T6E 5W1 General Inquiries: 780-427-1750 Sandra Thomson Reading Room Phone: 780-427-1056 Email: paa@gov.ab.ca

Jurisdiction	Parliamentary Library	Archives
British Columbia	British Columbia Legislative Library Legislative Assembly of British Columbia Parliament Buildings Victoria, BC V8V 1X4 Phone: 250 387-6510 Email: LLBC.Ref@leg.bc.ca Website: www.leg.bc.ca/learn-about-us/legislative-library	British Columbia Archives 75 Belleville Street Victoria, BC V8W 9W2 Phone: 250-387-1952 Fax: 250-387-2072 Email: access@royalbcmuseum.bc.ca
Manitoba	Legislative Library Legislative Assembly of Manitoba 100–200 Vaughan Street Winnipeg, MB R3C 1T5 Phone: 204-948-1312 Email: Legislative_Library@gov.mb.ca Website: www.manitoba.ca/leglib	Archives of Manitoba 130-200 Vaughan Street Winnipeg, MB R3C 1T5 Phone: 204-945-3971 Toll Free (Manitoba only): 1-800-617-3588 Fax: 204-948-2672 Email: archives@gov.mb.ca Website: www.gov.mb.ca/chc/archives/index.html
New Brunswick	New Brunswick Legislative Library PO Box 6000 Fredericton, NB B3B 5H1 Phone: 506-453-2338 Email: library.biblio-info@gnb.ca Website: www1.gnb.ca/leglibbib/	New Brunswick Provincial Archives Richard Bennett Hatfield Archives Complex Bonar Law–Bennett Building 23 Dineen Drive UNB Campus Fredericton, NB Phone: 506-453-2122 Website: http://archives.gnb.ca/Archives

Jurisdiction	Parliamentary Library	Archives
Newfoundland and Labrador	Newfoundland and Labrador Legislative Library PO Box 8700 St. John's, NL A1B 4J6 Phone: 709-729-3604 Email: legislativelibrary@gov.nl.ca Website: http://wpp.assembly. nl.ca/dbtw-wpd/catalogue.htm	The Rooms Provincial Archives Division The Rooms 9 Bonaventure Avenue, PO Box 1800, Station C St. John's, NL A1C 5P9 Phone: 709-757-8030 Fax: 709-757-8017 Archives Reference Desk: 709-757-8088 Email: archives@therooms.ca Website: www.therooms.ca/contact-us#sthash.nXqM9ovJ.dpuf
Northwest Territories	Legislative Library of the Northwest Territories Legislative Assembly Building PO Box 1320 Yellowknife, NT X1A 2L9 Phone: 867-767-9132, ext 12021 Email: vera_raschke@gov.nt.ca Website: www.assembly.gov.nt.ca/library	Northwest Territories Archives Prince of Wales Northern Heritage Centre 4750 48th Street, PO Box 1320 Yellowknife, NT X1A 2L9 Phone: 867-767-9347, ext 71211 Fax: 867-873-0660 Email: nwtarchives@gov.nt.ca Website: www.nwtarchives.ca/index.asp
Nova Scotia	Nova Scotia Legislative Library PO Box 396 1726 Hollis Street Halifax, NS B3J 1V9 Phone: 902-424-5932 Email: leglib@novascotia.ca Website: http://legcat.gov.ns.ca	Nova Scotia Archives 6016 University Avenue Halifax, NS B3H 1W4 Phone: 902-424-6060 Fax: 902-424-0628 Email: archives@novascotia.ca Website: http://archives.novascotia.ca

Jurisdiction	Parliamentary Library	Archives
Nunavut	Nunavut Legislative Library Box 1200 Iqaluit, NU X0A 0H0 Phone: 1-867-975-5134 Email: library@assembly.nu.ca Website: www.assembly.nu.ca/ legislative-library	Mr. Edward Atkinson Territorial Archivist Government of Nunavut PO Box 310 Igloolik, NU X0A 0H0 Nunavut Archives Program Department of Culture and Heritage Box 1000, Stn 800 Iqaluit, NU X0A 0H0 Website: www.gov.nu.ca/culture-and- heritage/information/archives
Ontario	Legislative Library Legislative Assembly of Ontario Legislative Building Queen's Park Toronto, ON M7A 1A9 Phone: 416-325-3900 Website: www.ola.org/en/ offices-divisions-branches/ library-catalogue	The Archives of Ontario 134 Ian Macdonald Boulevard Toronto, ON M7A 2C5 Phone: 1-800-668-9933 Fax: 416-327-1999 Email: reference@ontario.ca Website: www.archives. gov.on.ca/en/about/contact. aspx#sthash.ZMxGQmGC.dpuf
Prince Edward Island	Library and Research Services Legislative Library of PEI Coles Building PO Box 2000 Charlottetown, PE C1A 7N8 Phone: 902-620-3765 Email: lemorrell@gov.pe.ca Website: http://assembly.pe.ca/index. php3?number=1024559&lang=E	Public Records and Archives Office 4th Floor, Hon George Coles Building 175 Richmond Street PO Box 1000 Charlottetown, PE C1A 7M4 Phone: 902-368-4290 Fax: 902-368-6327 Email: archives@gov.pe.ca Website: www.princeedwardisland.ca/ en/service/search-public- archives-material-online

Jurisdiction	Parliamentary Library	Archives
Quebec	Library of the National Assembly Pamphile Le May Building 1035 des Parlementaires Quebec City, QC G1A 1A3	Bibliothèque et Archives nationales du Québec (BAnQ) 475 boul de Maisonneuve Est Montréal, QC H2L 5C4
	Phone: 418-643-4408 Email: bibliotheque@assnat.qc.ca Website: www.assnat.qc.ca/en/ bibliotheque/index.html	Phone: 514-873-1100 (région de Montréal) ou 1-800-363-9028 (d'ailleurs au Québec) Télécopieur: 514-873-9312 Email: archives.montreal@banq.qc.ca Website: www.banq.qc.ca/accueil
Saskatchewan	Legislative Library Legislative Assembly of Saskatchewan 234–2405 Legislative Dr Regina, SK S4S 0B3	Provincial Archives of Saskatchewan Room 91, Murray Building 3 Campus Drive Saskatoon, SK S7N 5A4
	Phone: 306-787-2276 Email: reference@legassembly.sk.ca Website: www.legassembly.sk.ca/library	Phone: 306-933-5832 Fax: 306-933-7305
Yukon	N/A	Yukon Archives 400 College Drive Yukon Place (Beside Yukon College) Whitehorse, YT Reference desk phone: 867-667-8061 Email: yukon.archives@gov.yk.ca

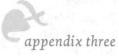

appendix three

Process of a Bill

Pre-legislative Stages
- Policy proposal is considered in Cabinet committee
- Memorandum to Cabinet is drafted
- If approved by Cabinet, legislation is drafted and introduced in Parliament

Parliament

First Reading
- Bill is introduced in the House or Senate
- Bill is printed

Second Reading
- Principle of the bill is debated in the same House as it was introduced
- House may decide to refer the bill to committee for further study

Consideration in Committee
- Bill is referred to a committee and examined by committee members
- Committee may:
  - Call witnesses to provide information on the bill
  - Receive written submission from the public on the bill
  - Examine a bill clause by clause

Report Stage
- ☙ Bill is reported back to the House by the committee
- ☙ Report is a copy of the bill

Third Reading
- ☙ Final debate and vote on bill as amended
- ☙ Bill is sent to other House for consideration (House of Commons or Senate)

Royal Assent
- ☙ Bill is sent to the Queen's representative, the Governor General, for assent
- ☙ The Governor General grants royal assent by signature or traditional ceremony
- ☙ A bill with royal assent is law and assigned a statute chapter number

Coming into Force
- ☙ A statute can come into force in four ways:
  - On royal assent
  - On a date named in the statute (usually found at the end of the statute)
  - On proclamation by the Governor General, which is printed in the *Canada Gazette*
  - A combination of any of the above in-force methods

Glossary

Dreidger's Modern Principle:

> "Today there is only one principle or approach, namely, the words of an Act are to be read in their entire context and in their grammatical and ordinary sense harmoniously with the scheme of the Act, the object of the Act, and the intention of Parliament."

Elmer Dreidger, *The Construction of Statutes*, 2d ed (Toronto: Butterworths, 1983) at 87.

Exclusionary Rule:

> The exclusionary rule had its genesis in British caselaw from the early eighteenth century. "Under the exclusionary rule legislative history of an enactment was not admissible to assist in interpretation ... as direct evidence of legislative intent."

Ruth Sullivan, *Sullivan on the Construction of Statutes*, 5th ed (Markham, ON: LexisNexis, 2008) at 594.

Extrinsic Aids to Interpretation:

> "Anything outside the text [of a statute] that might be relied on to assist interpretation."

Ruth Sullivan, *Sullivan on the Construction of Statutes*, 5th ed (Markham, ON: LexisNexis, 2008) at 573.

Intrinsic Aids to Interpretation:

"The elements that are part of the statute: preambles, headings, punctuation, text, definitions, marginal notes."

Stéphane Beaulac, "Parliamentary Debates in Statutory Interpretation: A Question of Admissibility or of Weight?" (1998) 43 *McGill Law Journal* 287.

Legislative Evolution:

"The evolution of a legislative provision consists of successive enacted versions from inception to current formulation or to its displacement or repeal."

Ruth Sullivan, *Sullivan on the Construction of Statutes*, 5th ed (Markham, ON: LexisNexis, 2008) at 577.

Legislative Intent:

"[L]egislative intention or 'legislative intent' is used by most interpreters to refer to the meaning or purpose that is taken to have been present in the 'mind of the legislature' at the time a provision was enacted. It is the meaning the legislature wished to embody in the legislative text or the purpose it sought to accomplish by enacting the legislation."

Ruth Sullivan, *Statutory Interpretation*, 3d ed (Toronto: Irwin Law, 2016) at 32.

Legislative History:

A legislative history includes "everything that relates to [a statute's] conception, preparation and passage ... from the earliest proposals to royal assent. This includes reports of law reform commissions, ... departmental and committee studies and recommendations; proposals and memoranda submitted to Cabinet; the remarks of the minister responsible for the bill; materials tabled or otherwise brought to the attention of the legislature during the legislative process including explanatory notes; materials published by the government during the legislative process, such as explanatory papers or press releases; legislative committee hearings and reports; debates ...; the records of motions to amend the bill; regulatory impact analysis statements; and more."

Ruth Sullivan, *Sullivan on the Construction of Statutes*, 5th ed (Markham, ON: LexisNexis, 2008) at 593.

Purposive Approach to Statutory Interpretation:

"The second (and slightly more common) version of statutory interpretation ... in that interpretation is driven by an enactment's
underlying purpose and not its literal textual meaning."

Geoff R Hall, "Statutory Interpretation in the Supreme Court of Canada:
The Triumph of a Common Law Methodology" (1988) 21 *Advocates Quarterly* 38 at 45.

Rule of Law:

"[T]he rule of law consists of principles designed to constrain the
exercise of governmental power and to ensure that power is exercised in a fair and efficacious way. The following rule of law principles are important in statutory interpretation:

a) No person can interfere with the freedom, security, or property
    of another person, except in accordance with the law. This prin-
    ciple applies to everyone, including government officials. For an
    act of a government official to be effective or binding, he or she
    must be able to point to a valid legal rule authorizing the act.

b) The law must be set out in advance and with sufficient clarity so
    that subjects can know what is expected of them and of others,
    can achieve a measure of security, and can plan for the future.

c) The law must be applied fairly, in a consistent and even-handed
    way, treating like cases alike."

Ruth Sullivan, *Statutory Interpretation*, 3d ed (Toronto: Irwin Law, 2016) at 34.

Index

*The letter **t** following a page number denotes a table*

About the Authors

Erica Anderson, BA, MISt, is the manager of digital and web content at the Legislative Assembly of Ontario and was previously a research librarian at the Ontario Legislative Library. She has worked in law firm libraries in Toronto and London, UK; was president of the Toronto Association of Law Libraries (2006–7); and was a member-at-large for the Canadian Association of Law Libraries Executive Board (2015–17).

Susan Barker is the digital services and reference librarian at the Bora Laskin Law Library, University of Toronto, Faculty of Law. She holds a master of information studies degree from the University of Toronto and a diploma in library techniques from Seneca College. She is the former editor and current associate editor of the *Canadian Law Library Review* and teaches legal literature and librarianship at the University of Toronto iSchool. She is also a contributor to *Legal Problem Solving — Reasoning, Research and Writing* (4th to 8th ed), and a coauthor of *The Ultimate Guide to Canadian Legal Research* (1st to 4th ed). In addition to her interest in researching legislative intent, she has also written on bibliometrics for legal academics.